A Dream Sets Sail, Part II

The Continuing Adventures of Amazing Grace

Kay Koudele

authorHOUSE®

AuthorHouse™
1663 Liberty Drive
Bloomington, IN 47403
www.authorhouse.com
Phone: 1-800-839-8640

Published by AuthorHouse 9/11/2012

ISBN: 978-1-4772-5208-6 (e)
ISBN: 978-1-4772-5209-3 (sc)

Library of Congress Control Number: 2012913715

Any people depicted in stock imagery provided by Thinkstock are models,
and such images are being used for illustrative purposes only.
Certain stock imagery © Thinkstock.

This book is printed on acid-free paper.

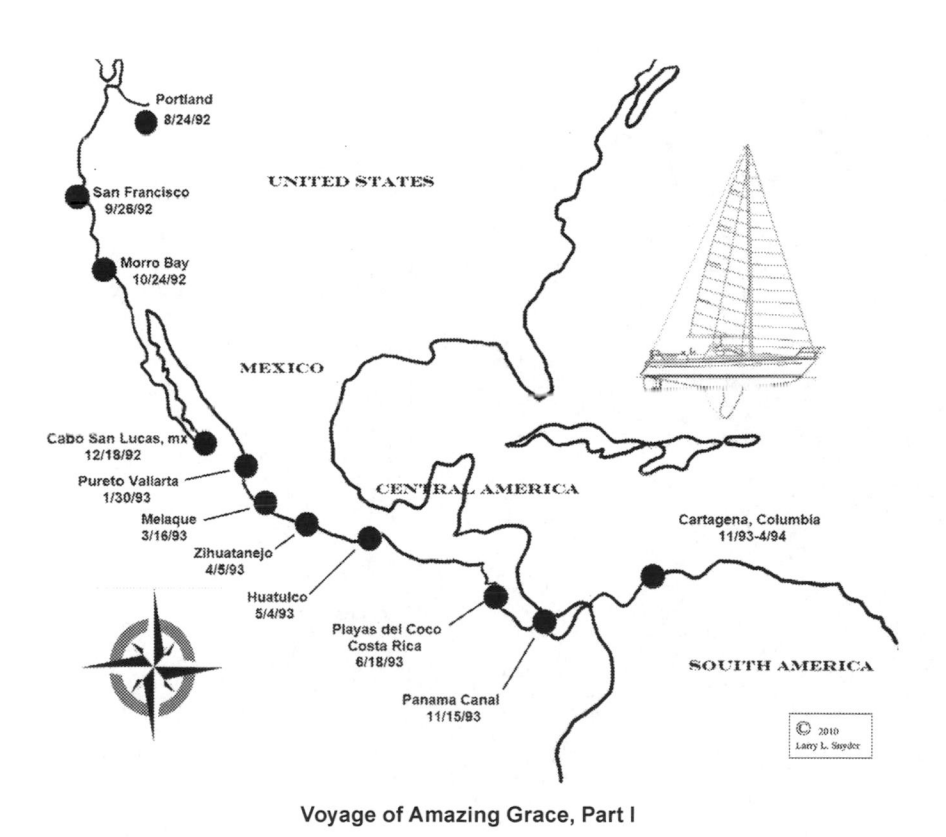

Portland
8/24/92

UNITED STATES

San Francisco
9/26/92

Morro Bay
10/24/92

MEXICO

Cabo San Lucas, mx
12/18/92

Pureto Vallarta
1/30/93

Melaque
3/16/93

Zihuatanejo
4/5/93

CENTRAL AMERICA

Cartagena, Columbia
11/93-4/94

Huatulco
5/4/93

Playas del Coco
Costa Rica
6/18/93

Panama Canal
11/15/93

SOUTH AMERICA

© 2010
Larry L. Snyder

Voyage of Amazing Grace, Part I

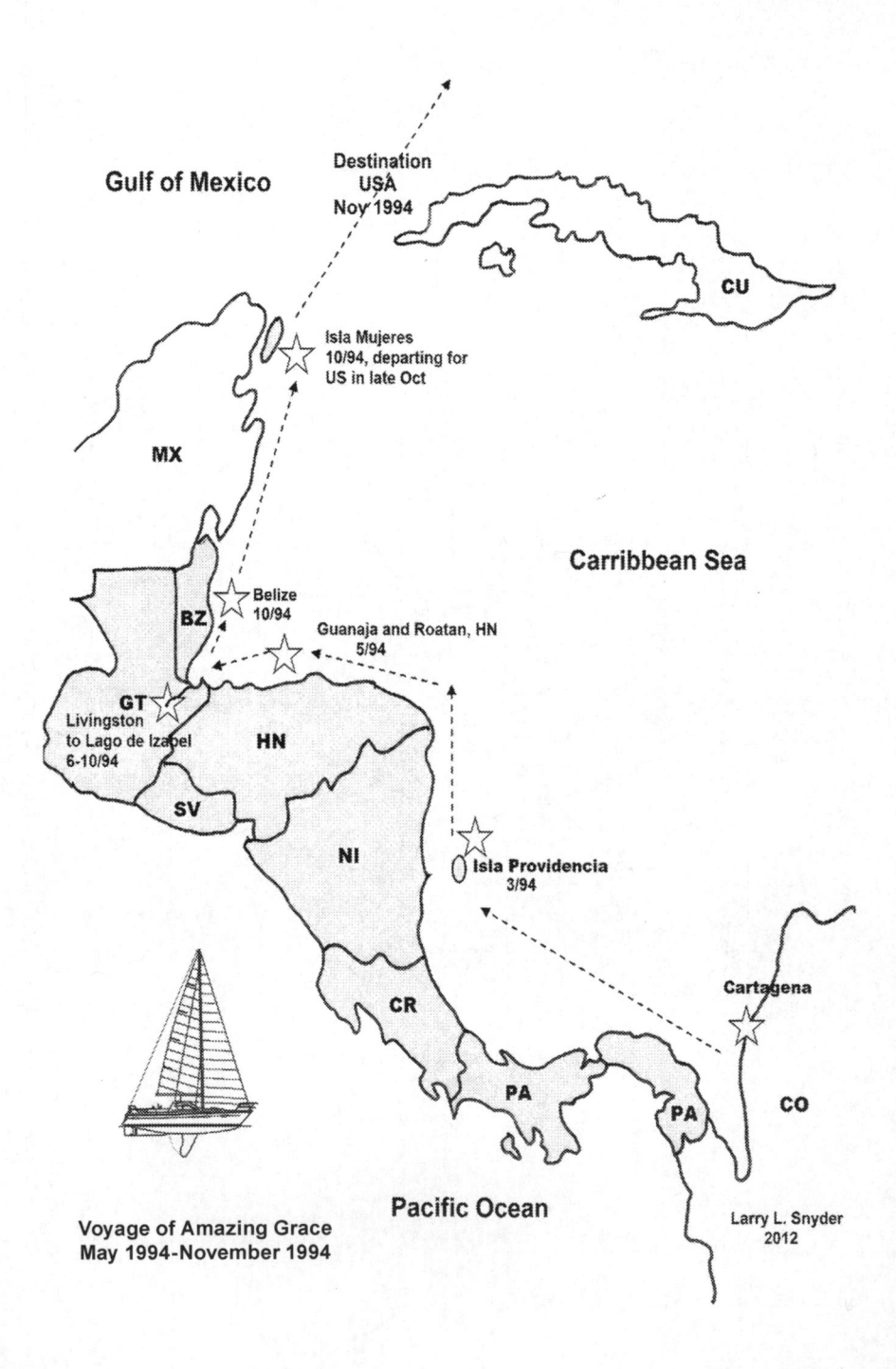

Gulf of Mexico

Destination
USA
Nov 1994

CU

Isla Mujeres
10/94, departing for
US in late Oct

MX

Carribbean Sea

Belize
10/94

Guanaja and Roatan, HN
5/94

BZ

GT
Livingston
to Lago de Izabel
6-10/94

HN

SV

NI

Isla Providencia
3/94

Cartagena

CR

PA

PA

CO

Pacific Ocean

Voyage of Amazing Grace
May 1994-November 1994

Larry L. Snyder
2012

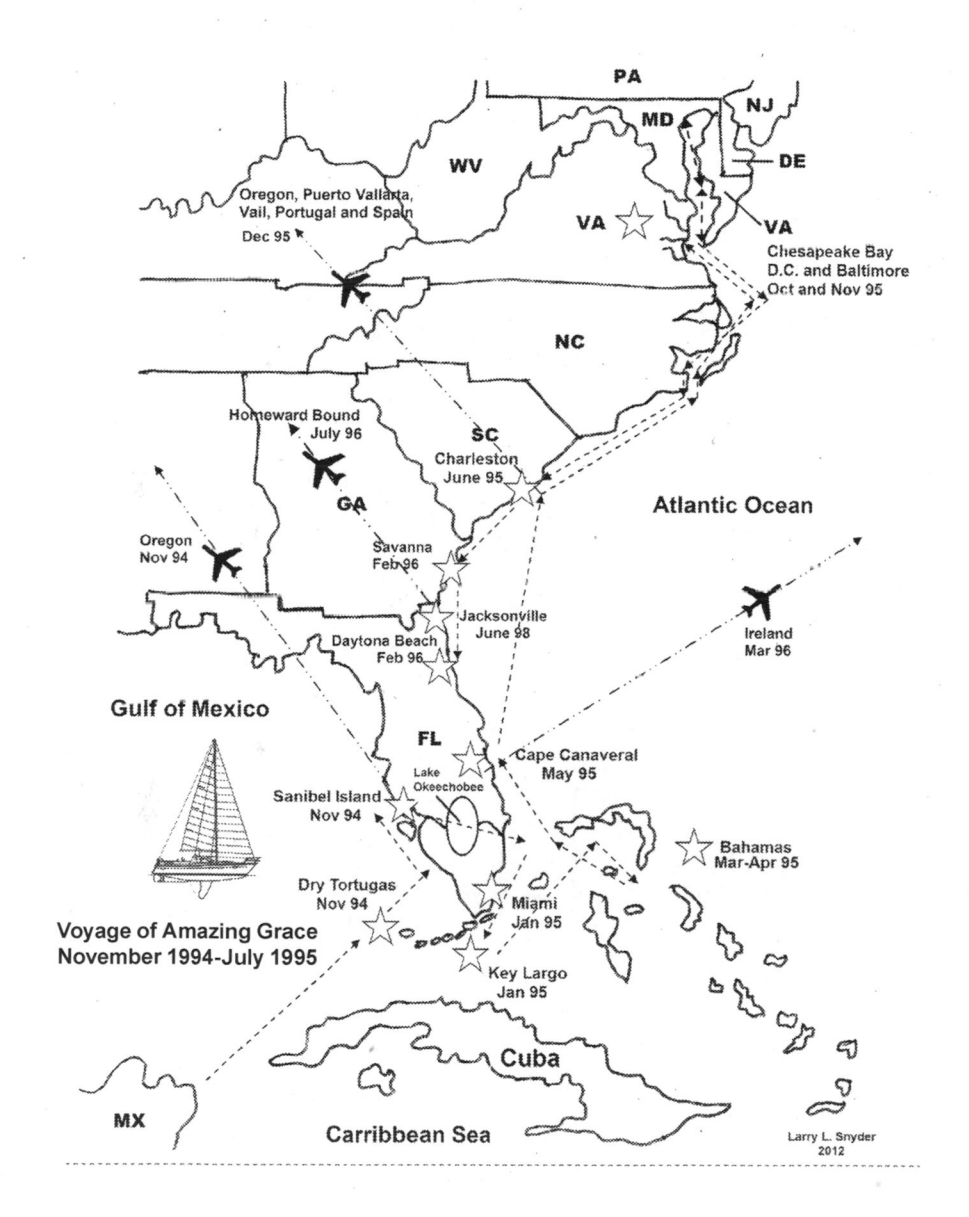

PA

NJ

MD

DE

WV

VA ☆

VA
Chesapeake Bay
D.C. and Baltimore
Oct and Nov 95

Oregon, Puerto Vallarta,
Vail, Portugal and Spain
Dec 95

NC

Homeward Bound
July 96

SC
Charleston
June 95

Atlantic Ocean

GA

Oregon
Nov 94

Savanna
Feb 96

Jacksonville
June 98

Daytona Beach
Feb 96

Ireland
Mar 96

Gulf of Mexico

FL

Cape Canaveral
May 95

Lake
Okeechobee

Sanibel Island
Nov 94

Bahamas
Mar-Apr 95

Dry Tortugas
Nov 94

Miami
Jan 95

Voyage of Amazing Grace
November 1994-July 1995

Key Largo
Jan 95

Cuba

MX

Carribbean Sea

Larry L. Snyder
2012

vii

Table of Contents

One

The Colorful Caribbean

By now, we recognized the familiar, pervasive symptoms. There was a vague restlessness, a yearning, a feeling that we were "chomping at the bit." Dreams of new places and new people were calling our names. My husband, Fred, and I definitely had it—the "itchy feet syndrome." The anticipation of ongoing adventures and the vagabond sailing lifestyle was crying out to us like the legendary Siren of the Sea, enticing us onward. After almost two years of international cruising in our 37 foot sailboat, *Amazing Grace*, we were anxious to once again see the sails filled with air, feel the motion of the waves passing under our keel, and seek additional experiences in new ports, different countries. With a conspiratorial shared nod of agreement, and grinning like two kids anticipating the delights of Christmas, we acknowledged that it was time to be "on the road again."

Since leaving our home dock in Portland, Oregon, we had sailed down the Pacific coast of the U.S., Mexico and Central America before transiting the Panama Canal, and then continued through the San Blas Islands, and over to Columbia, South America. Now, after almost five months in Cartagena, Columbia, a city of more than two million people, the winter winds were subsiding, the hurricane season would soon be upon us, and we were more than ready to continue onward.

"We've got to get out of here," I lamented.

We had been ready to go for over two weeks, but continued to wait, albeit quite impatiently, for favorable weather reports before attempting what promised to be a difficult passage from Columbia to Isla Providencia, a small island off the eastern coast of Nicaragua, in the Western Caribbean. The longer we waited, the more our anxiety about the trip grew as we continued to hear frightening stories about crossing this stretch of water. It felt a little like being pregnant for the first time, having passed your "due date," and impatiently but somewhat fearfully waiting to begin labor and delivery of that cherished baby.

"You're right. Let's take the boat to the Rosario Islands and wait it out down there," Fred said. "It's only fifteen miles from here, and we can begin our crossing just as well from the anchorage there."

Leaving Columbia and South America was not going to be easy. We had developed many friends in this country that had welcomed us with open arms. One of our main goals in cruising was to *experience* the culture of different countries, not just to *observe* it. Staying for an extended period in Cartagena had allowed this desire to become a fulfilling reality. We also had developed friendships with Columbians from different economic levels, giving us a broader understanding of this country and its people. It was sad to say goodbye to these folks whom we so enjoyed and would likely never see again. We had taken thank-you notes and candy to the staff of *Club de Pesca*, the private yacht club where we were moored, entertained all our Columbian friends one last time, and spoken to all those on the cruising boats at nearby *Club Nautico*, the local "hang out" for international cruisers. Our boat, equipment and navigation charts were prepared, fresh food supplies had been brought aboard, and everything was crossed off the "to do" list. We were ready to go!

After a restless night too full of anticipation to allow sleep, we were up at dawn, and made the last minute preparations to be able to leave the dock.

"I can't get our line off this piling," I yelled to Fred from the bow of the boat. "There are too many lines from the other boats on top of it. And it's like they're made of steel—they won't budge."

I was frustrated, and dripping with sweat from the challenging task. Then I saw Saul come racing over to help. Dear Saul (pronounced Saw-ule). He was our most cherished Columbian friend. Only 24 years old, he was a deckhand on the large motor yacht in the slip next to ours, so we saw him every day. We had even asked him to sail with us to Isla Providencia, and we'd buy a ticket to fly him back to Cartagena. But he hadn't been able to get a passport or arrange the time off work. It was especially hard to think of not seeing his smiling face and laughing with him every day as we struggled to learn Spanish, and he to learn English.

Several other club staff helped in the time-consuming process of getting *Grace* untied from the dock and pilings, and threaded through the crisscrossed mooring lines of the pie-shaped section of dock where we were moored. We had been wedged in tightly after strong winter winds had pulled and tightened the many lines holding all the boats. Finally, we were moving out into the bay and waved our bittersweet goodbyes. Tears welled up in my eyes as I looked behind to see Saul and the others standing on the dock, hands held high as they watched us leave.

The view from the harbor was amazing. We gazed fondly at the quaint setting of the marina amidst the charming architecture of an old Spanish fort. Many yachts surrounded the historical site. It had been constructed long ago with rough stone archways, multi-hued coral block walls, and rounded turrets that looked like something straight out of a children's storybook. High above the marina was the imposing structure of the massive San Felipe Fort, which blanketed the hillside and had stood guard over this remarkable city for hundreds of years. We couldn't help but be reminded of the colorful history and culture of this country and its very special people. We would never forget them and their kindness to us. Their friendship had greatly enriched our time in Columbia. We would so miss them. But we had work to do and that helped ease our sadness in parting. We quickly set about stowing the lines and fenders, set a course through the bay, and raised the mainsail. It was not long before we could feel the wind in our faces as *Grace* once again reveled in her freedom and her release from being captive to a dock and the shore. Once again did what she does best—sail!

"Wow," I squealed, "does it ever feel good to be *moving* again."

"It sure does, but I have to stop and think about everything before I do it. It doesn't just come naturally like before."

"Same for me. Isn't that weird? After almost two full years of cruising, you'd think it would be second nature by now. But I'm sure it will all come back quickly. Five months in a harbor is a long time."

We motor-sailed along in the huge bay, moving towards the narrow exit channel that would take us from the protected harbor into the open sea. Boat traffic was everywhere, and we dodged all the vessels moving swiftly about in the water. The watercraft ranged from huge freighters to single man dugouts. Few, if any, appeared to have a recreational purpose. Since we had initially come into the bay at night, and had traveled the nine miles up to the inner harbor area in the dark, we now enjoyed being able to see the city along the shoreline. As we moved away from the inner harbor and the familiar "Old City" section of Cartagena, we recalled the images of flower filled balconies lining the narrow cobblestone streets which we had walked and explored so many times. Now, we saw evidence of the commerce and industry of this metropolis. Smoke stacks poured out great black gritty clouds, filling the air with smells of grease, oil, and burnt rubber. Smog clogged the bright sunshine, turning the immediate area into a diffuse, ashen grey. The noise of machinery mixed with the insistent sounds of the hustle and bustle of cars, trains, trucks and boats. Every square foot of the surrounding hillsides was covered with small buildings or shacks that sheltered the huge population of this both modern, and yet ancient city. Viewed from the water, these densely packed districts appeared chaotic and teeming with life.

Forty-five minutes after leaving the dock, we suddenly realized that we had lost the GPS (global positioning signal) tracking. *Oh no.* Fred went below and worked for an hour and a half in the hot, stuffy cabin, but nothing he could do fixed the problem.

"We'd better head back to the yacht club," he said. "We don't want to proceed without it. I don't want to go back to 'dead reckoning' to figure out where we think we are."

While we could navigate using the old non-electronic methods, we had come to enjoy and depend on the reliability and ease of that little technological devise. Reluctantly, we turned around and radioed the club of our need to return. What a disappointment. Just before we were about to enter the marina back in the inner harbor, Fred managed to solve the problem. The all-important navigational instrument was once again working properly.

"Yahoo," I yelled. With a shared sigh of relief, we once again turned around and aimed for the exit channel. After several hours underway, we approached that restricted passageway and saw a huge freighter coming into the bay from the sea.

"I sure don't like the idea of having to pass that big guy in the channel," Fred said.

Besides being narrow, the channel had shoals on either side. We were proceeding cautiously, when suddenly the engine sputtered and died. *What next?* With just the main sail up and light winds, we again turned around to try to get to a wider spot in the bay where we would have more room to maneuver the boat while under sail. Fred thought there must be air in the fuel system from his previous work on the engine, and quickly began the process of "bleeding" the engine. In ten minutes he had the problem fixed, the engine was running, and we once again turned and entered the narrow exit channel. The massive freighter passed alongside us at a scant distance of about 20 yards. The huge, rusted steel walls of its hull towered many stories over us, making us feel small and vulnerable alongside it. The massive wake created by its propeller tossed us about like a toy in a swimming pool. The water foamed, churned and pulled at us as we struggled to maintain our course.

"Good grief," laughed Fred when we were safely passed. "The sea gods are really out to get us today."

"But think how much more difficult it would have been if the engine had died just fifteen minutes later. We'd have been right in the channel and not able to maneuver the boat. Even when the GPS went out, we were in a good place to turn around. And 'hat's off' to you for fixing the problems. We're being 'stretched' but those prayers are working as well."

Safely out of the harbor, we raised the jib, and began to make way towards the first small island in the Rosario's chain. It felt heavenly to turn off the engine and feel our *Grace* rush smoothly through the water. *Ah! This is it. A boat under sail!* The oppressive heat of the city and harbor gave way to the feel of warm sunshine on our skin, balanced by the cooling effect of the light ocean breeze, which ruffled our hair, filled the sails, and satisfied our souls. Fluffy white clouds danced above us, and the aqua-blue water of the Caribbean sang to us as it slid quietly by. The air was clean and refreshing. The noise of urban living and commerce had receded to a calming quiet, broken only by the sound of the waves and water.

Spotting the islands, we consulted our cruising notes and hand drawn charts as we cautiously approached the tricky entrance to the anchorage. There were no published charts of this area, so information came from other cruising and local boats. We went aground in several attempts to enter, before radioing another boat already at anchor there. It seemed we were in the *wrong* place to enter. *Holy Cow.* Thank goodness for that marvelous "swing keel." Whenever we found ourselves gently nudging the sandy sea bottom at slow speed, I would hurry to the galley area, and pump the handle of a hydraulic lift system. That would raise the keel and in a few moments we'd back out of the area. After almost five months at a dock, we were surely getting the kinks out of our systems—but it seemed that many of the kinks were *us.* Finally in the right place, we dropped the hook and rejoiced to be officially underway on our continuing awesome adventure.

Despite the frustrations and concerns of the day, we relished being in the solitude of the quiet, calm anchorage. After the noise and pollution of a huge city, and being tied to a dock, it was delightful to feel the boat swing on the anchor, turn herself into the wind, and bob gently in the breeze. Many trees and bushes surrounded this small sheltered place, and nowhere could we see any houses or buildings, or for that matter, any signs of civilization. It was *wonderful.* There were no sounds other than that of the water gently lapping at the hull, the occasional call of the birds, and the soft hush of the wind gently moving through the trees. We were in our very own oasis. Well, almost our own. We did share it with one other sailboat. But *no problema. Grace* and crew were free again!

Our general plan was to sail to Isla Providencia, and then on to the Bay Islands of Honduras. The plan was always flexible, for part of the adventure of cruising was the freedom to decide when and where we would go from day to day. The ideas could change depending on obstacles or attractions that beckoned us elsewhere. That was one of the most delightful aspects of this cruising dream, lending it such an exciting sense of anticipation. For now, the objective was to spend some time in the Bay Islands, and then to the islands off the coast of Belize, before going up into the *Rio Dulce* of Guatemala. That river was known to provide a great "hurricane hole" as it allowed cruising boats to go inland about twenty miles to wait out the major part of the hurricane season. Then, in late October or early November, after the worrisome season was past, we would likely make our way through Belize, up to the Yucatan peninsula of Mexico, possibly to Cuba, and over to the gulf coast of Florida. The possibility of crossing the Atlantic and venturing into European countries could commence from eastern Florida. There were also the options of crossing the Gulf Stream to the Bahamas, or going north, to explore the eastern coast of the U.S. via the Intracoastal Waterway. So many choices.

"I *don't* want to spend another holiday season without the family," I said that night, pounding my fist for emphasis.

"*I* don't *either,*" Fred had mimicked while dramatically pounding his fist as well, and we both laughed.

When I came out of the aft cabin the next morning I was greeted by a big sign hanging over the refrigerator – "Happy Anniversary!" *Had it really been 31 years?* We soon received a call on the ham radio from *Yobo*, and later one from *Pendragon*, both offering congratulations. How nice to be remembered by special friends on this special day. We had not been able to get clear reception on the ham radio while in the harbor of Cartagena.

"Time for celebration later," Fred said. "First, we need to clean *Grace's* bottom."

So much for romance. The water was clear and warm when we jumped in and began to scrub off all the yucky stuff that had grown on the boat's hull under the waterline when *Grace* had been moored in the marina. It was an extremely messy job, but it felt good to get it done, even though it took almost four long hours. Afterwards, I was quick to shower off all the slimy crud that had stuck to my skin. We checked each other's ears to make sure that no tiny critters formerly living in that crud, and who were now displaced, had taken up residency with us.

The fellow on the other boat in the anchorage rowed over to share a beer with us in honor of our anniversary. Later, we put on a cassette tape of Hawaiian music, reminisced about our wonderful honeymoon in that tropical paradise, and opened a precious bottle of Oregon wine.

"Hey, listen. It's the Hawaiian Wedding Song," Fred said. "Let's dance."

The two of us hugged and swayed together as we moved slowly around the galley (the only place in the cabin big enough for both of us to stand together) while that magical song transported us back to another very special time and place. I like anniversaries.

We waited three more days in the anchorage, struggling with the time consuming and frustrating process of making radio connections and obtaining the very limited weather information. Finally we heard a report from *Southbound II*, the amateur meteorologist who was so good at giving accurate information to cruising boats. Winds would be lighter and seas less turbulent for the next few days. While the report was not for "good" conditions, it was definitely more favorable than it had been for the last month. The prevailing winds, ocean currents, shallow shelf, and contour of the land made the area around Cartagena difficult to depart from at any time.

"Let's do it," Fred said after hearing the news.

"Aye, aye, Captain," I laughed. We were beyond ready. Last minute tasks were completed and we turned in early, although the sense of excitement allowed neither of us to sleep much that night.

Grey menacing looking clouds hung low over the matching grey sea when we pulled up our anchor shortly after daybreak. Everything looked dreary and rather threatening in the early morning light. It was such a contrast to the vision of "the dream" that I had held in my mind for so long. That image always had sunny skies, soft billowy white clouds, gentle winds and sparkling blue waters. The calm sea and wind changed quickly as we left the protected anchorage, and very soon we were in churning waves coming from several different directions and strong winds. White capped swells threatened to splash over the bow, and spray was blown horizontally over the water. The motion felt choppy and abrupt, unlike the slow rolling motion of the waves in the Pacific Ocean. No other boats or people could be seen, and I couldn't shake a rather ominous feeling as we continued out to sea.

Because of the clouds, we couldn't see through the water to find the channel through the reef that surrounded the island, so we moved forward slowly and went aground several times before successfully making our exit. How I wished for more accurate charts. Even after we reached the open sea, we encountered frequent shoals until we were many miles and many hours clear of the coastline. It was a tense time, and the motion of the boat was severe in the conflicting currents. We pounded up and down, back and forth, never knowing which way the boat's motion would send us next. Meanwhile, we kept a close eye on the depth meter for those shallow spots that would suddenly appear.

All that erratic and sometimes violent motion soon led to the "queasies" and we were glad we had been listening to my *SeaWellness* tape. After so much time in the harbor, we had known that there would once again be the possibility of becoming seasick. The self-hypnosis cassette tape I had made years ago was helpful in combating that cruiser's nemesis. Besides the stress of sudden shallow water and an unsettled stomach, we were being thrown about the cockpit or cabin by the short, steep waves.

By mid-morning, I found myself going to the bathroom every ten to fifteen minutes. At first, I attributed it to my anxiety, but after two more hours, I knew that I had developed another urinary tract infection. *Oh my.* From my background as a nurse, I knew that I needed to drink *lots* of water, but it was so rough and roll-y—it certainly was not conducive to drinking *anything.* When I made myself take a sip, I cringed when I smelled something awful. We had just begun to operate the water maker after it had been five months in a dormant state. In order to flush out the biocide that we had used to disinfect the system, we had run it for several hours. We had discarded that initially generated water before starting to fill our tanks. I began to think that we hadn't rinsed the system long enough. In a matter of minutes I was convinced that our water was tainted.

"Fred, I think our tanks are *contaminated,*" I groaned, my anxiety now escalating. "This water doesn't taste good and I can smell something bad. Maybe it's the biocide."

"Here, let me try it," he replied and took a drink. He thought for a moment before replying. "Tastes fine to me. It's likely just your imagination."

I wasn't satisfied. I also knew that I needed to take some antibiotics, but we had given most of our supply to Dawn when she had visited us in Cartagena and had become ill. I had forgotten to replace them. I stood on my head while digging through the lockers (which certainly didn't add to my stomach's state of well-being) and finally found some old medication from Mexico. The tablets were huge and the package was outdated, but at least it was something.

When I tried to swallow one of the "horse" pills, as we called them, it came right back up. By now, my anxiety, as well as my imagination, were off and running. I tried to rest and calm myself. But I worried about the safety of our water, about how few other fluids we had aboard, about the infection that could become a major health issue, about the effectiveness of the outdated medication, and about the potential difficulty of keeping anything in my stomach. Before long I was visualizing a helicopter medical rescue in the middle of the Caribbean! Never let it be said that I didn't have an active imagination. Once again, this idyllic dream we were undertaking had occasional *nightmare* components. Fortunately, I finally fell asleep.

"Stay down and sleep," Fred said when I started to get up for my midnight watch. "I can handle this."

"No way," I said as I pulled on my life jacket. "You're not Superman, you know. You need some sleep too."

But oh, how I longed to do just what he had suggested. I smiled to myself as I thought how typical it was of Fred to put my needs before his own. I was one *blucky* (blessed and lucky) lady.

Those "horse" pills did their job, and by the next day I was feeling better, and was finally convinced that the water in our tanks was safe. Nothing like a little drama to add to a dull (!) day. The wind was good, although a little stronger than I preferred, but we were taking it on the beam. That gave us good speed through the water, even though we bounced and rolled rather violently at times. The ominous grey clouds persisted, and the sea reflected the dismal color. The menacing motion of the waves was punctuated by the wild spray and foam of large whitecaps.

"I rather like the motion here in the Caribbean," Fred said from the helm. "I prefer the steep and choppy seas to those huge rolling swells of the Pacific."

"Not me. This is so wearing. I get tired just sitting here. I understand why they call it the 'washing machine' motion. We just get continually tumbled about and increasingly agitated. I guess everybody chooses their own poison."

We made 135 miles on each of the first two days, before the wind decreased. I continued to feel better and the wind vane held the course well, so we were very grateful that one of us did not have to constantly be at the helm steering. The auto-pilot might have held the course, but it would have used up precious electricity, and with the cloudy skies, we weren't generating many amps from our solar panels. Fortunately, the self-steering wind vane required no electricity. It would have been tiring to hand-steer the boat continually.

If at night, the sea and wind conditions were *stable* and it was our watch, we had long ago decided that we could choose to set the kitchen timer for fifteen minutes. Then we could sit in the cockpit, hold the timer in our hands, close our eyes and allow ourselves to possibly doze a little—but *only* if we had first set the timer so that we would not sleep longer than fifteen minutes. We needed to check for any ocean traffic at least that often in order to prevent any collisions. Commercial traffic that traveled at high speed, could be out of sight over the horizon one minute, and then at our position on a collision course within fifteen or twenty minutes. Many cruisers vowed to stay awake, but without intending to do so, some did succumb to sleep only to find themselves in disastrous situations. We sadly remembered our friend and his two young children that had been killed after their boat had been hit and capsized by a freighter in the Pacific. We prayed often for Judy, the wife and mom, who had survived the terrible ordeal, and for her healing. Another sailboat in our cruising community had also been hit by a freighter, and thoughts of those folks had us always watchful for those huge vessels. One night I jumped up to find a freighter only *four* miles away. We began to set the timer for ten minutes.

Sometimes at sea, I needed to talk, and with no one else around, Fred's ear got the brunt of it. He didn't complain, and we almost always found something to laugh about—often a laugh at ourselves. We often talked about the kids. When we thought of Dawn becoming a flight attendant, we began to consider the advantages for us. With the knowledge that we could fly free, thanks to "parent passes" from our "Delta Dawn," I suggested alternatives to long passages, like hiring a skipper to take the boat to the Azores, with the two of us flying there, most likely *first-class*. Standby, of course, and only if first-class seats were available.

"We can't do that," Fred said adamantly. "We can't leave *Grace* by herself. Besides, that's for wimps." But I think he secretly considered the idea.

"Land Ho," Fred cried. We had found our needle in the haystack. It was early morning and we were approaching Isla Providencia. The island is only ten miles long, and had a population of 4000 people of African heritage. It appeared in the distance as a very small grey mound in the vast expanse of ocean water. As if by arranged escort, we looked down in the water and found a pod of dolphins cavorting alongside our boat. At first they surrounded us, and then they swam to the bow where they jumped and frolicked in the waves generated by the boat.

"Wow, there's *hundreds* of them," Fred yelled.

He ran to the bow to watch the masterful swimmers jump through the air, then dive into the deep, dancing their beautiful ballet. He may have exaggerated a bit about the number, but there sure were a bunch of them. We sailed along with the delightful creatures whose presence instilled in us a very special connection with nature. We were continually amused and amazed at the speed in which they could dive under the boat and return to the surface, and marveled once again, about the wonder in God's creation.

We worked our way into a small, protected harbor where two other sailboats were anchored. Frustrated after making many attempts to get a good hold on the bottom, we finally managed to get a good set on our anchor. With the potential for wind and sea conditions to change drastically in the blink of an eye, having an anchor set firmly was always a priority for us. I was always amazed at how cool Fred remained in trying times, and just kept plugging along with whatever needed to be done. When I was tired and frustrated, I sometimes just felt like crying. It must be those hormones.

We savored our traditional and refreshing end of voyage tradition with a "Miller Time," (using a couple of cans of Columbian beer) and spent a few moments sitting and reflecting on the successful passage. Roy, from *Yankee Rogue*, a boat we had met in Cartagena, came over and offered to take us in to the Port Captain's office so we wouldn't have to set up our dinghy right away, but still be able to clear in to this port as required. Such thoughtfulness was greatly appreciated. We compared crossings with the other cruisers that evening, and the six of us decided to rent motor scooters to tour the island the following day.

Amazing Grace at anchor.

"Hang on," Fred yelled. "If the kids could only see us now."

I had climbed on our scooter behind Fred and we started out on our exploration of this small colorful and charming island. Everywhere we went, friendly people waved and shouted greetings to us. In the first half hour of our scooter caravan, I think I nearly tore Fred's shirt to shreds trying to hold on to *something* that felt secure. I finally began to relax and enjoy the trip. There were very few cars on the mostly dirt roads, but lots of scooters. It took only three hours to make our way all the way around the island, even with my backseat driving and frequent stops.

When we stopped and talked with the local folks, they were pleasant and welcoming. They appeared to have a laid-back lifestyle, although we found out that this was rather deceiving. In reality, they shared many of the same activities, concerns and economic issues that we faced at home, and worked hard to improve their way of life. They spoke English, although with a heavy "Caribe" accent, so that it was sometimes difficult to understand what they were saying. In conversation with the owner of a little hamburger stand, we learned about a good deal of political activism among the people. The islanders had voted not to allow any large tourist or commercial developments on their island—a courageous stand when they could have made a lot of money by selling to large resort corporations. The residents had also limited the construction of any new buildings to one story in order to protect the many small inns and family-owned restaurants. They wanted to preserve their familiar way of life and the small-town feel of the island.

Certainly, this was a very different culture and people from that of mainland Columbia. We were told that there were annual beautification contests, and every building, tree, pole, rock, or anything else they could find, was decorated with yellow, pink and blue painted stripes or any other combination of colors and designs. Along with the vivid hues of the brightly painted houses and businesses, the landscape took on a sort of magical rainbow appearance. We also saw lovely pearl white sand beaches with crystal clear water displaying the many different hues of the turquoise sea. They were "picture-postcard-perfect." This little island definitely had a lot to offer.

The other two boats in the anchorage continued on their way the next day, but we remained in the harbor by ourselves for a few more days. On Sunday we were thrilled to go to an *English speaking* little Baptist church and we were greeted warmly. What a treat! How we had missed being able to worship in our native tongue.

They asked us to introduce ourselves and tell where we were from. In the closing prayer, the minister asked for blessings for us and our travels in "this little sailboat that has come from so far away." We were touched.

The crystal clear water afforded some wonderful snorkeling. I finally found that if I pulled the straps on my goggles *very* tight, my mask would not leak. That gave me a headache, and left deep indentations on my face, but the snorkeling was much more enjoyable when I didn't get salt water up my nose. I loved the variety of colors of the fish. One was almost a fluorescent purple with a bright orange tail. Many were adorned with bright yellow or blue, or were covered with stripes and spots. I longed to identify all the many varieties. Because we floated in the water for extended periods, we were always careful to wear a T-shirt so that our backs did not become sunburned.

We also took in a local baseball game that must have had most of the island's population in attendance. The excitement in the crowd was palpable.

"These guys are really good," Fred said. "I sure wouldn't want to play against them."

"The crowd is really getting into it, too. I think the local rum adds to the enthusiasm."

A whole day was spent on preparing the charts and GPS for our next leg to Guanaja, Honduras, located in the Bay Islands. Needing a break from the paper work, we took the dinghy to town and tried to phone Page and Mom. More frustration. It took us two and a half hours. We knew that people at home had no concept of the difficulty and time it often took to make a phone call. Lines were busy, operators spoke no English, disconnects were common, and phones were often in direct sun, or stuffy cubicles full of mosquitoes. We persevered and were pleased to hear that Steve would take over the rental management of our house, as the renters were again behind in payments. *What is it with renters?*

We were also thrilled to hear that Lance would possibly join us in the Bay Islands. He was a "ski bum" in Colorado and on his way to spend his summer in the winter snow/ski season of Chile. That boy surely got around. Dawn was worried about leaving Grandma when she moved to New York, but basically there were no disasters – and that was always good news to hear. We knew that as much as the family prayed for our safety, we were praying for theirs as well. *Gracias a Dios*!

Two
The Islands of Honduras

The sea conditions and wind were good as we began our passage to Guanaja. We expected to sail about two days and nights to reach the first island in the chain off the coast of Honduras. With the conditions so mild, I even got out my guitar and played for a while in the afternoon, something I rarely did in the wild Pacific. The second day, early in the morning, we cautiously approached a specific area in the sea, which was charted as a cay (a very low *isla* that had a protective reef all around it). But in this instance, *no* land mass showed above the water level. It just looked like all the rest of the ocean. We carefully watched the depth meter as we worked our way into position and when the depths dropped to 15-20 feet, we threw out the hook.

"Wow—this is unbelievable. We are *anchored* in the middle of the ocean! There's nothing but water for as far as I can see."

"This *is* weird," Fred agreed. "And it's so calm."

The wind blew strongly, but the reef surrounding the cay broke up the sea motion, and we bobbed quietly in incredibly clear and calm water. We had to pinch ourselves to know we weren't imagining it all. I had never anticipated something like this in our cruising dream. We spent the whole day resting, reading, having a good meal, and a good night's sleep. What a joy.

We struggled the following day to get the right sail combination for a strong wind, and finally we were sailing "wing on wing." The mainsail was on one side of the boat and the jib on the other, with the wind directly behind us. We were really zinging along, sometimes obtaining nine knots through the water. *Grace* made an exciting *swishing* sound as she surfed swiftly down the waves, slicing through the water in a rushing motion. Our bodies could feel the momentary thrust, as if we had "floor-boarded" a car's accelerator. It was exhilarating going so fast, but not a very relaxing ride, as often the boat would begin to yaw (turn) around in the trough of the waves. That was a dangerous situation that needed to be corrected immediately as there was the possibility of jibing, with the wind powerfully blowing the main sail from one side of the boat to the other. An accidental jibe created tremendous force on the mast, boom and main sail as it slammed across the boat, and the outcome was seldom pretty. It was definitely something we wanted to avoid.

The wind vane was not useful at holding a course when running downwind, and we had switched to using the electric auto-pilot. It too, had a difficult time holding the course. It made a loud grinding sort of noise trying to correct the constantly changing course, making it hard to sleep in the cabin, which was also incredibly hot and stuffy. We dared not open any hatches while underway. For us, having everything closed up tight was a standard safety precaution when at sea. Even with the hatches closed, there was always the fear of that occasional "spitter" wave that could spill over the bow and dump gallons of saltwater into the cabin through the open companionway. Such occasions just made life miserable.

On my watch that night, I spotted a ship coming too close to us. My "Ready Freddy" jumped up to help determine if we needed to change the sails, something that was difficult to do with the wing-on-wing configuration. Again, at 4:30 am, we needed to jibe the jib, which again took the both of us. There wasn't much sleep that night for either of us. We had done six overnight sails in the past 12 days, so we were ready for some "R & R" when we approached

The Settlement (a town's unique name) at Guanaja, Honduras. Fred climbed the mast steps to the spreaders to direct our entrance through the reef, and we anchored in calm water despite the strong wind blowing.

"Look," I said. "All the houses are built on stilts over the water."

"You're right. It looks like an island of houses and shops—all attached. And there's no vegetation."

When we took the dinghy to town, we discovered that there were no vehicles, nor were there any streets in this place— only wooden walkways that weaved and twisted in meandering paths around the buildings that stood ten feet above the water. The elevated buildings not only made the homes cooler, but also kept them away from many of the insects that hovered over the water.

"I'm not sure how to get back to our dinghy," I said after walking for some time. "It would really be easy to get lost with all these winding boardwalks."

"Yeah, and if we ask for directions, I'm not sure we can understand a response. The English some people speak has such a strange dialect."

The houses we looked into as we passed were small, simple, and crowded together, but everything appeared neat and clean. The friendly people were descendants of African slaves, had very black skin and smiled broadly when they greeted us. We discovered that the standard of living was higher here on the islands than that on the mainland of Honduras. Because of that, many folks had moved here from the mainland for better jobs, and those folks spoke Spanish.

We found a travel agency and tried to get information on airline connections for Lance, as well as connections for me to fly back for Dawn's graduation from the Delta flight attendant training school. Since we had missed her ASU graduation, we wanted one of us to attend this event.

"Good grief, but it's *cold*," I said through clenched teeth. "And wet!"

"Hang on, it's getting pretty rough. Don't want to have to come back for you if you get bounced overboard."

When we were ready to go back to our boat, we had stripped to our swimsuits, and put our clothes in the water-proof bag we had brought along. It was a good twenty minutes by dinghy to the anchorage, and the wind was now "on our nose" and blowing hard. Going into the wind and waves made for a wild and wet ride. I didn't need another reminder to hang onto the sides of the dinghy as we pounded up and down. Our teeth rattled. Our bodies shivered. The sea spray splashed everywhere. Despite the heat during the day, it was now early evening and much cooler. Once we were wet, the wind made us feel surprisingly cold. But being cold was better than having wet clothes. When clothes got wet with salt water, it took a good deal of fresh water, which was always in limited supply, to remove the salt. If the salt remained, the fabric was stiff and scratchy in the daytime, and it reabsorbed moisture from the air at night, feeling clammy and sticky. Ah—the joys of cruising.

The waters of the Bay Islands are reputed to have some of the best snorkeling and diving in the world. We were anxious to see for ourselves. Along with Doc and Susan from *Manotec*, another cruising couple that we had met in Cartagena, we made our way around to the north side of the island through a very challenging narrow canal. We found that neither our charts, nor our cruising guide notes were always accurate, so we learned to depend on a good deal of local knowledge. Visual input also helped, but that was difficult to obtain if it was cloudy, raining or the sun was in our eyes. At those times, there was a definite "flair" to the adventure. Because of our swing keel, other boats always "graciously" allowed us to go first, while they followed (after we had determined the depths).

Slowly, we maneuvered our way through the restricted and uncharted waterway, and arrived safely to anchor along with one other sailboat in a lovely bay on the north shore of Guanaja. Gorgeous, clear turquoise water, soft white sand beaches, and gently swaying palm trees surrounded us and heralded our welcome to this island paradise.

"Well, it seems we've done our work for the day just by getting over here," Susan said on the radio, "so I guess we'd better get out there and start having *fun*."

We got the dinghies in the water, rode a short ways to a beach, and hiked about 45 minutes through dense jungle to a large waterfall that had a natural pool at its base. It was very hot and humid, and we were all sticky from sweat and the bug repellant that we had lavished all over ourselves. Jumping into the cool fresh water felt heavenly.

"It's too bad these islands have such an infamous reputation for bugs," said Susan when we prepared to return to the beach.

"Ah, yes. Paradise has one huge glitch," I responded. "Think of the money insect repellant companies must make here. If it weren't for those nasty little flying critters, this place would be an absolute delight."

We all had quickly developed the twice daily routine of "gooping up" with lots of repellant. We had seen tourists walking around with dozens of red circles on their legs and arms. We even had a few of our own. The no-see-ums, a type of flying sand flea, were the worst, and we thought that they were likely the reason there weren't more resorts and tourists here. Many of the nicer resorts raked their beaches daily to prevent the eggs, which were buried in the sand, from hatching. It was a constant "war of the insects," and they were winning. Fred was apparently not so attractive to the pesky critters, but they came to me like bees to honey. Although they were very tiny, their bite caused itching that lasted for many days or even weeks. In a local dive resort, we talked with a bartender about the spray we saw their clients using. He shared the recipe—one part water, one part DEET, and one part Avon "Skin So Soft" oil.

"Oh shoot," I groaned. "I've got the 'Skin So Soft,' but no DEET."

"Here," he said as he reached under the counter and handed me a bottle of it. An angel unaware. There are so many nice people in this world.

Snorkeling was everything we had heard it to be. The reef was often right by our boat, and we could hardly take in all the underwater delights. Before setting out on this dream adventure, I had been squeamish about swimming in places where there were lots of fish. I had never thought I would actually *enjoy* swimming in an aquarium, but that was just what it felt like. We swam every day, sometimes two or three times a day. We occasionally used our full body Lycra suits, and other times just swam with a T-shirt over our swimsuits. The water was so clear, that we could see underwater for great distances. Large schools of fish were everywhere. In one school they were all bright blue. There were *millions* of them. A unique fish had what looked like a huge eye near its tail. It made me think of the butterfly we saw in Costa Rica. It had a similar design on its wing. Should a predator attack, they would aim for the "eye" and the fish, or butterfly would be protected. There were so many different shapes and sizes of fish, and many with brilliant neon-like colors. We marveled again about the artistry, complexity, and intricate designs of God's creations.

"Don't you want to get out your Scuba gear and do some diving?" I asked Fred.

"Why bother, when we can see so much just by snorkeling or free diving?"

There were sponges, sea anemones, sea horses, tube-worms, conch – you name it. One entire area was covered with greenish, brown or yellow elkhorn coral. It looked like a dumping ground for antlers. Brain coral and fan coral looked just like their names implied. Often the ocean currents had the delicate and colorful fan coral waving gently, as if by a soft breeze. Shadows often revealed larger fish hiding under rocks. As we swam along, absorbed by the sea, often the silence of the water was deafening. At other times I heard eerie sounding melodies in my head that I wished I could record as music. I was fascinated.

One day, we did haul out our Hooka system and scuba gear. The air compressor had two long hoses attached to it, and floated on a small circular inflatable raft in the water. Fred used one of the hoses and dove 30 feet under the water, while I used the other air hose, but remained on the surface. I had no certification for diving, but I was beginning to think I might like to take the classes. While on the surface of the water, I could tug gently on his air hose if I needed his attention, or could, in theory, pull him up if there was a problem. He generally did not dive alone, as it was not a safe practice, so we did this only rarely. It was fun to watch all his air bubbles float upwards – there were hundreds of them in all different sizes. With the water so clear, I could easily see every detail of him many feet below me.

What's that? I thought, suddenly alert and tense. *Good grief! There's a diver right beneath me. He's coming toward me.* A moment later I laughed (a difficult thing to do with a regulator in your mouth) when I realized that the diver coming up was *me!* I had been watching my own reflection in the convex surface of an air bubble as it floated to the surface. The higher the bubble rose, the bigger the image became. It was as clear as looking into a mirror. Such wonders of the deep (and of the imagination).

When snorkeling, the fish seemed unafraid of us human forms, but they always moved away as I reached out my hand to touch them, or if I swam too close. But when I saw what appeared to be a five-foot long barracuda, I noticed that he didn't scamper away. He just sat there watching me. I hurried to get Fred's attention, but by the time I did, the fish was gone. *Had it really been there?*

Days passed quickly with all the water entertainment, and the usual social opportunities with other cruisers and people we met ashore. We talked to several European cruisers, but the number of boats in this port was less than in many of the other countries we had visited. One couple was leaving to go back to the States, where they had to sell their boat and go back to work.

"Do you think we'll sell *Grace* when we get home?" I wondered out loud to Fred later that night.

"*Sell* her? Sell *Grace*? Do you think we could *sell* one of our *family*? After all she has done for us?"

And he read aloud our favorite verse from that cherished and familiar hymn, which was written on a plaque that hung on the wall of our cabin:

"Through many dangers, toils and snares
I have already come.
'Tis Grace that's brought me safe thus far,
And Grace will see me home."

From "Amazing Grace"—An American Folk Melody

I never asked that question again.

When we sailed on to the island of Roatan, only fifteen miles away, we again rejoiced in being able to raise the sails as we had done virtually everywhere in the Caribbean. No more of the motor-sailing that was so prevalent in the Pacific, where the winds were inconsistent. Here they were strong and predictable. We had used the engine only to get in and out of a harbor.

We were also pleased about becoming increasingly confidant in our ability to enter into an island's lagoon when coming from the sea. With each passage, we knew more about what to look for as we approached the cut in the reef. Fred would put on his water/reef shoes or aqua socks to climb the mast to the spreaders where he could see through the water and watch for the rocks and coral. From there, he would yell directions to me, steering at the wheel, as we motored through the cut. It made me dizzy to look up and see him clinging on to the mast high above me, rocking great distances from one side to the other as the boat rolled in the ocean swells.

"Hold on tight," I often yelled to him—as if he needed to be reminded.

Shortly after arriving in a Roatan anchorage, we were approached by a fishing boat with two men selling lobsters. At first they asked twenty dollars for three lobsters, but when we were reluctant, they said ten dollars and a jar of peanut butter was fine. Yum. There'd be good eating tonight. The snorkeling was disappointing—mostly rocks and grass, so we moved on to another anchorage. I loved the short hops that required no overnight sail, and the islands of Honduras afforded many of these.

Exploring another anchorage by dinghy, we found a little beach, complete with a stake for opening coconuts. We had learned the trick for opening them, but hadn't yet found the secret for getting into the conch shells.

Coming back to the boat in the dinghy, we went aground, and after some frustrating minutes, ended up in a heated discussion (disagreement) about working together. Being together constantly, often in trying circumstances and having different ways of approaching problems or situations, sometimes led to friction between the two of us. Despite our compatibility, we were only human. Fortunately, these times were infrequent, and the "discussions" seemed to clear the air. We knew that because of our confined physical space, we needed to resolve or table these issues fairly quickly, as tight quarters were not good for festering emotions. Fred had occasionally offered to drag me in the dinghy and let out lots of line so I could have my space, but so far, I hadn't taken him up on the invitation.

It helped in times like these, to wrap up the discussion by trying to focus on what we could *each* do differently in the future, to avoid repeating the problem. That turned our focus to something positive, rather than negative. It sometimes surprised me that even after thirty plus years together, a marriage required constant work in order to maintain a healthy relationship. At one time, I had hoped we'd finally get to the point where we had covered all the hard stuff, and could just coast along. *Ain't gonna happen.* I now realized that besides our ongoing efforts, it also took a lot of grace for two people to live together harmoniously on a small boat—or anywhere else for that matter.

Back at the boat, I got things ready for dinner. I wanted to make a nice peace offering. Fortunately, it was leftovers—two big juicy lobsters. Life is tough—but somebody had to eat them.

We were anxious to do more snorkeling in these incredible waters, so the following day we motored around the lagoon in the dinghy looking for a good place. A dive boat was anchored at the far end, and we stopped to talk with a person on board.

"Why don't you tie up to us?" said Wayne, a laid-back Texan who was the owner of the boat and a nearby dive resort. "There's a good reef just a few yards north of here."

It was a good idea. Anchoring the dinghy was sometimes a problem, as we did not want to injure or kill the coral, since it was a living organism. Finding a buoy or something to tie onto was a better option.

"What do you think?" I asked Fred after we surfaced from exploring the underwater area.

"Well, it was good, but not as good as at Guanaja."

"I agree, but I'm glad Wayne told us about the remains of that pirate ship. That was cool. I wanted to dive down to look for hidden treasure."

Getting back into the dinghy from the water was always a problem for me, as it required significant upper body strength. Our dinghy had semi-rigid sides, which made it more difficult to climb aboard than the inflatable boats. Fred had made a loop in a line we dangled in the water, and we could step into it to help leverage ourselves up and over the side. Even so, I made many attempts before I managed to throw, wheedle and roll myself inside, often nearly tipping the dinghy over in the process. I felt rather like a beached whale at the time, and probably looked like one as well. Needless to say, it was not an elegant or graceful maneuver.

Sailing on to the next anchorage on the island of Roatan a couple of days later, we struggled to find the pass from the sea into the lagoon. We slowly motored back and forth, unable to detect the underwater cut in the reef. The cut was the only place that allowed a boat to enter. But going slowly also allowed the ocean waves to roll us significantly from side to side, making it difficult to stand up or hold onto the binoculars. It also made us feel "queasy" when looking through the glasses for very long. We were becoming increasingly frustrated when we heard a voice on the radio.

"Amazing Grace, Amazing Grace. Go north 50 feet, then turn east."

We didn't know who was calling us, but Fred climbed the mast, followed the instructions and found the cut into the lagoon. Going through it, we tried to maintain some speed so that the waves wouldn't knock us out of the channel, as the swells were significant. But going faster meant increased risk as well. I was at the wheel, while Fred was giving directions from above. My heart was racing and my stomach was in knots. *Where was that confidence we thought we had gained?* The water immediately flattened out as soon as we were through and into the lagoon, and I began to relax. After anchoring, we took the dinghy over to a dive resort, and discovered that it was Wayne's place, and it was he who had seen us in the ocean and directed us in. He had only one other guest at the time, so the three men decided to go scuba diving the following day. On the way back to our boat, we stopped to tour the little town in the lagoon, with its houses all on stilts at the edge of the bay. Everyone traveled by motorboats or dugout canoes. They were very friendly and would wave to us from their homes or boats. We saw children playing and swimming in the clear water despite the fact that the toilets in the houses nearby emptied directly into the bay. Stopping at a store, we found almost no fresh produce, as everything had to be brought over to the islands from the mainland.

Fred enjoyed the dive the following day, and was especially thrilled with "the wall" of the reef. The men had been diving in about 30 feet of water when the ocean floor suddenly dropped down several hundred feet. He told me that descending down the wall, or cliff, to about 60 feet and not being able to see the bottom far below, had his heart pounding, and he was using lots of air from his tanks. He was thrilled with the experience and decided to take me to snorkel the area the following day.

"Wow—that was breathtaking! When the bottom dropped away, at first I thought I was going to fall. Then it felt like I was *flying*. What an incredible sensation. You couldn't even see the ocean floor. It was like looking into a deep, dark blue abyss. It must be something like looking into outer space from the moon. And the colors of the reef as it descended into the deep. Those brilliant purples, pinks, yellows—all fading to only remnants of light and then the dark *nothingness*. Amazing!"

"Think about what must be deep down in those waters. It's a whole different world, and one that we still don't know much about. You're right. It is amazing."

We joined Wayne and Skip that night at the dive resort. I had enjoyed the chance to gussy up a bit as a change from our usual attire of swimsuits or T-shirts and shorts.

"Hey, Kay. You clean up real good!" said Skip with a slow Texan drawl and a whistle.

"How many times have I told you?" rebuked Wayne playfully. "That's no way to talk to a lady."

We all had a good laugh, put on aprons, and went into the kitchen to cook up a terrific Texas dinner of blackened chicken with seafood sauce. It was a real treat.

The weather was changing. One night we had no wind at all. The next, we had gale force winds. We heard thunder and awoke to rain that lasted for two hours. In the morning, I sat on my favorite perch at the inside nav (navigation) station, turned on the windshield wiper and looked out the water streaked windows at the dull, grey scene.

"Oh. It looks so familiar."

I was filled with nostalgia for Oregon. The rain also made it feel wonderfully cooler; a welcome respite from the constant heat and humidity. Rain at night, however, was not always so welcome. Since I slept closest to the hatch in our aft stateroom, when it rained I jumped up to quickly take down the large nylon wind-scoop which funneled air into the cabin and was desperately needed for air flow. Then I closed the hatches. That meant that I got up again to open them and haul the wind-scoop back up when the shower was over as it was stifling in the cabin with the hatches closed. With several showers each night in the rainy season, I was up and down, closing and opening, pulling up or taking down—not always with a smile on my face. No rest for the weary—or is it the *wicked*?

"Yippee Skippee," I cried after reading a fax we had received. "Lance is coming next week for sure. He's decided to take a side-trip and join us for a couple of weeks on his way to Chile for their ski season."

What have we taught our children? Dawn had moved to New York to work for Delta, Page was in Baker, Oregon doing a rural medicine rotation, Lance was going to South America, and we were in Central America. We were spread out all over the globe. We had found that faxes were often a better form of communicating with family than phone calls, although I missed hearing the sound of their voices. With a fax, we didn't have to worry if the kids were home, or if we had bad connections. It made life a little easier. Easy was nice. We saw that Lance planned to bring several snowboards and hoped that he could sell them in Chile.

"So he'll be traveling *light* again," Fred said with a chuckle.

We were glad that we had made a reservation at the French Harbour Yacht Club, as they had only seven slips available for transients. With all of Lance's gear aboard, it would be much easier to be at a dock where we could simply step off the boat, rather than the necessity of taking the dinghy to shore. We got ready to make the short sail over to French Harbour.

"Wouldn't you know," I complained. "Just when we need the sun, here comes the rain."

We were ready to come into the harbor from the sea, but with the torrential rain squall the visibility was now *zero*. We motored around in the ocean for almost an hour waiting for the rain to stop before we felt comfortable attempting the tricky entrance. Once inside, we motored to the yacht club. It was nothing like facilities in the States. It consisted of a little palapa building, and a small wood dock that held only a few boats. But it had a friendly staff, and good security. After we tied up, we decided to splurge and spend the extra two dollars a day to hook up to cable television. *English* speaking cable television. We stayed up half the night watching movies. One would think we had never in our lives seen TV.

The week passed quickly. One day we took a tour of Roatan by public bus and *collectivo* (mini-van) all the way to West End, an area that had the ambiance of a laid-back Hawaii. There were the usual souvenir stalls, restaurants, dive shops, and resorts. But unique to the these islands were the individual piers along the beach that led to small, covered, open gazebos that stood on stilts above the ocean water. These little structures were like mini-oases, and seemed the perfect symbol of the Caribbean charm and lifestyle. Their image could have been a travel poster for the islands. As you gazed at them standing out over the water, you could see behind them the billowy white clouds that floated in the brilliant blue sky over the incredible multi-hued turquoise water. The color of the sea was so different from the deep blue of the Pacific. The *palapa* roof of the gazebo provided welcome shade and relief from the bright sunshine that danced on the incoming waves. Here the ocean breeze cooled warm bodies and the structure's height minimized the invasion of those pesky insects. Hammocks beckoned from these places of refuge, enticing one to lazy hours of reading and naps that were the island's specialty. *Ah!*

No one seemed to get too excited or be in a hurry on this island. When we tried to get some stamps at the Post Office, we had to wait many minutes for someone to come to the service window, and even when they did, it was another few minutes before they asked what we needed in a slow, relaxed drawl. We had been told that three people were hired to do the work of one, so no one had much to do. Their pay was also so low that no one had any incentive to do more. But everybody had a job. Perhaps that was better than the U.S. system of welfare that was so demeaning to one's dignity.

Another day, we took the dinghy over to the elegant Fantasy Island Resort, the site of the popular TV program. They gave us permission to use the facilities, and we enjoyed the pool and *palapas* on a lovely groomed beach. It was a perfect place to lie on a lounge chair in the shade and read a book, and we did just that. On the way home we stopped at a well-stocked supermarket.

"Wow. Look at that. Heineken beer for 75% off the regular price. How can they do that? Let's get a bunch."

I loaded up our shopping cart and went to the check-out counter, delighted with our "find."

"Good price, eh?" said a store employee as we waited our turn to check out. "It has some sediment in the bottles, but it still tastes fine."

We looked more carefully at our "find." Upon seeing the little particles in the bottom of the bottles, we decided to return most of it to the shelves, and try just a few. I thought we could strain it, and the man said it tasted OK, but it had lost some of its appeal. But even in Central America I enjoyed a good bargain.

Along with relaxation, there was also lots of work to do—always. Finally, we had most of the necessary projects done and went to meet Lance at the airport. A small shack-like building sat in the middle of a sun-baked field that was devoid of any vegetation. We looked around for a place to wait that provided some shade from the sweltering sun. We started to worry when he wasn't on the scheduled flight, but we were assured that it was *no problema*. Fifteen minutes later another plane arrived at the little dirt covered airstrip, and there he was. It was easy to spot the "kid" with the long, platinum blond ponytail blowing in the wind. I couldn't get enough hugs.

"Bummer," he said, walking back to where we hunkered in the shade. "The bag with all my snowboards in it wasn't on the plane. They said it was *no problema* and would be on the next plane from the mainland."

We waited for three more flights, but still no bag. *Oh me*. He had *six* snowboards in that bag. We were assured that it would be there the next morning, and although Lance was upset, he handled it well and we returned to the yacht club. Our plan for his visit was to spend some time in the islands and then fly back to mainland Honduras with him. There we would meet Doc and Susan and all tour the Mayan ruins at Copan. Friends had told us that they were sensational to see.

"Hooray," Fred said the following morning after the club was notified that the luggage had arrived. He and Lance went to the airport to get it. Since Lance would be spending three months in Chile and hoped to find some work there, he wanted to improve his Spanish while he was here with us. We spent several hours studying almost every day, alternating with snorkeling, beach trips and public bus tours. He too, was mesmerized with the cable television, as he had no TV in Colorado. His living conditions there could well be described as "minimalistic." His bedroom was a closet with a sleeping bag on the floor. But his rent was cheap, he was having a good time, and that was fine with him.

The weather was still unsettled, often with 30 knot winds at night. Friends who were anchored in the lagoon, had drug anchor during those winds and had a difficult time getting the hook reset. We were glad to be at the dock. We thought it wise to delay our trip over to some neighboring islands and instead went by dinghy to the Fantasy Island Resort. Walking around the carefully manicured grounds, we found a gift shop that sold diving gear. Fred helped me select a new snorkel mask that fit properly and we went to the pool to try it out.

"Ah," Lance said as he fell into the pool with a funny grin on his face. "At last!" Luxury did have its place.

"Ah," I said. "No more water leaking in my face mask."

We spent a relaxing afternoon in the pool and swaying in hammocks under palm trees in the refreshing ocean breeze. Lance was again having a difficult time adjusting to the heat after the cool mountain air of Colorado. Unlike when he came to sail with us in Mexico, this time at least he had an idea of what to expect.

Lance has to work for a cool drink of coconut water.

When the boat was stationary at anchor or at a dock, we made considerable effort to keep things cooler. We attached shades to the outside of the boat windows, hung large nylon wind-scoops to bring air into the cabin through the hatches, and used multiple fans. We adjusted large awnings that we would attach to our cockpit bimini, and hung another awning over the bow area to keep the sun's rays off the deck of the boat. We may have looked a little like gypsies, but all these things helped cool the boat considerably. It was not so hot in the hammocks on the beach, and we all enjoyed the time of relaxation.

When the wind began to blow in earnest, we reluctantly began the several mile trip for home. The dinghy bounced roughly as we sped along and we got soaked from the spray of the waves caused by going into the wind, which had strengthened significantly.

"This is crazy," Lance laughed. He shook water off of his face and wiped his eyes. "I'm beginning to think you guys are *masochists*."

"Heck no," Fred grinned. "We're just *cruisers*."

At last the winds moderated and we left with *Manotec* for a 25 mile sail to Cayos Cochinos. It was difficult to stow all of Lance's gear, but we were glad we did, for the seas were lumpy and we bounced around for the first couple of hours. Everything not put away would have been tossed about the cabin. Then *Grace* caught a good wind, the seas flattened out, and we zinged along under clear blue skies and sparkling sunlight that reflected on the clear, Caribbean water. The boat had a gentle heel (tilt), the sails were filled and pulling well, and we slipped through the water effortlessly with only the sound of the hull slicing through the waves. Lance was loving it and *Grace* was too—she was doing what she was made to do.

"Hey, we're going to pass *Manotec*," Lance yelled. "Come on—let's race them."

"Son, don't you realize that *whenever* two sailboats are going in the same direction it's *always* a race."

"Hey, it's *Miller Time*," Lance announced after we dropped the hook in a lovely bay.

"Glad to hear you haven't forgotten our 'end of passage' tradition," Fred replied.

While enjoying our cold beer, we bought some lobster from a local fisherman who had paddled out to the boat. Lance had practically drooled when I asked him if he wanted some. A colorful and serene sunset filled the western sky with a kaleidoscope of colors while we ate a yummy dinner in the cockpit. It capped off a fun day of sailing. Lance was wilting a bit from the heat, saying he was ready for more *snow*, and I was frustrated with all the infernal flies we had brought with us from French Harbour, so we all went to bed early. I was almost asleep when I heard a loud slapping sound, and Lance yelled from the bow cabin.

"Hot dog. I win the prize. I got *three* of them with one blow!"

Snorkeling continued to astound all of us. One time we saw a small ray, about four feet long, gliding along the bottom of the bay. Another time we saw a piccolo—a fish that looked like a straightened Sea Horse. There were fish of every size, shape and color. We took the dinghy to several small islands, some of which had very primitive villages with no electricity or plumbing.

Going ashore was like entering a time warp, venturing into a culture of a hundred years ago. The homes, which were often little more than shelters, used an open wood fire for cooking, and were built of bamboo and thatch. The people stored rainwater for drinking, and washed in the ocean. But one significant difference from the past century—all the islands had Coca Cola. We bought three bottles, but it was warm, so it was not very refreshing to drink.

When we pulled our dinghy up onto a small beach at one little island, several children came running over, excited to see us. As I bent to secure the dinghy, I heard some young voices behind me.

"Es feo," (It's ugly) one little boy said. I turned around to see them pointing to our dinghy.

"Feo? *Feo!*" I said with exaggerated indignation. Two young boys immediately huddled together, looked embarrassed, and pointed at each other.

"El lo dijo!" (He said it) they both said. We laughed—kids are the same all over the world.

The wind and waves were up as we returned to the French Harbour Yacht Club, so it was another roller coaster ride. Fortunately, it only lasted four to five hours. We had two more days of dinghy trips through mangrove tunnels, diving "the wall," going to Coco View dive resort for more snorkeling, and doing laundry so that Lance would have clean clothes to take to Chile. There was also the need to get the boat ready to leave it unattended for a few days in the protection of the yacht club while we all flew to San Pedro Sula on the mainland of Honduras. There we would rent a car to drive to Copan to see the Mayan ruins. While getting things ready, we were also listening to the ham radio.

"Hey, listen to this. This guy's talking about spending the hurricane season in the *Rio Dulce* in Guatemala," Fred said. "It's where we want to go and he thinks it's a really great place."

"Some of the cruising notes say that it 'swallows up' cruisers," I told Lance. "People go up the river for a month or two, and never come back. They just stay there."

We listened to the man talk for about an hour. The *Rio Dulce* was a popular place for boaters, and we were hoping Page and possibily Steve, could visit us there. There was good hurricane protection in the river, twenty miles inland from the ocean. There was also fresh water, dock service and just about anything one wanted or needed could be obtained. There were lots of social amenities and it was a secure place to leave the boat to do some inland travel. Sounded good to me.

When we got to the airport the next morning, after lugging Lance's heavy bags up the hill to catch a taxi, we found that they wouldn't let him on the same flight as ours, as he had an international ticket. His flight would not be leaving for several more hours.

"It's cool, Mom," said Lance. "I'll see if they can move me up in the schedule, and meet you in San Pedro Sula."

We left, and upon arriving on the mainland, found Susan and Doc and a place for Lance's bags to be locked in storage while we toured the ruins. Thinking we'd have to wait four to six hours for him to arrive, we were surprised to soon see him walking down the terminal hallway.

"I just kept going up to the counter and asking if I could get on the next flight," he laughed. "I think they got tired of me pestering them and finally let me go."

The five of us picked up our rental car and drove about three hours to Copan, and a small town adjacent to the ruins in a remote mountain valley. Our hotel room cost only ten dollars per night; however, the electricity went off all over town every night from seven to ten. Of course there was no air-conditioning during those hours either. There apparently wasn't enough power generated for all day use. We walked about the small town with its cobblestone streets and many tourist places and shops when there was no electricity. That brought risks. The children besieged us constantly, trying to sell their souvenirs and wouldn't take "no" for an answer. And because it was very dark, it was difficult to see the many large pot-holes in the road.

After a *tipico* breakfast the following morning, we drove to the ruins, sometimes called the "Athens of the Mayan world," and hired a guide. Copan was reputed to be the best preserved of all the Mayan cities. Walking around the Acropolis and the Great Plaza gave us a small idea of what life must have been like so long ago. In the huge ball court, we learned that the losing team lost more than just the game—they lost their lives. Large monoliths, called Stelae, recorded the history of this civilization, as did the designs on the huge Hieroglyphic Stairway. Many art carvings adorned the structures, and there were bloody stories about human sacrifice in the temples. My imagination was having a "hay day." A museum tour in the afternoon completed the exhausting day. We sat outside after dinner and talked by candlelight when the electricity went off.

Lance was such good company and put up with the four of us old folks with no complaint. How precious was our time with him. He patiently listened, and had good, thought-provoking ideas to add to our discussions about the history and culture of this area, including the recent problems with the Contras. He was especially sensitive to injustices and shallow materialism and we hoped he would put these values into action in his life.

We had one full day to explore a little of Honduras before we needed to return to the airport. Driving down many dirt roads, we found ourselves a little lost and close to the border of El Salvador.

"I give up," Lance announced. "Somebody else can be the navigator." We drove through a few small towns, avoiding as many of the gigantic pot-holes as possible.

"These people obviously don't see many tourists," Susan said. "Look at how they turn and stare at us."

A little boy came running up to the car, yelling, "*Los gringos! Los gringos!*"

"I feel like I'm a fish in a fishbowl," Fred remarked.

We continued on through lush, green rural areas, all enjoying the cool of the air-conditioned car. Finding a town with a nice *economico* hotel, Lance and I enjoyed practicing Spanish with the staff. No lessons from books today. Later that evening, during the normal power blackout, we spoke with a local man sitting on the balcony, trying to stay cool. He spoke Spanish so distinctly and slowly, that we found we could understand almost everything he said. He was full of disdain for the corrupt government of his country and believed that there would soon be a violent revolution to overthrow it. When we suggested that he run for office he said that he valued his life too much to run for a political position. And he wasn't kidding. It was a rare snapshot into one man's view of his country and we were almost giddy with excitement at being able to converse about so much in Spanish. *Ah.* Finally, the electricity was working again, and along with it—the air-conditioning.

"Are you all right, Dad?" Lance asked the next morning as we left for the airport. Fred had a tight grimace on his face, and was unusually quiet.

"It's just an upset stomach, but it kept me awake most of the night."

Instantly, my anxiety soared. Both Lance and I were concerned, as it was obvious that Fred was not feeling well. He hardly ever complained about his health. Always, the fear of a major medical problem loomed large for all cruisers, and for good reason. Fortunately, this turned out to be not such a time, for soon after Susan gave him some antacid tablets, he was feeling a little better. Lance had been prepared to abandon his trip to Chile rather than leave his dad if he was truly ill. *Keep those prayers a-comin' folks!* We sent Lance on his way to snow country and new adventures, sad to see him go, but happy for this time and opportunity in his life. We flew back to Roatan for more adventures of our own.

On the short flight back to the island, we reflected on this time with our youngest child.

"He's so easy to be around. He's really a neat young man."

"Spoken like a true parent," Fred laughed, "but I agree. And Susan and Doc said the same thing."

At one point someone had asked Lance how old he was. He had laughed and said, "I'm twenty-four, but when I'm on the boat, I'm thirteen." It was a difficult thing for us to give up the parenting role, even when our goal was to do just that. And sometimes, even now as adults, each of the kids seemed to want to be the "special" child again, and get the extra attention and "TLC" of a parent. I guess everyone likes to feel special. It was almost time to land, and we summed it up with an expression made often throughout the years—"We sure make good babies!" I think we were beginning to appreciate all three of them even more as adults as we lived out our cruising dream.

What in the world? I heard a blaring obnoxious sound and looked at the clock. It was 2:30 am and through the thinning fog of deep sleep, I began to realize that the awful noise I was hearing was from our boat alarm system. Looking over at Fred, I saw that he was still sleeping thanks to those doggone earplugs, so I jumped up and hurried to the cockpit. There was poor Ramon, the night guard at the yacht club, standing in our cockpit, totally flustered and looking scared to death. He was so apologetic and embarrassed, that I felt sorry for him. I struggled to understand his rapid and frantic Spanish. His body language told the story.

Apparently, he was making his rounds and saw our companionway door open. He had not realized that we had returned from our trip, and he had come aboard to investigate. As soon as he had stepped onto the floor of the cockpit where our alarm pad was placed under a rug, the device was activated. This system allowed us to keep the boat open for the essential airflow when we were aboard, while still maintaining security. I tried to reassure him that I understood and was grateful for his watchfulness while I ran around trying to turn off the screaming alarm signal. Fred finally heard the commotion and came sleepily out of our cabin, wondering what was up. While I preferred that the "night watchman" position for our crew was a "blue" job, I recalled my previous escapades with *banditos* and middle-of-the-night crises in Costa Rica and Panama. Thus I acknowledged that because of those darn earplugs, I was likely stuck for life with the title of *Grace's* personal "wah-chee-mahn."

The next day we made phone calls to Page and Dawn. We learned that Dawn would be leaving Atlanta for New York the same day as her graduation and that flight arrangements would be very difficult to arrange for me to come to Atlanta. She encouraged me not to come for the graduation exercise. *Oh no.* Not *again.*

"It's not that big of a deal, Mom," she had said. "I want you to come when we can have some time together."

I knew it wasn't like graduating from college, but it was still an exciting time in her life, and once again, we would miss it. I was in a real funk, until Page later assured us that she would be coming to Guatemala and gave us the day of her flight. *Oh, oh.* It was *soon.* We needed to get going if we wanted to be there when she arrived. It meant that we'd have to override that cruisers' "rule" about not setting a specific time to meet someone at a destination that lay ahead. Doing that often meant rushing and taking undue risks with weather and sea conditions in order to keep the schedule. Well, it wasn't good, but the deed was done. The heart had overruled the brain, and the "rule" was ignored.

We went to Coxen Hole to check out of the country, did a little laundry, made some spaghetti that would be easy to warm for dinner while underway, and were ready for what we hoped would be a two day sail to Guatemala. Our earlier plan to spend some time in the islands of Belize was postponed. *Rio Dulce*, here we come.

Three

From Oceans to Rivers

The seas were steep and rough, throwing the boat every which way. The waves were coming at us so frequently that we had no time to adjust to the feel of the motion of one wave before being hit by another. Occasionally, there was even the feeling of a split second abrupt halt in our forward motion as we moved through the water. At such times, a wave would come from an opposing direction and this would momentarily interrupt our progress. It was unsettling and made it difficult to keep our balance. White caps surrounded us, and the occasional "spitter" wave coming over the bow deck had us ducking under the spray cover in order to avoid an unwanted saltwater shower. If we were too slow in taking cover, the wave was often followed by a few expletives from the crew. Sometimes when we were in the cabin, we could hear what sounded like a huge sledgehammer pounding on the hull, as those errant forces pushed at us. *Grace* would groan at the onslaught and continue on her way. We did the same, only from us, the groans were more frequent.

Had we not wanted to meet Page in Guatemala City, we likely would have delayed this passage until more favorable conditions prevailed. While it was uncomfortable sailing, we felt it was not truly dangerous, and pressed on. We bounced along, with *Grace* often rolling way over on her side with the impact of the larger waves and we scrambled to grab hold of something to keep from falling or banging into the boat's structure or equipment. Thank goodness for all the handholds down in the cabin. We didn't enjoy being in the cabin, however, as it felt incredibly stuffy and oppressive with the hatches all closed up tight. We both tried to spend most of the time in the cockpit, going below only when we needed to use the bathroom, adjust the navigational equipment, or do some chart work.

Finally the wind settled down and turned to come from behind us. However, this had the effect of reducing the sensation of the air on our bodies, since we were moving in the same direction as the wind. That increased our awareness of the heat. No more cooling breeze. It was hot—*incredibly* hot. The expansive, blazing sky seemed to be filled with a fiery, white-hot sun. Standing in its direct rays felt like being in a sweltering oven that had been set on "broil." *Would it be like this up the Rio Dulce where there would be no cooling air from the ocean breeze?* It wasn't a pleasant thought to consider.

The erratic motion of the waves with the wind behind us also made it difficult for either the autopilot, or the wind vane to control the boat's direction of sail. Once again, we tried many combinations of the sails and adjusted the ship's course line in order to find something that improved our ride and speed.

"I just hope the wind doesn't get any stronger," I said. "Anything up to 20 knots is OK from this direction, but this stretch is known for those gale force winds."

"I don't like getting thrown off course so much. Let's try taking down the main and just sail with the jib."

I knew that was a wise choice, but I also knew that in doing that, our speed would likely decrease. I started to worry about reaching Guatemala in time to make it to the airport for Page's arrival. It was the exact situation we had always known to avoid, and here we were—smack in the middle of it. We had warned her that there was a possibility that weather or boat problems could prevent us from meeting her flight. Even though I knew she was a capable and intelligent adult and could adequately handle that possibility, in my "Mama Bear" mind she appeared about eight years old, with suitcase in hand, standing alone, stranded and vulnerable in a foreign land. I willed the boat to go faster, and was pleased to see our speed remain adequate, even with only the jib pulling.

Despite the rough motion, neither of us had any "queasies," for which we were grateful. But we weren't hungry either, so we decided to forego the prepared spaghetti dinner, and snacked on fruit and crackers. During the night when Fred was managing to sleep a little, I saw a freighter coming toward us. I plotted its course on the radar, and figured it would pass a safe distance off our starboard side. I turned from watching the navigational lights of the big ship, to plot our position on the chart. Glancing up a few minutes later, I was shocked to see that the freighter had made a sharp change in course direction, had closed on us considerably, and was now heading straight across our bow.

"*Fred,*" I yelled, "*Fred! We're* on a collision course with a freighter! It changed course right in front of us," I rushed to explain.

The ship was moving swiftly and now about a half mile in front of us. I ran to start the engine. Fred hurried to shake himself out from a deep sleep and be oriented to the situation while he turned on our deck lights to make us more visible to anyone on the huge vessel. We quickly adjusted the sail and altered our course to avoid a collision.

"Good grief," I said when the danger was past. "I don't think anybody on that ship was even looking around. They would have seen us if they were watching. I think we'd have collided if we hadn't done something."

"Look here," Fred said, studying the charts.

We saw a faint dotted line indicating a sharp change in the direction of the shipping lanes, right at our present position. Neither of us had noticed it before. The vessel had likely been on autopilot, which corrected the course electronically, rather than manually. Not all shipping lines are straight lines, even out in the ocean. And those freighters frequently didn't have someone watching the sea from the bridge. Another lesson learned, and one I didn't think we would soon forget. Once again, we were grateful for the prayers of loved ones, and the amazing grace of God that sustained us, despite our frailty and errors.

When dawn came, we put out our fishing lines. We weren't catching as many fish in the Caribbean as we had in the Pacific. With the water shallower and warmer, perhaps our lure was too close to the surface, but it was always fun to try. We enjoyed our morning coffee in the cockpit, and soon made a turn into the Bay of Honduras, and aimed for the little town of Livingston to check into Guatemala. The bar of the *Rio Dulce* (sweet river), is over a mile long, and the entrance channel through it is very shallow. Most boats wait for high tide to traverse this area, and we were approaching a low tide. To wait for high water would mean a delay of several hours.

"Once again, we go 'where the brave dare not go,'" I laughed. "That swing keel sure is a blessing."

We lowered the sail, started the engine, pumped the keel about half way up, and started across the bar.

"But it would sure help if the water was clearer, like it was in Honduras," Fred said. He was hand steering from the cockpit wheel. "This water is so muddy, you can't see through it. That's going to make it difficult to find and stay in the channel."

To complicate things further, a strong wind hit us on the beam, pushing us to the side and out of the channel. It was a tense ride, but we made it to the anchorage off of Livingston. One other sailboat was there. We saw that the boat was from Florida, and heard the couple angrily screaming at each other as they tried to anchor. We never did see them set their hook, and they finally moved off somewhere else. We'd recalled many stories about botched anchoring procedures and how they stressed a relationship. Fortunately, we had eliminated many of those problems by using hand signals to communicate. So far so good.

"Look. Here come the officials," I said, pointing to a motorboat coming our way. "Goodness. There are seven of them. I wonder if they all plan on coming aboard."

Indeed they did, and we squeezed into the main salon to complete the necessary paperwork. We were tired, very hot, and anxious to finish the entrance formalities and get going up the river. Other cruisers had warned us that the local Port Captain wanted a bribe or tip, and it appeared that they were all waiting for a beer or some other *regalo* (gift). We normally would have liked the opportunity to talk more with them, but we felt like we were being coerced, so we offered only water. After some awkward silence they left, looking rather grumpy. We set up our dinghy and took our completed papers into the official in town, but didn't tarry. It was *siesta* time, everything was closed, and the heat on the sun baked dirt streets was oppressive.

Back at the boat, we took the outboard engine off the dinghy and hauled it aboard by a pulley system on the radar pole. Then we brought the dinghy onto the bow deck, using a three-point lift and the spinacher halyard. After we had removed the seats and transom, and stowed them below, we could fold the hull so that it was flat, and stow it on the bow deck. This arrangement made it possible to easily move about the foredeck and also to use our inside steering station, as we had an unobstructed view from within the cabin. With the dinghy stowed, we were once again underway.

The scenery unfolded before us as we wound our way up the river and inland. It was so different than sailing in the sea where we often could see only water. Sometimes the foliage on either side of us reminded us of being in the Columbia River in Oregon, and other times it thickened and appeared as if it would swallow us in dark, dense jungle growth. In those areas, trees, bushes and heavy vines overhung the banks and it was impossible to see more than a foot or two beyond the waterline. The river was wide, and its current was moderate, so navigating and up-river progress was relatively easy. Unlike the Columbia River, many areas had no rocks or beaches visible along the shore. It was about twenty miles upriver to Mario's Marina where we hoped to obtain moorage. We had heard from other cruisers that it was a good place to stay and would also be a secure place to leave the boat for a trip home for our "vacation" in August.

"Look at those thatched-roof huts just beyond the riverbanks. They're almost hidden by the jungle growth. It looks like a picture from National Geographic. I read that the indigenous Mayan people around here live like they did a hundred years ago."

"Here come some of the locals in those dug-out canoes. They seem to go everywhere in them."

"They're the same kind of boats that we've seen elsewhere, but they're called *cayucos* here. With no roads, they must be the main form of transportation. The people sure are friendly," I said as I waved and smiled in response to the locals' greetings.

With little sleep the previous two nights, we were tired when starting to traverse the large lake, *El Golfete*. We decided to enter a small bay adjacent to the lake and spend the night. It sure felt good to drop the hook.

"I'm anxious to find out about transportation into Guatemala City and the airport."

We were savoring our "Miller Time" and relaxing after experiencing the stress of making it in time to meet Page. We were now close to the marina and had three days to spare.

"It's still a long way from Mario's to the airport. And I imagine Page might be a little nervous about coming after hearing about the attack on those two American women."

There had been some unfortunate acts of violence against some U.S. tourists in the remote highlands of Guatemala, and the U.S. State Department had issued travel warnings to avoid this country. There had been no problems along the *Rio Dulce* that we knew of, but we wanted Page to be with us. Fred used the ham radio to put through a phone patch and we were able to contact her to let her know we were in Guatemala. But we still had to make it to the airport, so we told her to go to a certain hotel if we didn't meet her flight. We both felt better afterwards.

It was only seven in the evening when we fell into bed—it wasn't even dark outside, but that didn't matter to us. In the quiet and calm surroundings, we were asleep in minutes.

During the night, I was up several times opening and closing hatches when a couple of big thunder, lightning and rainstorms passed over us. It was the beginning of the rainy season.

"I'm going out to put our lightning cable in the water," Fred said after moving much of our electronic gear away from the nav station, thus hoping to protect it from a lightning strike.

"Do you think that cable truly helps?"

"Who knows? It's supposed to ground the boat, and we haven't been hit by any lightning yet. It can't hurt."

We also had ordered special cables built into the hull of the boat when it was under construction in England, as grounding protection. It was just an extra precaution that we hoped would ultimately protect us. We had seen holes punctured in boats after being hit by lightning, and knew that all the electronics aboard had been "fried" by the strike. It wasn't a pretty sight or thought.

The rain returned the following morning and continued most of the day. All about us was a thick cloud of grey fog, so we decided that it was best to remain where we were another day and work to clean up the boat. We raised the main sail so the rain could wash off all the salt, just as it was doing on the decks. The rain made it feel so much cooler, that I felt rather domestic and made cinnamon sticky buns. It was unusual to be able to use the oven in the galley without creating unbearable heat.

It took only about three hours to arrive at the marina after pulling up the anchor the following morning. Several folks came out and helped us tie up—a type of "Med Moor" technique, but with the bow to the dock and the stern lines around some pilings in the water. We had to climb over the bow and stretchhh the legs to reach the dock, but it worked. The marina managers were "Brits," ex-cruisers, and wonderfully friendly. When they heard we were from Oregon, the manager came over and spoke quietly to me.

"We love the West Coast people! By the time they get here, they really know what they're doing."

We hooked up to the shore power and I immediately got out our new, large oscillating fan. We had burned out our first one after using it 24 hours a day in Cartagena.

"Come on," I called to Fred. "That pool sounds heavenly."

Besides the small pool, the marina also had hot shower facilities, although they were somewhat crude. We were also cautioned that if the door was left open at night, you might find a snake inside them. *Maybe I'll shower on the boat.* There was also a nice bar/restaurant on the dock, and a large *palapa* with cable TV that showed movies three nights a week. They also had potlucks two nights a week, and a swap meet on Saturdays. But it was hot! As we had feared, there wasn't much wind in the marina. However, after a quick dip in the pool, we felt refreshed. It felt strange not to see people that we knew, but we quickly met new folks. Many were from Texas and the southern U.S.

"Come to the potluck tonight," our neighbor said. "The restaurant supplies the meat, and everyone brings something else." *Cool. I think I'm going to like it here.*

Amazing Grace (far left) at Mario's Marina on the Rio Dulce.

"Here comes our water taxi," I yelled to Fred.

There were no roads, paths, or walkways in the area around the marina—only jungle, so the river was our highway when going anywhere. We boarded a large, open launch or *panga* style boat that held about ten people. It had an outboard engine and in about ten minutes we arrived at *Fronteras,* a small village. Climbing up from the riverside, we walked a dusty road about a block to board a "chicken bus." The old recycled school bus took us and at least 50 others and often numerous animals, about 30 minutes down a rocky dirt road to a wide, modern highway.

"Do you think this is the stop?" Fred said, bending to look out the window of the bus.

We were assured by a number of friendly locals that this, indeed, was our stop. We got off and waited by the side of the road for the large, modern *"Especial"* bus that would take us to Guatemala City. The trip would take about five and a half hours. We waved our arms when we saw a bus approaching, and sure enough, it stopped for us. Pleased that so far, things had been proceeding smoothly on our adventure to the capital and airport, we settled back and enjoyed the scenery as we wound up and over mountains, through verdant valleys, and finally into the huge city. One more step—we had to find the right city bus to the airport. *Ah.* Sweet success. There it was.

Seeing our first-born come through the customs area brought tears to my eyes. There were lots of hugs, sighs of relief, and excited chatter as we made our way to a nice hotel for the night—a budget splurge for a special occasion.

"Here's your mail," Page said when we were settled in the hotel. "I know how thrilled you are to get that."

She also had brought all the ingredients for a dinner she wanted to prepare for the two of us as a belated Mother's and Father's Day gift. What a Sweetheart. She really had grown into a terrific young woman, and we were so proud of her. She appreciated everything, even when there were some uncomfortable hurdles to overcome. *Where did she learn to be so sweet?*

"You know," I said. "This is the first time we have had you all to ourselves for any length of time, since Dawn was born."

"And I'm lovin' it," she replied with a grin.

We stopped at the huge Central Market in the heart of Guatemala City for a little shopping on our way to the bus station the next day. Hundreds of stalls, on several floors of the large old building, displayed everything imaginable. One complete floor was set aside just for food items—from huge burlap bags filled with herbs and grains, to barrels of fish and unplucked chickens hanging by their necks from hooks on a string. Colorful vegetables and fruits, many of which were not familiar to me, were artfully piled high on endless counters. We were especially interested in the floors that displayed the native handwork and weaving which were made with brilliant colors, including a deep, rich purple that was so typical of this area.

"Boy, these sales people don't take 'no' for an answer, do they?" Page groaned.

With so many stalls, all the owners were working hard to snag a potential customer, and it took some time to make our way down the narrow aisles. We couldn't ask "how much?" without a lengthy discussion developing, as the assertive folks would try to engage us in a bargaining process for the item. It was colorful, chaotic and noisy—not to mention *hot!* The long ride home on the bus wasn't much cooler, and poor Page was wilting as her body tried to acclimatize. She never complained, however, and made the best of each situation, even when we arrived in *Fronteras* and found that we had missed the last water-taxi of the evening that would allow us to get to the marina. *Oh my.* Fortunately, Fred was able to find a boat going downriver, and they agreed to give us a ride. A new experience—"hitch-boating."

We took it easy for a couple of days in order to help Page adjust to the heat, making quick dips in the pool at least four or five times each day. We also explored the area with the dinghy, and went to Casa Guatemala, a nearby orphanage located just across the river.

"Those children *engulfed* us," Fred said when we returned. "Each one wanted to talk with us or be picked up. It was overwhelming."

"Think how starved they must be for affection and attention," I added. "So many needs."

"I really enjoyed talking with that young physician from England," said Page. "I wonder if I'd ever consider doing something similar when I'm through with medical school."

"And she said so much of the donated medication and equipment that is sent to her really isn't helpful. Like laxatives! Can you imagine? In a country like Guatemala, that's the last thing she needs. And the things she really needs, she doesn't get."

"Yeah. I wonder if we could bring her a nebulizer and medication for it," I said. "It was heart wrenching to hear how she holds those little ones in her arms when they are having an asthmatic attack, and her frustration in having nothing available to treat them. And vitamins. She always needs vitamins. I bet we throw away a ton of those when they get outdated back home."

We began to make a plan of how we might be able to help. We had changed our planned dates for returning home in August, to returning with Page after she had told us that our renters were in the process of being evicted for non-payment. Steve said the place was in pretty rough shape and would need lots of work to make it ready to rent again. Silly me. I had thought that we had finally found some responsible renters. It looked like our "vacation" at home would be a lot of work *again*. But perhaps we could bring back some supplies for the orphanage when we returned to Guatemala.

"You know, sometimes it seems as if God has set a virtual 'smorgasbord of needs' before us in these countries," I said to Fred as we lay in bed that night. "There are so many."

"I know what you mean. The hard part is figuring out how, where and to what extent we can respond to them. And choosing which ones to help is probably the most difficult of all. We can't help them all."

It was not easy to fall asleep after trying to balance the awareness of our many blessings with what we felt were opportunities for grateful responses.

Page wanted to call her husband, Steve, one evening while we were attending a Happy Hour party in a neighboring village. We had not been able to get good reception on our ham radio for her to make a phone patch call from the boat.

"Well," said Fred, "there's only one phone booth for making long distance calls, and it's outside in a town square. It's only open for limited hours, and then only if there's electricity, but we can sure give it a try."

There was a long line of local folks waiting to use the phone when we got to the hot, dusty, mosquito infested square. Two hours later, Page finally got her turn to use the phone. After several frustrating attempts, she finally made contact with Steve.

"I said I'm yelling as loud as I can," shouted Page into the phone after he repeatedly asked her to talk louder.

Those waiting around the square smiled at the *gringos* and all the hollering going on. At least she was able to learn that he had been accepted into the College of Oriental Medicine where he had applied to enter in the fall. We were all pleased for him, and decided it was worth the hassle and long wait. And the itching.

"Tonight, you two sit back while I fix my special dinner," Page announced one evening.

She brought out all the goodies she had packed, including a wonderful bottle of Oregon wine. It made us remember the complete Thanksgiving dinner we had taken to her and Steve when they had lived in Japan. While we sat and talked with her, she cooked, but in the process she accidentally turned off the propane stove. As I went to relight the oven, I inadvertently upset the balance on the gimbaled stove (which swings back and forth in order for cooking pots to remain level when the boat is moving) causing several quarts of boiling water to spill. Fortunately for me, the water spilled toward the back of the stove, rather than going forward onto my face and body. Only the tops of my barefoot feet were dumped with the scalding water. Page and Fred raced to help me get them into ice water, which cooled the pain of the burns considerably.

"Maybe we should reconsider our trip to Tikal," Fred said when we had all settled down.

"That's right, Mom," Page said. "I'm not sure you'll be able to wear shoes."

"We'll worry about that if it happens," I replied. "Right now it's OK, and I can wear sandals for most it. I want to see those Mayan ruins. Everyone says they are incredible."

I took some medication for pain, and we continued to enjoy the wonderful meal Page had prepared. I went to bed that night, wondering if our touring plans would truly be possible, but oh so grateful that the burns were not worse. *Gracias a Dios*!

Because we intended to leave for the States with Page at the conclusion of our inland excursion and would not be returning to the boat before our departure, there was much to do to get everything ready for us to be gone for a month. We felt good about the attention *Grace* would get in the marina, as they provided a service of cleaning and airing out the boat, which helped prevent mildew formation. They also provided good security. Staff would observe the boat carefully to avoid any potential damage such as that created by a dysfunctional bilge pump. We packed bags not only for our tour around Guatemala, but also for our trip home.

The following morning, I was pleased to find that I was able to wear my sandals, so we loaded all our gear into the water-taxi and started out on our odyssey into the jungle to see the marvelous Mayan city of Tikal. To get there we took *seven* different modes of transportation—all in one day. The first leg was returning to Guatemala City. Riding the "chicken bus" from *Fronteras*, Page was sitting with Fred and another woman in the seat behind me, while I sat with two other folks. We all bounced on the hard seats while we rode down the rocky, pot-holed and dusty dirt road.

"Oh. *Oh*!" I heard Page say in a shaky voice just above a whisper. I turned to see her folding her arms tightly across her chest. "It *bit* me," she said.

I saw that the woman sitting next to her, had a duck in her arms, wrapped in a towel. It had not been evident when she sat down. The duck had poked its head out from under the towel, and given Page a little nip on the arm. It wasn't strong enough to harm, but sure enough to startle.

"Well, I guess we had it wrong. Instead of 'chicken buses,' from now on, we'll call them '*duck* buses,'" Fred said, and we all had a good laugh.

Arriving at the bus station in Guatemala City, we placed the luggage we were taking to the States into lockers, and again found the city bus to the airport. Upon arrival there, we boarded a large plane for a flight to the town of *Flores,* near the Tikal ruins. Then a mini-van took us into the town for the night, and another took us up into the jungle the following morning. There was one small, new hotel adjacent to the ruins, and we arranged for a room there for that night, before finding a guide that spoke English.

We spent a fascinating day touring this "grandest" of the ancient Mayan cities, established in 700 BC. What a civilization it must have been. Climbing to the top of the huge pyramidal Temple of the Great Jaguar, we surveyed the city and the verdant jungle canopy surrounding the site. That jungle constantly encroached upon the structures and threatened to again swallow up the city as it had done in the past. The dense green vegetation grew quickly in the intense heat and humidity, creating an organic barrier wall of tropical forest. The thick canopy cut out much of the sunlight to the tightly packed undergrowth, which hid myriads of animals, reptiles, birds and insects. It was formidable, to say the least.

By afternoon, my feet were beginning to hurt, and we returned to our hotel. Taking off my tennis shoes, I saw that the tops of my feet were covered with blisters. I decided to forego the late afternoon nature walk, but was content to lie in our cabin and listen to the musical orchestration of multitudes of tropical birds, and an occasional monkey, or was that a *gorilla?* Or maybe a *jaguar?*

"Oh, oh," Fred said. "This is not looking so good. No telling what little critters can come through this hole."

The hotel room windows had no glass, only screens, which

allowed needed ventilation. Fred took some tissue and stuffed the one inch hole he had seen in the screen, and we left for the restaurant that evening. Coming back in the dark, we hurried along the little path to our cabin, keenly watching for what must surely be menacing nighttime jungle life hiding only yards away, and waiting to pounce on their prey.

"Oh *no*," Fred said when we entered the room. Looking at the window screen, we saw that the tissue was gone, and the hole was now about four inches wide.

"What do you think did that?" I asked. Page and I looked at each other apprehensively.

"I have no idea, but we have about ten minutes to find it before the electricity goes off for the night," Fred groaned.

Once again, there was no electricity from 10 at night until 6 in the morning. We all began a furtive search under beds, behind dressers, in the bathroom, in the closet—anywhere we could think of, not knowing what we might find. Finally, Fred saw a five-inch long scorpion high up on the wall. He took off his shoe and climbed up on the bed.

"I don't know if this is the culprit, but I know I'm only going to have once chance to get it," he said. The clock showed we had two minutes of electricity left. Fortunately, his aim was true and we grabbed for our flashlights just as the lights went out. We gooped up with insect repellant and tried to sleep, but the uncertainty of what else might be in the room with us lingered. It was not a restful night.

When we returned to "Guate," as the locals called the capital, we picked up a rental car and drove to *Antigua*, the charming colonial city we had visited with Lance when we were on the Pacific side of Guatemala. Here there were cobblestone streets and buildings with charming old-style architecture, as well as clean and tidy homes. The cooler and less humid climate, and abundant shopping opportunities were such a contrast to the jungle setting of Tikal. Fred and I began to consider returning to this historical city later to attend a Spanish language school. There were dozens of schools here that used the immersion techniques. Students lived with a Guatemalan family and were encouraged to speak Spanish for the duration of their study. Many European college students came here for this experience.

We found a travel agency and purchased the plane tickets for our return to the States, but were disappointed to not be able to take the same flight as Page. After two busy days of exploring *Antigua,* we drove up into the highlands to see the famous market city of *Chichicástenango.*

"The market in this town is said to be the largest clothing, artisan and handicraft market in Central America and has been running continuously for over a 1000 years," Page said.

She was reading to us from our guidebook as we climbed the winding roads up into the mountains. As we gained elevation, we frequently saw stone terraced fields, looking like giant stair steps on the steep hillsides. Every inch of useable land was being cultivated.

"Look at all these folks hand-tilling the crops," I said. "They are all wearing their native dress, even in the fields. Such beautiful colors and fabrics." It was another "Kodak moment" and made us feel as if we'd stepped back in time.

The city and market were a huge tourist attraction, and we met some cruisers from England among the many visitors that wandered the streets. It was odd how we could spot like-minded souls in a crowd. They gave us some tips for shopping, and we got up early the next morning, ready to give "due diligence" to this historical extravaganza. Block after block spread out before us holding hundreds of stalls that sold wonderfully made handcrafts, masks, fabrics, serapes, bedspreads, beadwork—the list was unending. Walking through the myriads of aisles, the vivid colors bombarded our eyes. It seemed as though we were looking through a giant kaleidoscope. We tried to be discreet in taking pictures of the natives and asked their permission before doing so. Some believed the camera would capture their soul so objected to any photography.

"Look at that old woman," I said to Fred. "She'd make a terrific photo. I'll ask her if it's OK, and look at her lace tablecloths. You can take our picture."

I had no intention of buying one of her articles. But after taking her picture, the woman followed me for blocks. She continued to drop her price, going from 150 to 40 quetzals. I felt sorry for her, and finally bought one. She was a tenacious saleswoman.

Page too, bought a number of items and we were all exhausted from the negotiating process. I had given up on being able to buy a gorgeous purple wool embroidered fabric that I would love to have had for a bedspread. I had returned three times to the stall, but the owners wanted a good deal of money for it, and wouldn't reduce their price. We reluctantly started to leave the market, when I felt a tug on my sleeve, and looked down to see the young son of the stall owner. He had followed me for several blocks, and told me that they'd take my last offer. Yippee.

Fred and Kay shopping at an artisanal market.

On the largest square in the city, stood the Santa Tomas church, built in 1540. We were fascinated at the mixture of Roman Catholic and ancient Mayan rituals performed there, and watched the natives chant their prayers while swinging incense on the steps of the large stone structure. *So much to see; so little remaining energy.*

"Look at that sign in the window of that tavern," I said as we sat in the car, waiting for a road construction traffic delay. We were passing through a small town on the way to Lake Atitlan.

"That's funny. It says 'Free Beer Tomorrow,'" said Page. "And in English. Somebody has a sense of humor."

"Sounds like just the place for us," Fred said and pulled out of the traffic. As we sat and enjoyed a cold beer, we talked with the owner about the problem for tourism after the beating of the American women by the natives in a rural area not far from here. The village people thought that the Americans were stealing the native children and selling them for body parts for organ transplants.

"The indigenous in the highlands are very superstitious," he said. "They are very poor and their children are all they have, so they are fiercely protective. They are also ignorant and suspicious. It's best for now, that you stay in the popular tourist areas."

Hearing of the problem, we decided we needed to change some of our behavior. I loved to talk with the local children and compliment the parents on their precious little ones. But due to the current situation, we avoided any special attention to *all* the children. How sad. As we sat waiting two hours for the traffic delay to clear, we got a glimpse of *real* life in the highlands, not the image that was often projected in the popular resort areas.

"Life looks pretty basic here," Fred said, "and hard. Look at those men building the road with pickaxes. Those others are down on their knees placing one brick at a time."

"And the work in the fields is done by sickle or hand. No motorized equipment here."

By the time we arrived at Lake Atitlan, reported by some to be the most beautiful lake in the world, it was late afternoon. The deep, rich blue of the water reflected the cloudless sky in the clean and cool air at 5,000 feet elevation. Three dormant volcanoes towered over the lake. It was a perfect place for some relaxation. We found a lovely lakeside hotel that was a bit of a splurge on the budget; not at all like the usual sparse and basic room we used when traveling. What a delight to spend a couple of days absorbing the quiet surroundings before we needed to return to the bustling "Guate." We enjoyed the warmth of the sun in the daytime, and the cool of the evening which even allowed a fire in the fireplace of our hotel room.

"Page gets plenty of looks from the locals with that cute little figure. And that long blond hair is a real novelty in these parts," Fred said. "I think I better stay close by," he added with a grin. We watched her sunbathing by the lake.

"Now, Papa Bear. I think she can handle herself," I laughed. "Think of what she's done without our help. What an excellent physician she will be. It's fun to hear all her stories about medical school. She obviously wants to be a good doctor, but also to have more in her life. That seems to be such a good balance."

We were really enjoying our time with her. We shared our world of the past two years, and got a little caught up on hers. It was soon time to return our rental car in Guatemala City. Unfortunately, we later discovered that we had inadvertently left our camera in the glove box.

"Oh no," I moaned. "We had a whole roll of exposed film on that camera—36 of them. Finally, we remember to take some pictures and now we've lost them all. All those remarkable sites and people." Taking pictures was definitely not our forte.

"Well, we have lots of memories," Fred said and gave me a consoling hug.

The small inn where we stayed in the capital city, was in a very modern area close to the airport. Looking around us, we thought we could have been in any large city in the States. What a contrast to the highlands. Again it reminded us of the mixture of subcultures in every country, making generalizations impossible and misleading. Certainly here in Guatemala, we had seen the old and rugged as well as the new and sophisticated. Boarding the plane for our flight home to the U.S., we realized how ready we now were for the normal and familiar, and looked forward to seeing friends and loved ones. We were almost giddy with excitement as we anticipated our three-week "vacation" in Oregon.

Four

Variety in Guatemala

Our trip back to the States little resembled the "vacation" we had anticipated. When our flight from Guatemala City arrived in Dallas, Texas, we were startled when hearing our names paged on the airport speakers. We were immediately apprehensive. We soon learned in a phone call from Steve, that Chuck, Mom's husband, was in the hospital in intensive care. Despite several flight delays, Page and Steve were waiting for us when we arrived at the Portland airport. We had the use of Dawn's car to go directly to McMinnville, where Mom and Chuck lived in a retirement home. The next seven weeks were hectic and sad.

Chuck had struggled with medical problems for many months. We often felt relieved that they lived in a comprehensive health-care facility where he could receive care, and Mom could continue to be in her own apartment within the same building. Chuck gave up his long fight to survive a couple of weeks after we arrived home. It was bittersweet. We were glad that his ravaged body didn't suffer any longer, but there was also deep grief for those left with the loss. We were glad that God had called him home at a time when we were able to be with Mom.

It had been something we had often discussed while we were

on the boat—the illness or death of a loved one, and our being so far away. Perhaps we didn't need to worry so much about things we couldn't control. We were ever so grateful for this time of being in the right place at the right time. The airlines gave us an additional month before we needed to make our return trip to Guatemala, which was also a blessing. *Gracias a Dios.*

"This business of being a landlord sucks."

We were once again camping out in our vacant house and sleeping on a mattress on the floor. Long days were spent cleaning up, repairing, and trying to get our home and yard presentable to rent again.

"I agree, but that monthly check makes the cruising possible. I guess I'm not all that surprised that renters don't take very good care of a place, but I sure wish they'd make their payments."

"On the 'plus' side, it has given us a place to stay while we're here in Oregon, and we're close to Mom as well as Page and Steve," I said. "And Dawn is flying back from New York again. I love that her schedule allows her to spend time with us and she can fly back and forth for free."

We had also talked on the phone with Lance in Chile. He was living life "on the edge" as usual, but having a great time. Mom was doing well, and had lots of support and caring from the folks who lived in the retirement home. While we didn't get to see Fred's mom, we talked with her several times and she was doing well in Nebraska.

It was backbreaking work getting the yard in shape and the house cleaned up. Our efforts paid off however, and we found some renters before our return to *Grace.* Leaving for the boat was easier this time. If all went well, we hoped to return to Oregon for Christmas in just three more months. The plan made it ever so much easier for both my mom and I to say good-bye. We were anticipating "spending" those free Delta parent passes even before we got them.

After going over business details with Page and Steve, we left for the airport and our return to Guatemala.

"It feels like a *beginning* again, with the same sense of excitement and anticipation," I said to Fred. "I'm almost as giddy as we were when we started this journey."

We were savoring the perks of free drinks and a good meal on the international flight, knowing we'd soon be working hard on the boat.

"But there's not that same sense of anxiety about the *unknown*," he replied. "Sure, there's much ahead of us that's still unknown, but we have a much better idea of what we're getting into. It feels good."

While we were in the States, we were able to collect a large amount of vitamins from local pharmacies and a nebulizer machine with medication for it from our local hospital. We planned to take the supplies to the doctor at the Casa Guatemala orphanage. We had packed everything carefully in our luggage, but we were more than a little concerned about getting it all through customs. Would the officer believe that all those pills were truly vitamins? After disembarking from the plane in Guatemala City, we nervously headed for the custom inspection desk.

"Try to look normal," Fred said.

"You mean hot and weary?" I replied with a smile.

We pressed the "stop/go" button at the desk, and breathed a sigh of relief to see the green go-ahead light pop on. We were able to walk through without any inspection. Yippee Skippee!

After spending the night in Guatemala City, our innkeeper took us to the station to board the bus to *Fronteras*. As we relaxed on the big modern bus, we watched the countryside roll by and marveled at how different this country was from our own. We were amused to listen to the loud and animated chatter of three young Italian women sitting behind us. Finally, they implored the bus driver to stop so they could get off to go to the bathroom. Running into the bushes, one of the gals accidently stepped on a piece of glass and cut her foot. Blood was dripping all over and the girls were becoming hysterical, waving their arms about, and all yelling frantically at the same time. I got off, told them I was a nurse, and offered to clean and dress the wound. By then, almost all the passengers had come out to watch the proceedings.

"Boy, those Italians can talk fast," laughed Fred after we continued on our way.

"But they were grateful for our help. They're going to *Fronteras* too, and hope to catch a boat going downriver to Livingston," I replied. "It seems there's always some excitement somewhere."

After catching a water taxi and arriving back at Mario's Marina, we were thrilled to see our beautiful *Amazing Grace*. We were *home!* We loaded all our luggage and packages aboard and quickly changed into our "uniform" of shorts and T-shirt. Hearing some loud commotion coming from the dock by the restaurant, we walked over to see what it was all about.

"Look. It's the same three Italian women," I exclaimed, "and they're all wet."

Wet luggage was strewn all over the dock, and once again the young women were jumping about hysterically and yelling at a boatman they had apparently hired. His boat had sprung a leak after leaving *Fronteras* and nearly capsized, barely making it to the dock at Mario's. The girls were angry and demanding their money back, while wildly flailing their arms and shouting colorful invectives in Spanish, English, and Italian; all screaming at the same time.

"Why don't you just give them their money?" Fred yelled to the boatman, trying to make his voice heard above the vociferous complaints, general commotion and the rapidly increasing throng of spectators.

"I will," he said, "if they would just stop yelling."

"But they're *Italian*," Fred said with a laugh, "and besides, they've had a bad day."

Such was our welcome back to Guatemala.

Grace looked wonderful. The marina staff had opened the boat daily to air it out, and had her cleaned both inside and out. Our luggage and gear from home lay scattered about wherever we could find a place to put it. We needed to reorganize in order to stow everything that had been previously cleared out of the bow cabin to make room for Page and her things. It also seemed oppressively hot and humid.

"Thank goodness for that pool," I sighed after jumping in for the fourth time on the first day at the dock.

"It's going to take a little time to get used to the heat again," said Fred. "Let's not rush it. Just take it slowly."

There were several new boaters in the marina. We knew none of them, but had some mutual friends with a few. Many of those now here, were from Europe. There were always people visiting and sharing stories in the large *palapa* bar/restaurant/lounge at the end of the dock. It was rather like a clubhouse and meeting place. This was definitely a pleasant, social, safe and secure place to be on the river.

"I understand now, why it's said that the *Rio Dulce* swallows up cruisers," I said walking back to the boat after yet another dunk in the pool.

"True. Folks sure like to stay on here," Fred added. "With potlucks, swap meets, movie nights, Monday night football, races, karaoke, celebrations—there's always something going on. But a lot of the interaction is with other cruisers. There's not much exchange with the locals. I miss that part of cruising. There's still a lot of places for us to see. Especially if we are going on to Europe."

"Oh, I hate to give up the karaoke," I laughed.

Fred rolled his eyes and shook his head recalling my delight in singing until the wee hours of the morning. Listening to "wannabee" vocalists was definitely not his cup of tea.

Amongst all the socializing, there were always the chores—the maintenance and repair jobs that took so much of our time. Well, actually *Fred's* time for most of the "fix-it" projects. I was continually amazed to watch him tackle one problem after another, spend some time thinking it through, and with infinite patience, figure out a way to repair whatever was needed. Sometimes that took a lot of ingenuity, rubber bands and chewing gum (or so it seemed) but he got the job done. *How had we ever managed without duct tape?* We had brought a number of books along with us, and one or two had a wealth of information about fixing broken boat parts and systems. It was always a "Hallelujah" time when a project was completed and the "whatever" worked the way it was supposed to. I was not nearly as impressed with the mess he made as he tackled those tasks. He sometimes just threw things aside in a helter skelter manner, until it was almost impossible to walk the length of the boat. But I must say, he put it all back in place when he was done.

"Why the frown?" I said one morning as Fred hunched over our pedestal compass in the cockpit.

"This compass is leaking fluid, and I can't figure out a way to open it up. It likely needs a new membrane and the oil replaced."

"Why don't you ask on the 'net' to see if anyone has any ideas?" I timidly suggested.

I recalled the stereotype of how reluctant men are about asking for instructions, help or directions. The morning radio net was an exception and a great way to get information one needed about virtually anything. It was one of the ways cruisers helped other cruisers and nourished that strong bond of friendship and interdependence. With a vast variety of backgrounds available to draw from, there was a wealth of collective knowledge that was often put to good use. It was also an important safety factor, as information about navigation, weather, chart discrepancies, security measures, etc. was shared. Fred took my suggestion, discussed the problem on the net, and arranged to have another boater come over to help fix the compass. After all, that's what *family* is all about.

We talked again about our interest in attending a Spanish language school in *Antigua*. Perhaps the word "our" is misleading. It was primarily my desire; Fred was more or less going along for the ride. While he had taken a year of Spanish in college, he was quite content with my trying to communicate in Spanish when necessary, with my limited vocabulary, no grammar, and lots of pantomime. Since it was so easy, secure and inexpensive to leave the boat at Mario's, we decided to "go for it." We had gathered as much information as we could, and with a mixture of excitement and anxiety, planned to return once again to Guatemala City via the water taxi, chicken bus, and *Especial* bus. From there we'd go to *Antigua* via a city bus and commuter bus. You could go anywhere in Central America on a bus. Having been to the charming old city with Lance from the Pacific coast, and with Page from the Caribbean coast, we knew we'd enjoy the place. The Spanish school experience was an unknown.

"You know, quite a few folks who have been to the language schools were not very happy with the homes they stayed in," I said. "They said they were not much more than shacks, they only had rice and beans for dinner, no privacy, and had no place to just relax when they wanted."

"Yeah. And some were frustrated that no one would speak any English at the school or in the home. Sometimes they never could figure out what was being said," Fred replied.

We decided that since the school arranged the home stay, we'd ask for a family with whom we had a little something in common and an instructor for Fred that would occasionally speak English if necessary.

Bob, our friend from Holland, rode with us into the city. A severe toothache had bothered him for about a week, and his face was badly swollen. He hadn't slept for days. He'd managed to arrange an appointment with a dentist in Guatemala City, but dreaded the long ride to get there. He was grateful for the company and our help. I had shared some pain medication with him to enable him to sleep the night before we left. Two other cruisers were also very sick and the local doctors didn't know what was causing their illness. We were once again mindful of the great blessing of health and we, along with the entire cruising community, were concerned about Bob and the others.

Finally, after riding on all the different buses, we arrived in Antigua. For ten dollars, we spent the night in the same hotel we had stayed at previously and set out to find a school for us amongst the 50 to 60 located in the city. Hustlers on every street corner tried to get us to attend their respective schools. Of course they got a commission if we signed up so they were persistent salespersons and were reluctant to accept our "no thanks."

After talking to folks in six places we finally found a school which agreed to have an instructor for Fred who would speak English if necessary. They placed us with a family that consisted of a widowed mother about our age, and three adult children. One daughter worked in a bank. Since Fred had been a banker, that was our "something in common." We met the family and they were delightful, but spoke no English. Our bedroom was modestly furnished, but the home was charming, and built around a central courtyard. We shared a bathroom with two others. The house and family were obviously of a higher economic level than many of the homes for students. Three other students stayed in the home—one was Japanese, one was German, and another came from Portland, Oregon. Our lodging cost 50 dollars a week per person, and included three meals a day.

"Going back to US prices will really be hard after those in Guatemala," I said.

"Yeah. But let's hope that we have more than just beans and rice to eat," Fred replied.

We had one more day to move in and explore the city before classes started. We tried for some exercise by going for a run, but the cobblestone streets made the footing tricky.

"I love this rainy season," Fred said as we huffed and puffed our way up a hill. "It makes it so much cooler. And the rain doesn't last very long."

"And there's so little humidity. The cool mornings and evenings makes me think of home," I managed to say. "But we have really gotten out of shape. This running is hard work."

That night we attended an English speaking worship at a Catholic church. It was led by two nuns. The service was publicized as something for all Christian denominations.

"What a great experience," I said as we came out of the church afterwards. "It really was an inclusive ecumenical gathering—so spirit filled. Definitely a 'G.E.' (Guatemalan Experience) memory. I love it every time we discover that we have *family* in a different country."

"And when the power went off, it was even better when we finished by candlelight," Fred added. "But with no street lamps, I'm not sure where to go now."

We cautiously made our way back to our new home along the uneven cobblestones of the very dark unlit streets, hoping we would find and enter the right house.

"I feel just like a little girl on her first day of school," I said in Spanish at the breakfast table the next morning.

Everyone laughed. As on previous occasions when people laughed at my comments in Spanish, I wondered what it was that I had said, or if they had understood what I had intended to say.

Arriving at the school, Fred and I were each assigned a teacher that we met with in a small, private study room. There was one staff member for every student. For four hours each morning, we conversed in Spanish. Although we could also go for walks or sit in the park during this time, I liked the minimal distractions of the classroom and chose to spend my time there. Our instructors spoke slowly and distinctly and corrected our pronunciation or choice of words when necessary. I worried about the experience for Fred, but he reassured me at the break time that he was doing fine and liked his teacher. Both of our teachers were young women in their senior year at the university. We were "pumped" as we made the five-minute walk back to the house for lunch.

"Wow, this food is great," Fred exclaimed after dinner. "We are sure getting more than rice and beans." So much for hoping I'd lose a few pounds these two and a half weeks.

The goal of the immersion program was that we would speak only Spanish in the home and at school, but sometimes we five students would become "brain dead" after struggling for many hours with Spanish, and since we could all speak English, we'd lapse into that for awhile. It felt like a bit of a student rebellion in breaking the "rules." One night at the dinner table we were talking in English when someone had asked me about our kids.

"We only had one child at that time," I had responded. "Dawn was only a gleam in her father's eye."

"Let's hear you translate *that* into Spanish for our host family," our German friend had quickly challenged me with a laugh.

After many sputtering attempts, and lots of hand gestures, I saw the *senora* grin shyly and nod her head, and could only hope she had "got it" and that I had not offended. It was good for a laugh for the rest of the table. Humor can be difficult to translate.

Our time in Antigua passed quickly. Afternoons we spent walking about the town, visiting museums, playing basketball in the park or, for me, studying Spanish. The people of the community all spoke slowly and clearly, making it much easier to practice what we were learning. Our instructors were pleasant, educated young women, and it was interesting to learn about their lives and hopes. It surprised us then, that both would express belief in what we would call "old wife's tales" or superstitions. We sometimes struggled with what we learned about some of the vast differences in our cultures, things that were not readily apparent.

"It's hard to imagine that Sylvia really believes that babies are stolen, their hearts are cut out and the bodies returned to the parents with notes saying the body parts are being used for surgical transplants in the U.S.," I said one night to Fred. "She believes that if you have enough money you have the power to buy *anything*."

"That's apparently the way it works here," Fred replied. "They say that all the government officials and even the common people accept bribes for everything. They assume it's the same elsewhere. And they don't believe that Guatemala or most of Central America is a real democracy. Money is power. Those who have it are in control. It sure creates a feeling of hopelessness in a lot of the people."

"And a feeling that they are always the victim," I added. "Sylvia couldn't believe the power of the press in the U.S. I told her that it exposes much of the corruption there, and that everyday people do have power. Remember the woman who sued McDonald's for the burns she got from spilling her coffee? She couldn't believe anything like that was possible."

As we learned more about the people of Guatemala, we sometimes ached for them, and perhaps in different ways, they sometimes did for us.

Guatemala's Independence Day was only one week away and it was a national holiday and local celebration. One tradition leading up to the festivities, was to have students of different schools run from neighboring villages into Antigua's central plaza each day, with a lead runner carrying a torch. Fred and I thought it would be fun to take part with our school and had been training in earnest by running each morning before class. We thought it was to be about five to seven miles, but each time we asked someone about the distance, we got a different answer. A couple of miles here or there meant nothing to those who weren't running it. *No problema!*

"Hey. Slow down," I yelled as Fred ran up a hill.

"Gotta get in shape," he yelled back. "I don't want to be embarrassed by all those 20 to 30 year olds."

Most of the other folks at our school were college students from Europe. *Good grief.* He was the personification of competiveness. He was going to kill us both.

On the day of the run, about 25 of us piled into the back of one small pick-up truck, standing wherever we could find an inch or two of floor space.

"This is *crazy*," I laughed. "We're packed in here like sardines."

"Hang onto me," Fred said. "This guy is driving like he's in the Indie 500, and he's not slowing down on the curves. We might not have to worry about finishing the race—we'll be lucky if we make it to the starting place in one piece."

We entered a little village, everyone climbed off, someone lit the torch, and we all started back to the city. Fred was right out there in the front with all the "studs" but I couldn't keep up with their pace, and began to fall to the back of the pack. A truck followed to pick up those who were running out of steam.

"You want to ride?" a young man yelled down to me as I puffed my way along the dirt road.

"No thanks," I said and tried to smile. "You go on ahead."

I was determined to run the whole distance. The truck fell back and waited for me to chug along. Intermittent showers cooled off the sweltering body, which was by now soaked in sweat anyway. Occasionally the group stopped when the rain extinguished the flame, as they needed to relight the torch. At those times, I could catch up with the bulk of the runners who by now had greatly diminished in number. The truck was getting full again, and the passengers all looked happy and content to ride.

"Thank God for the rain," Fred gasped. "I need the breaks."

We all took turns carrying the torch, and people alongside the road clapped and yelled for us. Many were delighted to see the *extranjeros con torcha* (foreigners carrying the torch). It felt like we were in the Olympics. Finally, we wound our way around the town and into the plaza and stopped in front of our school. I didn't think I could go another inch and leaned on Fred, gasping and wheezing. When Fred and I walked inside, everyone stood and clapped and yelled for us. The owner of the school came over to congratulate us for finishing the race, and said to Fred, "*Su esposa—buen constitucion!*" I guess he had expected Fred to finish, but not me.

The day was not over, however. The school was having a dance in the evening, so we gratefully drank a cold *cervesa* and hurried home to shower and return.

Looking back, I think that the dancing did me in more than the running.

"I don't know how those folks can keep up with those fast Latin dances, one after another," I said on the way home. "That really takes stamina."

"But it sure was fun when they started playing the old rock and roll songs," Fred laughed. "They all liked the music, but weren't sure how to dance to it."

When we, along with a German couple, had started to do the

Twist and then swing dance, everybody stopped dancing to clap, whistle and watch us.

"It was good for laughs, but I am dripping in sweat," I laughed as well. "I'm glad we didn't stay very long. Anymore and I think I'd have collapsed. But we sure showed those young whippersnappers that we 'old folks' were still *cool*, didn't we?" I guess Fred wasn't the only one who was competitive.

So much was going on with the holiday celebration—fireworks, parades, music everywhere, folkloric dancing in the park, marimba bands, concession stands. It was a great peek into some of the historical culture of this colorful country. Other peeks were not as pleasant. It was not uncommon to see a man urinating in the street. One night we saw a man doing just that behind a car in the street. When we passed by he looked at us, smiled boldly and said a hearty, *"Buenas nochas!"*

We decided to forego the opportunity to climb the active volcano close to the city. It was continually erupting and created a spectacular light show at night. However, the trail was slippery with mud from the rain, and difficult to descend in the dark. Besides that, there were reports of frequent thefts of the tourists, even when they were being escorted by a guide. Maybe another time. Despite these incidents, we could easily have stayed a month in this charming city. We were so pleased with our improvement in understanding and speaking Spanish, but we were starting to feel a little "overdosed" and could hear *Grace* calling us to return. We said our goodbyes to our host family and new friends and made our way back to the huge and bustling Guatemala City.

"It's really beautiful," I said. "But it's so expensive."

"But it's an investment and I think it will bring us a lot of pleasure," Fred replied.

We were in a large modern gallery of an artist in Guatemala City. We had first seen his works at Lake Atitlan when we were there with Page. She had encouraged us to buy one of the unique paintings. They showed the traditional folkloric design of dress, but in a modern, heavily textured style. We made our selection, arranged to have the artwork and frame shipped to Page and Steve, and were assured that it would arrive safely. What wonderful memories it would bring us.

Before catching the bus for the long ride back to *Fronteras* and the *Rio Dulce*, we spent the night in a small hotel and went across the street to an inexpensive restaurant for some Chinese food. We were waiting for our meal when we heard some commotion and saw the restaurant owner grab a man who was obviously intoxicated and throw him out onto the sidewalk.

"Hey, look. The drunk's not going to leave. He's trying to come back inside," Fred said.

"Oh my goodness! The owner pulled out a gun."

I was more than a little alarmed. The confrontation lasted several more minutes. Everyone else in the diner seemed not the least bit interested in the drama unfolding, and just continued to eat and talk. Another peek into what was perhaps, "big city" Guatemalan culture.

"Wow," I said when we walked down the row of boats to where *Grace* was moored. "The river has really risen from all the rain. With this fixed dock, that's a *big* jump to get on the boat."

We found a crate to place on the dock next to the bow, stood on it and cautiously passed our gear and bodies across the intimidating span of river water in something akin to a gymnastic feat. While doing all of this, we were keenly aware that too many times in the past, we had sadly been reminded of that old sailor's warning: If it *can* fall into the water, it *will*. Fortunately, we beat the odds that day.

"Boy, does it ever feel good to be back home," Fred said.

"I'll say. But I'm sure going to miss having those three wonderful meals made and served to us each day."

It was not long after unpacking that we began to make plans for continuing the dream, leaving this river oasis on the *Rio Dulce*, and making our way north into Belize and the Yucatan of Mexico. As navigator, it meant many days of immersing myself in cruising notes, charts, books and articles about the waters and places we would soon be covering. Just learning the names and locations of the new places that lay ahead was daunting. It was too overwhelming to study and prepare for all the places we eventually wanted to go to, so we took one geographic segment at a time. Even so, I could feel the tension rising as I initially tried to get a handle on so much information. After a few hours, I began to get a general feel for Belize, had found the right charts, and was definitely making progress and feeling less stressed.

The waters of Belize are protected by the largest barrier reef in the western hemisphere, second in the world only to that in Australia. Traveling inside the reef required navigating in many shallow and coral filled areas. But it also provided opportunities to stop at numerous islands and cays and sail in calm, protected seas. Many sailboats felt the water was too shallow, and went out into the open ocean. Our boat, with its swing keel, was perfect for this kind of sailing. However, it was vital to have a good working knowledge of the area that we would be traversing.

"I'm more than a little worried about the rain we've been having lately. It's not just at night anymore. In a downpour, it would make it almost impossible to spot the coral heads when we are sailing in those shallow waters."

"Yeah. If we hit one when we're really moving, it would be dangerous," Fred replied. "It's probably why many boats don't try it inside the reef."

"You know, we are pushing it if we try to go north in October," I said one night. "Hurricane season lasts through November. What if one comes up when we're out on the banks in Belize? There'd be absolutely no protection out there."

"I agree it's a risk," Fred replied, "but I'll be watching on the weather fax for tropical storms and depressions that could become a hurricane. Those things don't spring up instantly. Hurricanes develop over time. We can learn of their coming and plot their course. If one looks like it will come our way, we'll find someplace to duck into."

It sounded simple, but we both knew that a good "hurricane hole" wasn't all that easy to find in many places and getting to a protected one could take some time.

"I know it's really a balancing act to head north between the close of hurricane season and the beginning of those infamous 'northers.' They start rolling down from the Gulf of Mexico as early as November, or even late October. I've heard lots of 'horror' stories of the seas they can create. It would also be so much worse when we would be going right into the wind and waves, rather than having them behind us. I definitely want to avoid an 'up close and personal' bout with that stuff." I was getting on a roll in my lament. "And the guide books are all written for folks coming from the Gulf and heading south. The currents and seas going north will be much more difficult."

"Hey, that's part of the adventure, right?" Fred said with a grin. I was not to get any sympathy that night.

The following morning I announced on the local net, a meeting for all those traveling north. We met in the palapa and everyone that attended shared a great deal of information. Those who lived in the south or southeastern parts of the U.S. had a lot of local knowledge of the areas where we would be going in the States, as well as Mexico, Belize and Cuba.

"All of the information was useful," I said later to Fred. "It's good to know about ports where it's easiest to check in and out of the countries, and especially, the places *not* to go."

All through our journey, we had learned that *local knowledge* was indeed precious and sometimes even conflicted with what we had read in books. While I prepared most of the navigational information, Fred continued to ready the boat. He found that it would cost about $100 to fix our compass. We could buy one cheaper than that in the states, but it would mean waiting some time for one to be delivered. We decided to go with the repair.

"So I guess we're not going to go to Cuba, right?" I had our charts laid out for that destination.

"Boy. It's a tough decision. I'd sure like to go, but we've heard so much feedback that makes it a very questionable stop."

We knew that it was against U.S. law to spend any money there. We had also heard from many cruisers that if they did have any significant interaction with the local people, it often meant that those Cubans were put in jeopardy with their government because of the contact. It was also extremely difficult to purchase any food or other items, as everything was bought with ration coupons. With a good deal of regret, I plotted a course bypassing Cuba.

Staying on the *Rio Dulce* was so pleasant and easy that it was sometimes difficult to think of leaving. Still, the lure of the unknown continued to beckon to us, although with ambivalent feelings.

"You know, this leg will likely take us back to the States," I said one night.

"I know. It's bittersweet, isn't it? Being out of our country has been such an adventure, but if we want to consider going on to Europe, we need to do that from the east coast of the U.S."

"Yeah, but we've learned so much not only *about*, but *from* the Latin American countries. I'm afraid we won't have similar experiences back in the States."

"Ah. But think of the *conveniences;* the familiar; the ease of contacting the kids and moms. And I'm sure there's a ton of things to learn about our own country by spending some time on the east coast. We've only known the west coast from the water perspective."

"And we can be with the kids for the holidays. Yippee, skipee!" That thought sealed the deal.

We stayed three additional days, after deciding to have the local young men who worked on the docks, wax the hull and deck. They only charged a dollar an hour, which was well worth it for working in the sun and heat. We also had a special treat in the clubhouse palapa during that time, when a cruiser had set up his Karaoke machine and speakers. It turned out that there were more than a few "hams" amongst us, and I led the pack. What fun. Sometimes Fred would tire of it all, and head back to the boat, shaking his head in disbelief at my enthusiasm. Once again, I was aware of how much music and singing added to my life. One night I was even toasted as the "chanteuse of the *Rio Dulce*."

"What's a chanteuse?" I asked Fred as we walked back to the boat.

"I have no idea, and don't think I want to know," he laughed.

Wanting to begin our journey to Belize in one more week, we decided to first head upriver into Lake Isabel for some exploring. Getting out of the marina was a challenge as there were many lines behind us from other boats tied to us or neighboring boats. The dock staff helped us untangle the mess, and using a motor launch, pulled us backward and away from the dock. We were *free* again. After almost three months harnessed to the marina, *Grace* was ready to go.

"Look at everybody waving like crazy," I laughed.

"It's really an occasion when someone leaves," Fred said smiling and waving as we motored alongside the marina and headed out into the river. "Get ready—here it comes!"

I covered my ears just in time. A loud blast pierced the air from a cannon up by the marina office. It made our leaving official—a sort of local ritual salute for departing boats. Mario's was indeed a fun place to be and we had met some wonderful friends there whom we would miss. But for now, we were "on the road again" and did it ever feel good.

A short distance upriver, we passed through a narrow stretch of water that had an old small Spanish fort standing alongside the shore. It was one of the most restored structures we had seen in Guatemala. The pink toned coral walls with their tall round towers and turrets at each corner, the carefully concealed cannon placements and solid upper ramparts triggered my imagination. I was reminded of the pirates and battles that occurred along this river many years ago. We anchored, took the dinghy ashore and explored the nooks and crannies of the fort and the park surrounding it.

"Let's cool off with a dip in that pool," Fred suggested when the heat became too much.

"I think it's just a wading pool for the kids," I said, looking around at a number of small children and their moms.

"Who cares? It's hot."

There were more than a few giggles by those observing the crazy *gringos* cavorting in the water with the little ones.

By afternoon we were in the lake and anchored close to *Finca Paraiso* (Paradise Ranch), a place reported to have hot waterfalls. When we set the hook, we thought we had found a good location in shallow water behind a rocky point that we hoped would shelter us from the night wind that can move across the lake. We enjoyed a refreshing swim in the warm, although muddy waters of the lake. It was dark by 6:15 pm, and with the stress of getting underway, we were tired and turned in early.

"So much for planning," Fred said the next morning. The wind had shifted during the night to the opposite direction from what we had anticipated, and it was a bouncy chop that had us rolling much of the time. *Ah...the joy of cruising.*

Going ashore, we paid a dollar apiece to a caretaker and were told the way to the waterfalls. The trip was a delight to the eyes as we hiked up a path that took us alongside lush farmlands of oranges, corn, and bananas. Cows grazed in green pastures. Soon we began a steeper climb with denser trees and vegetation drawing us further into the jungle. We saw the thatch huts of a small village across a small stream, and bare breasted women washing clothes in the pretty clear waters, while naked children splashed and squealed. A small boy rode on the back of his slightly older brother as they crossed the stream and both eyed us warily. Many places provided welcome shade from the relentless sun, but the humidity grew as we traveled away from the lake into the interior. By the time we reached the waterfall we were ready for a swim in the deep pool at the base of the cascading hot water. Unlike the lake below, here the water was crystal clear. Strong currents prevented us from swimming directly under the falling water, but we enjoyed the swim immensely. We crawled around the huge rocks surrounding the pool and marveled at the quiet and lovely tranquil setting shared by only the two of us.

"Well, I understand why they called this Paradise Ranch," Fred said. "It feels like the set of some tropical island movie."

"I know. Me Jane. You Tarzan," I laughed.

As we sprayed ourselves with insect repellant before our hike back through the jungle to the boat, I couldn't help but wonder how Jane had handled all the mosquitos.

One night we were bombarded with hundreds of tiny flying gnats. They didn't seem to bite, but they were *everywhere*. We turned out all the lights to see if they would leave, but that still didn't help. When we went into the aft cabin to go to bed, they covered the pillows and sheets.

"That does it," Fred growled. "I'm spraying."

Well, it seemed to do the trick. But now, instead of flying gnats, we had hundreds of dead gnats covering every possible surface inside the boat. *Yuk.* It was quite awhile before we got the mess cleaned up and could finally get in bed.

It continued to rain a lot during the night. I was up and down, opening and closing the hatch in our stateroom. One night there was a real deluge. Fearful that the dinghy would again fill with water and sink, but not wanting to get out of bed *one more time,* I seemed to have "accidentally" woken up Fred, who got right up to go outside and bail out the dinghy. I felt more than a little guilty as I confessed my ploy.

"That's O.K.," he said. "You can be the 'watcheemahn' and I will be the 'bailer.'" I think I got the better deal.

We continued to keep an eye on the weather fax map. A tropical depression was moving over Guatemala, so it looked like our trip to Belize would be postponed for a while. We decided to leave the three other cruising boats with whom we had been anchored, and move up into a small river by ourselves. The river was deep, but often narrow, allowing just enough clearance in the center for our mast to slip through the tree limbs and vegetation along the riverbank. Birds were abundant, including a large flock of parrots. We could hear the howler monkeys making their loud, fierce growls that sounded to me like gorillas, but we couldn't see them. It sounded like they were angry that we had invaded their space. The river water was muddy from all the rain, and I fantasized big, ugly crocodiles and man-eating piranhas just below the surface.

"Wow. This is beautiful. Look at all those water hyacinths along the shore. Those huge clumps that broke off the main plant look like small islands of flowers as they float downriver. But it's also a little intimidating up here. We're really isolated."

"I doubt that many boats try to come this way. Perhaps we've gone far enough. We're really enclosed by the jungle, so we'll likely have lots of *guests* tonight."

We spent more than an hour preparing for the potential onslaught of bugs and snakes. We had anchored right in the middle of the river. Fred prepared a diesel soaked rag to wrap around the anchor chain to hopefully stop any snakes from crawling up it and into the cabin. Then we got out every screen we had, and covered every hatch and vent.

"Let's enclose the cockpit with that great big screen I made," I suggested. "That way we can sit outside and still be protected."

We took an early shower and lathered up with insect repellant, lit the mosquito coils, and settled down to savor our efforts. Sure enough. Just about dusk, while I was sitting in the cockpit playing my guitar, the blitz began. Flying insects clamored all over the outsides of our screens, aggressively trying to enter our domain. There were *thousands* of them. Maybe *millions*. We laughed in delight, as our defense perimeter held. We had won the battle! It was the highlight of the day.

Back in the lake, we went to a little town for some groceries. From the reaction of the villagers, we thought they must not see many *gringos*. As in most of the villages, the children were anxious to make some money, and ran toward us as they saw us coming to shore. They offered to help us tie up the dinghy, or protect it from *banditos* (likely their friends), or carry our garbage or groceries.

Sometimes we had to separate things into two bags so each child could have something to carry.

At Denny's Beach, we were warmly welcomed by Denny, a friendly Canadian who had a Guatemalan wife. Friends on a Dutch boat came in shortly after we did, and anchored close by. We all ate at the beach bar that night, and Denny insisted we take the three-hour horseback tour the next morning.

"I don't know," I said. "I've only been on a horse once before."

"Not to worry," we were assured. "You'll love it."

With some trepidation, I decided to give it a try. As we waited on the beach at eight the next morning, I realized that I needn't have worried. The man with the horses never showed up. He'd gotten drunk the night before, so decided not to come. It was another G.E. (Guatemalan experience).

Gunk-holing around the river and lake was fun but we were starting to get antsy about moving on to Belize. We worked our way back to *Fronteras* and anchored by Mario's. There we were able to install the compass, now fixed correctly, and find the charts we were missing. We borrowed them from another cruiser, and made four copies of a part of each page, taping each section together so that we had a complete chart. I was much relieved to have the additional information. The fuel tank was filled, laundry done, frozen meat and groceries brought aboard and we were ready to go—all this interspersed with frequent dips in Mario's pool.

"But you can't leave tomorrow," a friend implored. "That's the big Going Away party for Denise and Lane."

Never wanting to miss a party, I joined the effort to convince the captain to wait.

"What's one more day?" I said to Fred, who knew he was in a losing battle. "And it will give us a chance to make a phone call home." Ham radio reception continued to be spotty in the river.

The following morning we took the dinghy over to *Fronteras*, arriving at 8:30, hoping there would be no line for using the phone. No such luck. There were three folks in front of us. An hour and 45 minutes later it was our turn. But we got more bad news about the renters, there was a long delay that made conversation very difficult, and I found it almost impossible to learn much of what was happening in our children's lives. It was so frustrating.

"I'm so mad at that rental manager," I said as we made our way back to the boat. "And I didn't get any of my questions answered about Page and Dawn. And I sure wish Lance would let somebody know where he is."

"Maybe he feels the same way about us," Fred replied calmly. "But at least we put a lot of effort into trying to communicate."

I was still disgruntled as we made our way over to the party that night. It was a fun send off for a couple that had been the managers of Mario's. But every time we talked with anyone from Florida, or Texas, my anxiety escalated. They were all sure this was not the time to head north and had horror stories to prove their point.

"You know, we've heard this all before," Fred said. "In virtually every port we've been in, there seems to be some who pass on scary stories to those who want to move on. It seems to be a kind of group hysteria that somehow justifies staying in one place."

"I know, I know. 'A ship in a harbor is safe, but that's not what ships are built for,' right?"

"Right. We're ready, and we're going."

Five

Hiding Out from Hurricanes

"I can't stand it any longer," I said as I put the engine in neutral. "I'm going to jump in to cool off."

Fred watched while I jumped overboard into the river. We were making our way downriver the 20 miles to Livingston. Once in the water, I quickly discovered that although the boat had been moving slowly, there was still a moderate current, and despite my swimming at full speed, I was losing ground and couldn't catch up to *Grace*.

"Unless you want to stay in Guatemala, you'd better grab onto the dinghy," Fred laughed.

I really wasn't worried that he would have left me behind, but I was glad to climb back aboard, exhausted but cooler.

Once we arrived in Livingston we went through the tedious process of checking out of the country. We made our way to the three separate port offices in the stifling heat, hoping to complete the paperwork before everything closed for *siesta* time. At one point, I was so hot that I thought I was going to be sick. *Where was that ocean breeze?* Fortunately, we found it back at the marina, and settled into some hammocks. While there, we met more boaters from Texas. They had been hit by lightning only three weeks previously when they were up the river. It had "fried" all their electronics, and punched six holes in their hull. We were reminded that it's not just that it *can* happen, it *does!*

The following day we crossed the bar, relished being out in the open ocean, and sailed a short ways to enter a port in Belize and again go through the paperwork shuffle to enter the country.

"Despite the two towns being so close, the people here are much different appearing than the folks in Guatemala."

"For sure. Their skin tone is so black, like a beautiful ebony, and they have a strong Caribbean accent to their English."

Once again, it was incredibly hot in town, and we hurried to get back out to the boat and underway. We later anchored at a little palm-covered cay about three in the afternoon.

"Well, the snorkeling was a little disappointing after that of Honduras," Fred said after we explored the waters around our anchorage. "It'll likely be better on the outer islands."

"But did you see that school of fish with the yellow tails? They were almost transparent. Weird. And whenever I changed directions, so did they. They stayed right with me for quite awhile. Was I watching *them*, or were they watching *me*?" I laughed.

Snorkeling in Belize.

Sometimes at night, we would sit in the cockpit and observe the "laser light show" in the distance, created by distant thunderstorms. Large sections of the sky would suddenly illuminate behind the huge silhouette of clouds above the horizon. Other times, the lightning strikes would appear as huge flashing streaks that raced to the ground or tore sideways across the sky in their erratic and powerful pattern. It was almost like sitting before a fire, watching it dance amongst the logs—it was mesmerizing. Less enjoyable was when the lightning appeared all around us. Sometimes I would lie in our bunk, watching through the hatch at night. It was awesome! I could even "see" the flashes through my eyelids when my eyes were closed.

"Are you asleep?" I said quietly one night. "Come and look at this."

Also unable to sleep through the noise of the rain and thunder, Fred got up and followed me into the main salon. I had gotten out of bed to close the main cabin hatch, as the rain was ferocious, when I saw the strangest white lights, flashing and dancing; swirling around the very top of the mast.

"What *is* that?"

"I have no idea, but it must be something to do with the lightning."

After watching for some time, we began to think it might be birds that we were seeing. Our suspicions were reinforced, when we found a dead bird on the deck the following morning. But we didn't know what caused them to circle the mast. Wonders never cease.

One day a good sail took us to the outer cays. We had our fishing lines out, and caught three small skipjack tunas, but threw them back, hoping for something better.

"Whoa. Look at that. Something bit off our hook and broke the rubber stubber on our line. That had to have been *big!*" Fred said excitedly when examining our line.

"The other line is the same way," I said. "Maybe just as well. I think its better that we didn't land those suckers on the boat. *Too* big."

We soon were at the cay where we wanted to anchor, and tried unsuccessfully for over an hour, to find the entrance through the coral. The water was clear, but it was very difficult to determine how deep those corals head were that we saw looming under the water. Finally inside and anchored, we were amazed to look out upon the huge expanse of open ocean. We were on the eastern shore of the cay and the water was calm all around us, broken from the ocean swells by the reef about 25 yards away.

"It took us so long to get in here, let's stay another night," I said that evening.

"Good idea. We can get good reception on the ham radio here, and I need to work on that water maker and see if I can get it going again."

We had learned by now, that gremlins invaded the electronic gear when it hadn't been used for a while, and it took some troubleshooting to get things functioning after any prolonged time in a marina. I marveled again, how successful Fred was in fixing things, and how proud of him my dad, who was also a wonderful "fixer," would have been.

With our work for the day done, we decided to try snorkeling on the ocean side of the reef. That meant swimming in about two foot depths of water for a short distance to get across the top of the reef. But shallow water snorkeling was not my cup of tea. I knew it had great potential for getting painful stings from the anemones that lay on the sea floor. I gingerly floated over the area willing my body up to the surface of the water as much as possible. My gloved fingertips carefully pushed on the sandy or rocky spots of the ocean floor, and I sucked my belly in until I was sure it touched my backbone. I prayed that my stomach or legs wouldn't touch any of those beautiful but painful stinging tips of the sea anemones that nestled amongst the rocks. They were *everywhere*. Once we were in the outside ocean waters, we were astonished to view the coral as well as the fish. There were some huge angelfish—larger than any we had ever seen, and some jellies with their trailing stinging tendrils that we carefully tried to avoid. But some of my enjoyment in what we were seeing was overshadowed by knowing that I would have to swim back over the reef in that shallow water.

In the afternoon we took the dinghy across the lagoon to another cay. It was very hot and there was only a slight breeze at the time, so I brought along our large beach umbrella so that we could sit in the shade it provided while we threaded our way through the water and the coral heads.

"You know," Fred admonished while pointing to the umbrella, "that looks a little 'prissy.'"

"You know," I replied after a moment's thought, "I don't see you moving out from under it." Touché.

When it was time to leave the anchorage, we waited until the sun had risen high in the sky so that we could see what dangers lay under the water, and started the tricky exit. We must have found the correct channel on our first try, as we easily slid out into deeper water. Our next desired anchorage was found and entered without problems, but it then took us *two* hours to set our anchor. What a mess. We finally tried using our stern anchor, which had a different shape. This meant digging into the depths of the cockpit locker and hauling out 40 feet of chain and 100 feet of line, as well as the anchor, and taking it all up to the bow to deploy it.

"I'll dive down again, and this time, I'll see if I can hold the prongs into the bottom, while you back it off with the engine," Fred said after many dives to check the contact. He was getting his exercise today.

Finally, we were reasonably certain that the anchor was set and began to relax. No more than five minutes later, we saw a small local boat leaving a nearby buoy, and asked the man if we could use his buoy.

"Sure," he replied. He would not be coming back that day.

So we pulled up our painstakingly set anchor and proceeded to motor over to the buoy and grab the float line that marked the buoy with our boat hook.

"Oh *no*. The line to the buoy broke," Fred cried. "It must have been rotten. Now all we have is the float. See if you can find the other end of the line."

We motored around in *Grace* for many minutes, looking for the broken buoy line with no success. It had likely sunk. We were back to "Square One." So once again, we went about the laborious task of setting our anchor. Fred dove so many times to check each effort, that he surely must have been waterlogged. With it finally set, we got in the dinghy, and I towed Fred behind while we went around the lagoon and he looked with a snorkel mask for that elusive buoy and line. *Nada* (Nothing).

"I think we're O.K., but I sure wouldn't feel secure if a big wind came up," Fred said as we climbed back onto the boat, "because we're surrounded by reefs."

"Why don't you rest for it bit," I suggested. "I think I'll do a little snorkeling."

The luck of the Irish! (Well, I'm partly Scotch—that's close enough.) Within three minutes I had found the buoy, which was a large industrial engine on the ocean floor, and had a rotten line tied to it. *Yahoo.* Once again we pulled up our anchor and motored over near to the buoy. We attached the float, and then tied on to a ring of the engine with the largest line Fred could find aboard. What a fiasco this job had become. It had taken all afternoon.

By evening, the winds had started to increase and during the night they were up to gale force strength. We were up and down several times checking our location, but all remained fine as we safely bobbed up and down on that big engine buoy. Despite getting little sleep, we were ever so grateful to have found the buoy and sure we would have drug had we still been at anchor. *Gracias a Dios!*

Upon arriving in Placentcia, a small town on the mainland of Belize, we took the dinghy ashore to explore the area.

"Look at this sidewalk," Fred exclaimed with wonder. "The base of it is all conch shells resting on the sand, with just a little layer of cement covering the top. Now that's ingenuity."

"And it's the only sidewalk in town. This place is really different from the other places we've been. Let's go watch the cricket game. That has to have come from the British influence."

We were intrigued to see a large number of Rastafarians living here. They often had ferocious reputations as fighters, but they were very friendly and waved or greeted us. Another difference was the clothing of the women. Unlike many of the Latin countries where women wore skirts or dresses, here they all had on T-shirts and shorts. I felt overdressed in the sundress that I normally wore ashore. We tried to get a few groceries and ice, but were unable to get bread, because "John, the baker man" was out all day. We would have enjoyed staying ashore for the evening Columbus Day celebration, but had not left our anchor light on, and being in the sun and wind all day had tuckered us out. I guess we were getting old.

"Now this is more like it," I squealed.

We had left early in the morning, as we had entered a deep channel and didn't need the sunlight to view the ocean bottom. We also did not need to worry about shoals and coral heads—those bothersome things that could suddenly appear, punch a hole in the hull and really ruin your day. Finally, we were having a great sail.

"Going five knots against a strong current, and one tack (direction) all day," Fred replied with a smile, "and we're even pulling the dinghy."

Life was good. We'd even been able to reach my mom on a phone patch through the ham radio. She needed a little coaching to remember to say "over" at the end of a transmission, but otherwise did fine. How exciting it would be to just pick up a phone and make a call when we arrived back in the States. With the wind consistently from one direction, I even got out my electric piano and played awhile—something I had not done for a long time. Music was always good therapy for me.

We were again feeling more confident about entering the lagoons and cays. But we didn't want to get cocky, knowing anything could happen "just around the corner." Another great sail took us to Garbutt Cay. Many of these anchorages were quite isolated, with no towns or villages nearby. Occasionally we would see fish camps on shore, and local fishing boats. One afternoon we were approached by Austin, a local fisherman. He wanted to trade lobsters and conch for some meat. The only meat we had left in our food locker, was a two pound can of ham, and two cans of Spam. In return, he and his friend gave us five small lobsters and started dumping shelled conch in a sack for us. We kept telling him that was enough, as we had no more meat to trade, but he waved our protests aside.

"Can you believe it? There are 26 conch in here."

"Besides the five lobsters," Fred added. "He must have been out fishing for a long time and mighty tired of eating seafood."

We worked all afternoon cleaning and skinning the conch; something we had not done before. It wasn't an easy job. But the eating that night was marvelous.

"Man, oh man. We're really eating 'high on the hog' right now," Fred said.

"Now there's an expression. How do you think you'd translate that one into Spanish," I replied and we laughed at our attempts.

Each morning when we were out on the cays, Fred would get up early, so that he could get the latest weather information on the weather fax machine at six o'clock. While it provided little useful data for local conditions, it was good for seeing the big, overall picture. Fortunately, all continued to look benign; no tropical storms were developing. We'd sigh with relief, knowing we'd not be hurrying to find a place to hide from a possibly developing hurricane that day.

"I'm ready to move on, but it looks so cloudy and threatening this morning," I said as we sipped our morning coffee. "I'm concerned about getting into the next cay without the sunlight."

"There's a small beach restaurant at the next stop. I'll see if I can raise anybody there on the VHF radio."

When Fred did so, he was successful in talking with the owner, a colorful character named Finn. We had heard about him from other cruisers. In a heavy, lilting accent, he assured us that he would watch for us, and help us into the anchorage.

We pounded into the wind, which was coming right "on the nose" under dark, grey clouds that appeared ominous and ready to burst with a deluge of rain. Because we were still inside the outer reef, we had no large build up in the seas, but it was choppy, there were lots of white caps and it was less than pleasant sailing. Finn was waiting for us, and we spent a fun afternoon with this unique fellow. He loved to talk, knew all the different kinds and makes of boats and remembered each of the "yachties" that had stopped at his cay. He showed us a book with all their names and cards. He'd been a cook since he was fifteen, so we simply *had* to go back to his restaurant that night for a terrific dinner.

The following morning we had Finn out to the boat for a cup of coffee as he had wanted to see our English boat, one that was unfamiliar to him. As we talked, he shared a wealth of information about going on to Europe from the U.S. I tried to take some notes. It seemed he had been everywhere and had done it all.

"You know, it's the 'Finns' of this world that make life such a treasure," I said that evening.

"You're right. For me, I think that the *people* we've met in this dream, are even more memorable than the *places*."

Well said.

It was going to be another gorgeous sunset, although it was only 5:30 pm. Fred was hauling a beach chair to the bow of the boat.

"Just call me Lance," he laughed.

While we usually sat in the cockpit, Lance had always settled comfortably in a chair on the bow deck, never failing to "stop and smell the flowers" by taking in the glorious and colorful artwork in the sky at sunset. We often tried to emulate his respect and appreciation of nature and the visual gift we were given at close of the day. I turned on some classical music, and joined my hubby for the show.

It was four in the morning, and we were both up after being woken by the unusual motion of the boat.

"What's happening? It feels like we're at sea."

"The wind switched to the south and it's a good blow. But it looks like the anchor's holding well."

"*South? The south?* They told us it never blows from the south." One thing we could always depend upon—the weather was truly undependable.

By morning, the wind had eased some, although it was still strong. Unlike so many of our anchorages that were in shallow water, this time we were in over 40 feet of water. That meant we had let out a *lot* of chain. Fred really had a good workout pulling it all in, while I tried to counteract the opposing pull of the wind on the boat using the motor. We were going to Belize City, where a friend of ours was living, and we hoped to make contact with her.

In order to meet with Pam we decided to go into a marina, although we would have preferred to stay at anchor where it was cooler, free, and had far less bugs. After many unsuccessful attempts to reach her by phone, we took a water taxi into the city, looking for a place to cash a one hundred dollar bill.

Belize was a much more progressive country than many others in Central America. It had a healthier economy and a 93% literacy rate. As we looked around, we could see that most of the homes were quite substantial, and although some were run-down, they were charming in their gingerbread style and brightly painted colors with fancy, lace-like scroll work adornments. They were also built on stilts above the ground. People were friendly, and it was easy to find our way around when everybody spoke English. The supermarket we found cashed our large bill, although many smaller places would not have accepted it. The store looked like any big supermarket in the States. But it was *hot*. And we still were unable to contact Pam. I was frustrated and feeling a little sick from the heat, so we headed back to the boat.

"I've got so much goop on my body, I'm afraid I'm going to slip right off the boat," I complained that night. The bugs were fierce in the marina. "But thank goodness, your eye is better. Now *that* could have been a real problem."

Fred had developed an infected gland on his eyelid. We had watched it for several days, and had finally started treating it with antibiotics, as well as frequent warm packs to the area. If necessary we could have seen a doctor in Belize City. Bug bites were a nuisance, but an infection, particularly around the eye, was a concern. *Keep those prayers a comin', folks.*

We had met an American couple that were living in Belize and had a chartering service on their sailboat. They were going to the outer islands, and asked us if we wanted to follow them to get through a narrow, and tricky channel. Before doing that, they first took us in their car to the several necessary offices, separated by long distances, to complete our required check-out paperwork. They even took us to the supermarket. Small kindnesses really made our day. We had finally managed to contact Pam on the phone, and she was going to meet us in San Pedro in a couple of days.

"It was easy following *Sting Ray* through that first cut, but I sure wish they were here now," I said, looking at the depth meter that registered *four feet* of water.

"Look at that white track on the bottom," Fred said. "I bet that's the mark they told us to watch for—it's a boat's keel dragging through the sand. Let's follow it."

Sure enough, the track took us to deeper water and the channel out. *Whew.* Thank goodness for that crystal clear water. But once in deeper water, what a sail we had. We yelled with delight like kids in a playground, as the fifteen knot wind came across the beam in a constant speed and direction, the sails filled, the sun shone, the pale turquoise water sparkled, our bodies cooled and our spirits soared. Ah...*this* was cruising!

San Pedro was another charming and unique place. It was a small town that had recently developed into the number one tourist attraction in Belize. The big draw here was diving, and there were dive shops on every corner.

"I feel like I'm walking down the streets of a ski resort," I laughed. "It has the same cozy feel of a community that caters to a particular sport. It even looks like a mountain town."

"It really does in some ways. With the streets made of packed white sand, you can almost imagine it's snow covered. And the shops and hotels are all small, not gaudy or pretentious. I like it. It's relaxing."

"And I like that all the vehicles here are sand dune buggies or golf carts. Fun."

As we got ready for bed, we both checked the anchor and agreed that it was dragging. Thank goodness for the full moon and warm wind, which made the task of resetting the hook much easier. But it was a restless night as we continued to get up to check for further drag.

We met Pam and spent an afternoon finding out about her exciting life as a single American woman living on a ranch in a sparsely populated area about 25 miles from San Pedro. She seemed to know all the local folks, and told stories with drama and flair about both the country and her experiences. They were certainly not the kind of things we read about in the guidebooks. Because roads were not good in this area of Belize, and her boat was not big enough to cross the bay, she had flown up from Belize City by seaplane to see us. Our visit was short as the plane had to return before dark, but we were so pleased to see someone from our hometown, and Pam certainly knew how to entertain.

We had one more day to finish preparing for the next big leg of our journey. We got right to work and pulled out the jib sail, lowered it, and greased the roller furling mechanism that had been getting stuck in strong winds. It could have been a difficult job to do when we were at anchor if the wind had come up, but all went smoothly. We also continued to check for additional weather information. Fred had noticed a small disturbance in the northwest part of the Gulf of Mexico. That could become problematic as it was in the region where those "northers" originated. We wanted to keep a close eye on it.

Our plan was to sail north to Mexico, stopping first in *Bahia Ascension*, and then moving on to *Isla Mujeres*. From there, we'd enjoy the eastern coast of Mexico, one of our favorite countries, and wait for a good weather window to jump across the Gulf of Mexico, stopping at the Dry Tortugas on our way to the west coast of Florida. *Florida.* Just the sound of the word brought bittersweet and ambivalent feelings to mind.

It helped to keep busy. That old familiar gnawing anxiety had snuck up on me and raised its ugly head. I had come to expect it, knowing that it often accompanied our anticipation and preparation for those likely rough offshore passages. By now, it had become sort of an unwelcome guest, something that was really more of a nuisance than a real threat. But on the other hand, there was also a large part of me that tingled with the excitement of a challenge and identified with that classic children's story— "The Little Engine That Could." I acknowledged the former, and embraced the latter, and that seemed to work—until Fred told me that the disturbance in the northern gulf was moving. Decisions, decisions. *Would it come our way? Should we wait until it passes, or would it just be the first of a long string of expected weather patterns? Could we get to Bahia Ascension before it was upon us?* The conditions at San Pedro were great. The disturbance was a long way north of us. We decided to go for it.

Lordy, lordy! Let me off this infernal contraption. We were pounding into heavy seas and strong winds right "on the nose" in one of the worst passages we had yet encountered. The waves were incredibly steep and choppy, slamming the bow and hull with terrific force as we attempted to make forward progress. Sometimes I feared such continual punishment would destroy the boat. *Grace* would sometimes be momentarily motionless, then shudder and groan as she plowed onward. Tons of churning, green water poured over the bow, often splashing into the cockpit, drenching the unfortunate souls who found themselves there (us!) despite the fact that it was not raining. The sound of the wind on the sails, the sea as it roared by, the impact of the water on the hull and deck—all engulfed us in the feel of nature's power and fury. The wind vane self-steering managed to hold our course, allowing us to spend some time in the cabin, for which I was very grateful.

"I thought cruisers never went 'to weather, (into the wind)'" I yelled to Fred over the noise in the cockpit. "Maybe it would be more comfortable and less tiring on us, if we lowered some sail and went slower."

"We could do that," Fred yelled back, "but then we'd likely not get to *Bahia Ascension* until dark tomorrow. I'm not sure I'd want to attempt that entrance then, and I sure don't want to go on in this if we can get out of it."

We'd already spent one night in this mess, and I dreaded the thought of two more. Both of us had been seasick, but fortunately had thrown up only once. My waterloo came after putting on my life vest, which had been so long down in the locker that it smelled horribly of sweat, mold and mildew. That was all it took.

It was my turn on the night watch, and Fred was attempting to rest on the settee in the cabin. After several minutes of checking things outside, I went below. What I found there horrified me.

"Fred, Fred!" I yelled. "There's *water* on the floorboards in the aft cabin! There's several inches of it."

"We need to find where it's coming from," Fred said as he jumped up, every fiber of his being alert and in motion. Taking on water was a life-threatening problem. We both started pulling up the floorboards and checking the bilge.

"Maybe it's the engine seacock," I said fearing the worst.

"I bet it's coming in from that anchor well. We've been taking a lot of water over the bow."

He continued to tear up the entire boat, as he checked for all possibilities. As he suspected, he saw a wall of water streaming down from the deck through the opening for the anchor chain. Before we had left Oregon, he had made a plug for this hole for just these conditions, but it would have meant unfastening the anchor chain in order to use the plug, and we wanted to tuck into the first anchorage possible. As he considered how to "jury rig" a solution to the problem, I continued to bail like crazy. I wasn't keen about what he decided he'd do, but we both knew it needed to be done. We went out into the dark cockpit after donning our life vests and lifeline tethers.

"Please be *very* careful," I pleaded unnecessarily.

We eased the sails for a slightly less violent ride, and Fred slowly and carefully made his way to the bow of that "Buckin' Bronco," making sure his safety tether was attached at all times. But there were a few dangerous seconds, when he unclipped from our jack line to re-clip onto the lifeline in order to reach the bow. During that time he was not clipped on to anything secure, and thus vulnerable. The bow had more motion than anyplace else on the ship and was heaving up and down, fiercely at times. The wet deck made footing potentially slippery. I prayed mightily as I watched him from the cockpit with our large floodlight in hand. The thought of trying to fish him out of the water in these conditions at night, was simply too overwhelming to consider, but I knew that I must be ready and act should that be needed. I thanked God for the full moon that made it somewhat easier to see. Finally arriving at the anchor well, he plugged the hole with of all things—*Silly Putty*! It was one of those ideas we had read about as we contemplated this "dream/nightmare" adventure and fortunately it seemed to work. He had a wild ride up there in that bouncing bow, but made his way back to the cockpit safely, and we both began to breathe again.

We were no longer taking in water, so began to relax a little, only to soon find ourselves in a squall with 30 plus knots of wind. Again we went outside and wrestled to take down the jib. There truly was no rest for the weary (or maybe it really *is* "wicked"). By morning the seas had moderated, we put the jib back up and had a fast sail. We made it to *Bahia Ascension* in good time.

"Good grief," I complained. "What timing. Another of those darn squalls, just when we want to enter through the reef."

"Like we need some more excitement," laughed Fred. "Maybe it'll keep us from being seen by the guys in that Navy base here.

If they board us and find we haven't checked into Mexico, they'll likely tell us to leave, just like they did to Susan and Doc."

"And if they do, they'll have a fight on their hands," I said with righteous indignation. "I'll say we're claiming 'Port of Refuge.' After that last storm, we need to make repairs—the boat's a disaster inside. Most of the things in the bow cabin, and a lot from the aft cabin are wet, and the jib sail has a big rip in it." Nobody was going to tell me to leave—even if they carried automatic weapons!

Bahia Ascension is a huge bay. We motored in safely, but it was quite a distance before we could snug up behind a little island on the farthest shore. It appeared to be a secure anchorage and we were out of sight from the base. Fortunately, we had no contact with the Mexican Navy and both of us gave a huge sigh of relief as we threw down the hook. It was definitely a *Miller Time.*

There was much to do the next day as we cleaned up, dried out, and put away. After hand sewing for several hours, I had the jib repaired. I was grateful for the opportunity to repair it, as it likely would have continued to tear. We also talked with friends on the ham radio. They were one day ahead of us and had tried to go north but were turned back by the same wind and seas. They were waiting for us at Cozumel. Another good night's sleep brought a day with a decent weather forecast, and we gave it another try.

"Darn, the seas are better, but that wind it still on the nose."

"And with the waves breaking on the bow, we're still taking in water. I fixed the area where I thought it was coming in. Apparently I didn't have the right spot."

Our concerns continued, and we adjusted our heading to try to limit the impact on the bow. It was not long before our anxiety climbed yet again.

"Listen! Did you hear that noise from the foredeck?" I said.

"I did. That didn't sound good. I haven't heard that before."

After much troubleshooting, Fred feared there might have been some structural damage to the deck, hull or rigging and we took in the jib to lessen any stress on the forward part of the boat. *Oh me.*

This was not fun. We said we'd continue cruising as long as it was fun. Maybe it's time to quit.

As we passed Cozumel, we radioed our friends on *Babe* and *Manotec* and they sailed out to join us. Having company felt comforting, especially with the worry about possible damage to the integrity of the hull or rigging.

About five in the morning, I was on watch sitting in the cockpit with Fred down in the cabin trying to sleep. The sky was just beginning to lighten in the east, allowing me to see the faint outline of Cancun as we sailed by about a mile or so offshore. At first I thought maybe I was dreaming and had been transported to another planet. The scene passing by looked like something I could imagine on the moon. All along the beach were *hundreds* of huge hotels, side by side. They appeared to be never ending. But I could see no trees nor any kind of vegetation—all seemed totally sterile and completely flat. I felt like I was observing a movie set of an alien world. This was not the Mexico we remembered and had so enjoyed.

By eight in the morning, we were tied up in a marina on *Isla Mujeres*, a charming but definitely tourist-oriented small island. Boats filled with vacationers arrived hourly from the mainland. These folks often spent the day on the island and then returned in the evening.

"It seems odd to see all that summer-time apparel, knowing we aren't going to be needing that stuff much longer. It's going to be cold where we're going," I said. We were observing the tourist shops as we walked about to complete our check-in. "It feels rather sad—like the dream is over, even though I tell myself that there are lots of new things ahead."

"Yeah. It's rather bittersweet, isn't it? But then again, if we can't fix the boat, we may be here indefinitely."

Back at the dock, Fred continued to twist and turn his body into a human pretzel in order to squeeze into the anchor well and bow to investigate our problem. He finally found what he was convinced created the seawater intake—two open spaces on either side of the anchor chain between the hull and the interior hull liner.

"That's a relief. I can't find any structural damage. But we need something to fill those spaces and that's going to be tough." We collaborated on ideas of what we could use for solving the problem.

For several hours we tried to fiberglass a board in place, but were not successful—other than creating a huge sticky mess. We then searched for and found a single can of foaming insulation material at the only hardware store in town. Since the store had only one can, we hoped it would be enough to do the job. To our dismay, the can was so old it wouldn't dispel the contents. *Oh me.* To add insult to injury, something broke as we tried to pull up the blade on the wind vane. More fixing needed. This just wasn't our day. But the weather map Fred brought up that afternoon looked really good. So good in fact, that our friends came over to look at it, and despite our plans to spend a few weeks in this country that we so enjoyed, we all decided to seize the weather window for a favorable opportunity to make our "jump" to Florida.

We did manage to enjoy a good Mexican dinner that night, and tried not to think of it as our last in Mexico. Our check-out the next morning reminded us once again of the Mexican love of paperwork as we worked our way around the various governmental offices. Unlike other ports, one of the officials tried to charge me an extra twenty dollars. We had heard many stories of minor extortion in some ports, but until now had not encountered any.

"We do not need to pay that," I said firmly, "but if you insist, I must have a receipt with your name on it."

"All right, all right," came the reply after I repeated myself several times. "Make it ten dollars."

Knowing I didn't need to pay it at all, I did just to hurry the process along. At the other port office, I gave the officials T-shirts from Oregon, told them we appreciated their kindness and thanked them for not trying to "fleece" us.

Six

Next Stop—U.S. of A

Although we left *Isla Mujeres* in the company of *Babe* and *Manotec,* it was only a short time before we lost sight of both boats. Each of us had chosen our own route, but we continued to check in with each other via the VHF radio. Thankfully, the sea was calm and the wind was light. How I hoped that it would stay that way. (In retrospect, perhaps I should have been more careful about what I wished for.) A beautiful blue sky with a few fluffy white clouds smiled down on us, and we felt relieved to be underway on this notoriously difficult late autumn passage. We set the sails, and although the wind was still close to the nose, and an occasional wave splashed over the bow, we were no longer crashing into violent waters. Still, my stomach felt queasy and I knew it likely was just apprehension. We also felt frustrated when we discovered that the problem with taking in seawater had *still* not been solved. It was apparently not coming in at the anchor well as we had thought and had worked so hard to correct. *Would it create further problems?* I tried not to think of that possibility.

"Wow. What happened to the wind?" I said as I came out of the cabin the following morning after taking a nap.

"It dropped to almost nothing during the night," Fred said. "We've been motor-sailing for a couple of hours."

"Who would have *thunk?* I guess its feast or famine."

By mid-afternoon, the wind was so light that we had to rely on the engine to make any forward progress. The sails were really no help at all. What little wind there was, was coming from the northeast, rather than the southeast, as forecasted. *But of course.* Our desired course was *northeast.* All day we had searched for the elusive Yucatan currents that fed into the mighty Gulf Stream, but we could find no sign of any currents except for the relatively strong one that was flowing directly *against* us. I began to wonder if we'd have enough fuel to reach Florida.

We commiserated with our friends on *Babe* and *Manotec,* as they were feeling the same frustration. We were all inching our way northward as we looked for the favorable current, but moving only about two knots *or less* over the ground. It was an agonizingly slow process.

"I wonder what it will be like to spend Christmas floating around out here," Susan said with a sigh. Since that was almost two months away, it wasn't a delightful thought.

"When I'm sailing in these winds," said Adam, "I can go very slowly either to the northwest or the southeast, when all I want is to go northeast." Adam didn't have a working engine, so he truly was at the mercy of the wind. He had made only ten or twelve miles progress in the previous 24 hours.

"The forecast is for even lighter winds," Fred told the others after pulling up new information. "If we don't find the current or get some wind, we really may not have enough fuel to hold our course to Florida."

As if to cheer us, a tiny sparrow had accompanied us for a couple of days. It appeared especially curious when watching Fred take his cockpit shower, and then twice flew right into the cabin.

"I finally caught this little fella," Fred said bringing the bird out to the cockpit in his hands.

"Listen to him scold you," I laughed. "For being so tiny, he sure can make noise. He really is indignant about the whole thing." It was nice to have company and a diversion.

Hooray! In the middle of the night, we found it—the Gulf Stream. Almost immediately we began to zip along at seven to eight knots over ground. Unfortunately, after we had struggled so mightily to make any northward progress, we now found that the current carried us in the opposite direction—southeast. That hidden "river in the sea" had us in its clutches. Despite a number of efforts to adjust sails or motor, with the wind so light we could not alter our heading. We were going wherever that current was taking us—like it or not.

"Well, we'd better just sit back and enjoy the ride," Fred said. "It's really weird to be moving this fast without the sails. I rather like it." He was like a kid amazed with a new toy.

"I guess we'll not be going to the Dry Tortugas as we planned," I sighed.

"Yeah, well we're headed directly for Cuba, also not as planned."

We knew that the Gulf Stream would eventually turn east, then northward, and we could make landfall in Miami. But we had not wanted to go to the east coast of Florida, as Dawn had arranged for us to have flight passes from Fort Meyers, on the western Gulf coast. *Daggone.* We knew that we shouldn't have said we'd be in a certain place until we got there. *Will we never learn?*

Just before dark, the wind came up, we raised the sails and found that we could change tacks, and head due north. With the current's push, we were actually going northeast—just where we wanted to go. None too soon—we were only twenty miles off the coast of Cuba.

"Look at this cold front that's coming into the Gulf," Fred said after checking the nightly weather report.

"Oh dear. Adam is going to get hammered. He right in the middle of that 'norther' and all the big seas that it'll generate.

Thank goodness we're out of its reach." It was difficult to enjoy our own position, when we were concerned for our friend.

During the night, the strong winds died again, creating a sea that was like glass, but we were still able to make good progress by motor-sailing. With the exultation of the rising sun came a beautiful calm morning and we were thrilled to arrive at the Dry Tortugas, about 70 miles due west of Key West, Florida. We had expected our passage to take about two days, but instead, it had taken five. It seemed we were continually being given lessons in developing patience. Unfortunately, I was a slow learner and the lessons did not seem to improve my frustration tolerance level. There was a large reef around the seven "keys" ("cays" in Latin countries) or islets that formed the Dry Tortugas. Once inside, the protection of the reef provided calm, clear water. Wonderful.

"Look at those huge fish. They must be over six feet long."

"Since this is a National Park, the marine and bird life is all protected. It must be why they grow so big."

After anchoring, enjoying our "Miller Time" tradition and lunch, I encouraged Fred to take a nap. He slept so little on these ocean passages; I knew he had to be tired. While he slept, I decided to try to set up the dinghy on the foredeck. It was an easy job for the two of us, but neither of us had ever done it by ourselves. It was a challenge and I struggled to do it quietly so as not to wake Fred. I was so proud when I finally finished the job; I could hardly wait for him to wake up.

"Ta Da! Look what I did while you slept," I said when he awoke and came out into the cockpit.

Blinking in the bright sunlight, looking confused and rubbing his eyes, he looked at me with disbelief after glancing back and forth from me to the dinghy.

"How did you *do* that?"

I pranced around and giggled with delight. After all these years, I could still surprise him.

Fred later decided to dive into the water to free up our knot meter, which was stuck again. He wasn't in the water very long, when he hurried up the swim ladder.

"Those big fish are barracuda, and they have huge mouths and sharp teeth," he gasped.

Although supposedly safe to swim with, we decided to forego any snorkeling for the time being.

Because we couldn't bring any fresh meat, fruits or vegetables into the States, that night we used up the last of the beef tenderloin in the freezer, opened a bottle of wine, and savored the lovely evening. *Yum.* Boy, did I love these landfalls—it was so good when you finally arrived. It almost made the going worth it.

Weather fronts continued to go by us, so we spent several days in the area and took our time exploring the huge old Fort Jefferson. It was built in the 1800s but never finished. Its most famous use was as a prison for several men convicted of conspiracy in the assassination of President Abraham Lincoln. It seemed odd to now be touring a part of the U.S. The thought of being in our home country had both of us excited with the anticipation of being with the family for the holidays.

We had helped a couple of young men the previous day who were delivering a sailboat to *Isla Mujeres*. Since they too, were stuck here due to the frequent fronts passing through, they were anxious for weather information. One of them was also concerned about his mom, since he was unable to contact her due to the delay. She had been so worried about his safety in taking the sailing journey. We offered to show them the weather information we had onboard and made a ham phone patch for them. They were very grateful (as well as their moms). They had so reminded us of Lance and his spirit of adventure. I hoped that he would make the same effort to contact us if he thought we were worrying about his safety.

One rainy day I spent baking on the boat. I looked forward to more baking in preparing a Thanksgiving dinner with Dawn, Page and Steve in Nebraska at Fred's mom's house. And just the idea of making Christmas cookies with the kids back in Portland made me smile. It was sharing the simple things of life with them, as well as the special times, that we so missed. We were anxious for the weather to improve so we could be on our way.

"Did you feel it turn last night?" I asked when waking the next morning.

"I did. I did," came the enthusiastic reply. "Hot dog. Winds are out of the *south*."

"If we can get to within 50 miles of the Florida coastline, we should have some protection from the big seas that next front will bring. Let's go."

It was a glorious, sunny day. We were zinging along with a nice wind just aft of the beam—almost perfect conditions. We were feeling mighty *blucky* as we had anticipated that we'd have another beat with winds and seas coming from the northeast. Since our problem of taking on water was not resolved, we were especially grateful for the favorable wind direction. It had almost eliminated any water coming over the bow. All during that day we heard warnings on the radio of severe thunderstorms and waterspouts, but they were either north or south of our location. Towards evening the wind dropped enough that we fired up the "iron genny" (diesel engine) and continued to motor-sail into the night.

"Holy cow. That lightning is striking more than once per second. I've been counting it. Sometimes there's multiple flashes each second. I've never seen anything like this."

With the storm many miles south of us, the wind had increased and we had been able to make good progress under sail alone. It was thrilling to watch the lightning—from a distance. The spectacular "laser light show" lasted several hours. Great jagged streaks of dazzling light sped across the blackened sky, crisscrossing with numerous other brilliant flashes at odd angles in a frantic, chaotic pace. Sometimes clouds would be illuminated from behind, casting eerie images, as if a giant searchlight was shining through them. Not all the strikes went to the sea, but when they did, the power they displayed was frightening. I looked up at our mast, standing so tall above the water and thought about how vulnerable it was. Nothing else projected into the night sky for miles and miles around us. But since we were a relatively safe distance from the storm cell, I found the display fascinating. Finally the show was over as the strikes slowed and stopped altogether.

About midnight, Fred was sleeping. Another thunderstorm had developed some miles south of us. I watched it awhile, and began to think that we may be directly in its path. Definitely worrisome was that it appeared to be getting closer. *Oh me.* I certainly did not want an up close and personal encounter with that sucker. I turned on the radar to track the storm's direction and speed. It wasn't a large cell but I realized it would likely be directly over us in less than an hour. I quickly started the engine.

"What's up?" said Fred, coming into the cockpit. The sound of the motor had awakened him.

"Look," was all I said as I motioned at the approaching storm. "And it's coming our way."

We pulled in the jib, adjusted the main sail, and made a 90-degree turn to the west. Fred gunned the engine into full speed. *Did we have time to "run for it" far enough to get out the storm's path? Grace* wasn't moving nearly fast enough for my liking. *Come on, baby!* It was frightening to consider that evil looking monster from Hell passing directly over us.

About 45 minutes later we had managed to put five miles between *Grace* and the center of the storm cell as it passed behind us. It punched us with strong winds, but had no lightning strikes in our immediate surroundings. The sound of the thunder had been deafening at times, and instantaneous with the ominous, blinding flashes that were only a short distance away. I was sure that the boat was vibrating from the cracking and crashing of the thunder's sound waves. My ears were definitely ringing.

"And to think I thought the adventure would be over when we got back to the States," I laughed. "I forgot that being in a boat on the water is *always* an adventure."

It was a beautiful sunny morning when we motored into San Carlos bay on Florida's western coast. We were definitely experiencing a major case of culture shock as we gazed around us while finding our way to a marina on Sanibel Island. Huge, multi-million dollar homes lined the waterways, complete with private docks holding lavish motor yachts suspended out of the water by lifting hoists.

"Everything around here is beautiful, but it *reeks* of money—lots of it."

"Well, the cost of the marina is no exception. I'm afraid Florida will be a heavy hit on the cruising budget."

"Jeepers. We've only been back in the States for an hour, and I'm already wanting to return to Central America."

It was a mixed bag. True—the excitement of living in foreign countries and encountering different cultures was gone. But after picking up a phone that worked, flushing the toilets, drinking the water, buying familiar items, eating familiar foods, and taking a very long hot shower, we knew that we were enjoying the comforts and *conveniences* of being back in our own country.

It was *so* good to call, hear the voices of the kids and talk about being home for the holidays. At the same time, we reflected on the sadness of leaving so many of the relationships with cruisers with whom we had so much in common. *Manotec* had gone on to Key West, and *Babe* was still somewhere out in the Gulf. It was not only sharing the struggles and joys of what we experienced, but also relishing the bond that so quickly developed with all types of personalities that venture on this kind of adventure. *Fools of like mind?*

We were saturated with such a contrast of feelings and thoughts. It all felt a little "crazy-making" and being tired surely added to the mix. We had gone for a walk to find a grocery store and had become a little lost. While gazing around me, I accidentally ran into a stop sign and nearly fell over in the process. *Oh me.* Tomorrow was another day. There were more plans to be made, surely more adventures to undertake. Would those take us on a "jump across the pond" to Europe and points beyond? Perhaps the eastern coast of the U.S.? After savoring a big juicy *real* hamburger, we wearily turned in.

"Are you still awake?" Fred whispered some time later.

"The boat is so still, I can't sleep."

"Neither can I. It feels so unnatural."

Our efforts now included researching for a safe place to haul out the boat and leave it for two to three months. We would be using our new parent passes, courtesy of our "Delta Dawn," for a trip to the Midwest and Oregon, perhaps even on over to Europe. We started up the narrow channel in the river that led to Fort Myers. We found that our yacht club had reciprocal privileges with the Royal Palm Yacht Club there, even though we still had to pay $21 a day. When arriving there, we found a friendly place with a small marina and a huge clubhouse. In the information packet we received it said that for the clubhouse "gentlemen are required to wear jackets after 6 pm."

"I guess we won't be going there for dinner," I said, "unless your foul weather jacket qualifies."

"What happened to that sport coat I started out with?"

"After a year and a half it in the locker it got so moldy, that I finally threw it out."

We decided to walk to a pub for a beer instead. When we got back we found the security men looking for us with a fax to call Page. I was filled with anxiety. *Why would she be contacting us? Was it the thing we had so dreaded?* Sure enough. Page carefully told me that Mom had experienced a small heart attack and was in the Cardiac Care Unit in the McMinnville hospital. My emotions roller coasted. Page told me that Dawn had already arranged for me to get an emergency pass so that I could fly home. With concern for Mom, and amazement at how the girls had handled all the details, I arrived at the Fort Meyers airport at six the following morning. Talk about job benefits. Here I was, flying free in First Class and I wasn't even the employee. *Gracias a Delta!*

My brother, Kent, picked me up at the airport and took me

to Page's to get Dawn's car for the drive to McMinnville. It was so good to see Mom and find her in good spirits—even enjoying all the attention in the hospital. She had wonderful care from staff and doctors. Four days later Mom returned to her residence, although first for a short stay in the Assisted Living component, rather than her own apartment. How good it felt to know she had ample, good, loving care and that Fred and I would be returning in only a few weeks. I marveled at the timing as well as the outcome of this crisis. Was it coincidence that we had just arrived back in the U.S.? And that we had told the girls where we would be only one day before? And that we were in a place where they could contact us? And that I could get to an airport to come home quickly? *I think not.* We were indeed *blucky,* and we were surely in good hands. How I counted my blessings. *Gracias a Dios!*

Returning to Fort Meyer after being gone a week, I was overjoyed to see Fred come walking down the dock. We had been together almost 24 hours a day for nearly three years, and when we were apart, I had missed him terribly. He had kept busy with many projects, but still had not been able to find the source of the water leak in the bow of the boat.

"What have you had to eat?" I asked suspiciously.

"The usual," he replied with a grin.

"How can anyone survive on peanut butter sandwiches, hot dogs and beans. Let's go get some *real* food."

Like two kids on Christmas morning, we reveled in the moment, practically skipping down the street.

In the midst of many work projects, we needed to go to a boat supply store. As we stood on the sidewalk looking at a bus map, a bus driver stopped in the traffic across the street and motioned us over. He told us to board, and then explained how to get to our destination. In the process, we had the whole front half of the bus laughing and talking with us. Before we had gone cruising, I doubt that would have happened. Something had changed in the way we responded to or interacted with people after having met so many new folks in so many new situations. While I had never been the shy type, I could see a huge change in Fred and I liked it.

"Let's get off this boat and have some fun," Fred said. "We are always *working*. Let's go to the mall."

Oh my goodness. Dawn would absolutely love it—her dad wanting to go to the mall to play. Part of the appeal was that he had discovered that the malls were *air-conditioned.* Coming back that night, we belatedly learned that the buses had stopped running. A kind driver was going back to the bus barn when she saw us standing at the bus stop looking perplexed, and offered to take us to within a half mile of the yacht club, even when it meant going out of her way. The world is full of nice people.

"On the road again," I sang with relish. We were on our way once again. It always felt so good to be underway after having been dock-bound for even a short time. There was something about that breeze in the face and the sound of the water slipping by that invigorated. We enjoyed warm, sunny days and cool, calm nights in a couple of quiet anchorages as we began traversing the Okeechobee waterway. It crossed the southern third of the Florida peninsula from the Gulf of Mexico to the Atlantic. Our plan was to have the boat hauled out in the protected but isolated (read "inexpensive") boatyard of Glade, and fly home. But the peaceful weather and relaxing days didn't last long.

"Did you hear that? Tropical Storm Gordon is headed our way, and may very well become a *hurricane* tonight!"

"As if to prove that the adventure's not over just because we're back in the States. Let's find us a good hurricane hole."

There wasn't any good "hole" nearby, but we found a spot that appeared reasonable for riding out the impending storm. Unfortunately, a number of other boaters had found it too. The dock was full, which was OK with us, as we preferred to anchor. After finding an isolated spot, we dropped the hook, taking great care to see that it was firmly set and put out many extra feet of our all-chain rode.

"Good grief. This is not good," Fred said while watching some smaller recreational boats that were likely on a weekend trip come into the small bay. "Look at the way they're anchoring—they just throw the anchor in, and have only rope rode. They're not even setting it. And they're way too close to us."

"You're right. They'd drag down right on top of us. Boy, that would really screw us up. Look. That guy has his cocktail in hand and is laughing. They seem to think that this is some kind of a party."

We watched more boats come in, looking for a place of refuge. Observing the seamanship skills and anchoring techniques would have been funny if it were not so potentially dangerous. One couple kept screaming at each other as they tried over and over to anchor. Soon the anchorage was more than crowded with many boats surrounding us.

"Let's get out of here," Fred said.

"But where will we go? It's almost dark, and I can't see any other suitable place on the chart."

"Just about anyplace would be better than this," he mumbled as he began to pull up the anchor.

"Hey, *Amazing Grace*. Where are you goin'? Don't you know a hurricane is coming?" yelled one of the boaters as we motored toward the exit. Indeed we did.

Back in the river, we had only gone about 100 yards when we saw a narrow tree and bush lined entrance to another little cove that looked ideal, but no one was inside. It didn't appear on the charts. *Why was no one in it? Was it too shallow to access?* We tried to enter and immediately went aground.

"Pump up our '*miracle*' keel," Fred yelled.

I did, and we entered easily in three and a half feet of water to find good holding ground in about ten feet of water. It was almost completely surrounded by mangroves, making an excellent hurricane hole.

"Can you believe this?" I sighed. "Boy, are we ever *blucky*." *Coincidence? No way.*

We took all equipment off the deck, tied down the sails with additional line, and felt we had the boat as ready as we could make her, before scooting for the cabin. Gale force winds came that night, as well as the next three days and nights as Hurricane Gordon, in a very unusual pattern, zigzagged back and forth over southern Florida. No one seemed to know where it would go next. Throughout it all, we remained "snug as a bug in a rug" in our protected little corner in our very own cove. Fred had set a second anchor, so we felt relatively secure. We bobbed, jerked and swayed to the boat's pull on the hooks, occasionally rolling to the side with the intense gusts. Sometimes the howling of the wind and the haunting, whistling sounds it made as it tore at our rigging was intimidating. Rain came in torrents and blasted the windows and decks with a barrage of bullet sounds. It was so noisy that it was hard to hear yourself think. Thank goodness for ear-plugs at night.

I had started crocheting some Christmas ornaments, so that helped pass the time, and we watched some television—something we hadn't been able to do for a long time; a perk of being nearer to modern technology. The radio transmissions were full of "Severe Weather Warnings," so we tried to be patient with being where we were. We even enjoyed the periods of gentler rain and cooler weather, particularly when we didn't have to be out in it. We called the boatyard on the radio about our delay, but since they could not haul us out in these conditions, arriving later was not a problem. And having flight passes meant that we could fly any day, unlike having a ticket for a certain flight on a specific day. All the drama was even a little exciting. The winds never did reach hurricane strength in our area, but they did elsewhere and they certainly gave us a good ride.

Watching threatening storm clouds approach.

"Oh...I hate to see our *baby* hanging up there high above the ground with only those two slings holding her," I moaned. "Taking her out of the water always makes me nervous."

"Yeah, she looks so vulnerable. But other than being dirty, the hull looks good. That's a plus after all that time in tropic waters."

We had arrived at the boatyard and the haul out had proceeded smoothly. *Grace* was lying in a wood cradle, with support beams on the sides. She truly looked like a "fish out of water." Until we flew home, we would be staying and working on the boat in the dusty dirt packed yard. That meant that it was necessary to climb high up or down on a ladder each time we went to or from the boat. Supplies or equipment also had to be carried up the ladder. It wasn't exactly convenient, especially when needing to go to the bathroom in the middle of the night. A number of other boats stood nearby, looking rather forlorn, dirty and out of place in this terrestrial environment. And it was hot and dusty. Thank goodness for good showers in the little office building.

The boatyard was located in the middle of a large cow pasture, miles from anywhere, with no bus service to a town. Acres of dry, brown grassland, thick grey/green trees, a highway and a river surrounded us. Other than the yard office, there were no buildings in sight. Finding a ride to the airport became a priority for me.

"Finally. I found a card on the bulletin board from a neighbor lady who said she'd take us in for $50. Taxis don't like to drive out this far. We'll have to leave about 4:30 am, as it's an hour and a half drive."

"Great. Let's get this boat ready to leave. We're going *home for the holidays.*"

Seven

Wintertime in Florida

Almost eight weeks went by quickly as we traveled across the country by plane and car, spending time with family and friends. We flew first to Nebraska where we spent two wonderful weeks with Fred's mom. Her terrific sense of humor and positive attitude never changed. Page, Steve, and Dawn joined us there for Thanksgiving. We then rented a car and drove to Colorado with the girls to join Lance in the ski resort of Vail. He had not been able to get time off work to come to Nebraska.

"Hey, it's the original 'Fabulous Five' back together," I said.

"And all it took was driving through a *blinding blizzard* across the entire state of Nebraska. Is he really worth it?" added Dawn, always on the ready for a playful jab at her brother.

We all enjoyed the snowy Bavarian style ski village, learning about Lance's world and just being together. When the girls flew home, Fred and I skied the mountain with our son, who had made the switch to snowboarding. As he slid effortlessly down the sunny slopes, his long blond hair streamed out from under his hat, allowing everyone to recognize and call out to him. He was in his element, surrounded by "his" jagged, awesome and majestic snow covered mountains. Being a "ski bum" suited him well. But all of life is not a utopia. The kids shared that there were problems too, for each of them, in varying degrees. Whenever they were hurting, I so wanted to "kiss it and make it better," as I could when they were young. But I had to trust that as parents, we had given them some skills and values to work out those pains and problems, and they had developed character on their own. We were glad that they told us about their struggles as well as their joys.

We flew on to Portland and rented a house in a mountain resort for Christmas week with my mom, Page, and Steve. Dawn, working on the holiday, was able to fly in from New York a day later. To be with family was even more special after having been alone the previous year in Columbia. It was also different to not be in our own home.

New Year's Eve found us with two other cruising couples that we had met in Mexico. They were back living in Portland again, and how we enjoyed seeing them. Once more, we marveled at how the special relationships that developed while cruising endured over time.

We also babysat two days/nights with our new "grand-dog"—a darling little seven-week-old Lab puppy that Steve had given Page for Christmas. They had gone to Tacoma to be with his parents for a couple of days. Listening to the pup cry the *whole* night long, reminded us of what work a puppy can be. But what fun too, after she adjusted. We hated to leave her.

It was also heart-warming to be with our church family one Sunday before we said sad goodbyes to everyone, not knowing when we would be back again. After a long flight, it was dark and late when we wearily arrived back at the boatyard in Florida.

"Oh. Oh! Doesn't she look good?"

"Better than good—fantastic." We were so glad to be *home*.

The following morning we were sound asleep when we heard someone knocking on our hull. Stumbling out of bed, we staggered out to the cockpit to find a couple standing on the ground below us. Their boat was also in the yard.

"Oh, good," they said when they saw us. "We were worried. We hadn't seen anybody moving about this morning, and were afraid that you might have inhaled that mildew gas stuff you put in your boat before you left."

How nice to have concerned neighbors. It was a little *early*, however. They had forgotten our body clocks were on west coast time, three hours behind theirs.

The boat was moved from the storage yard to the work yard, to begin some big retrofit and maintenance projects. There were several other boats there, mostly from Canada and Europe doing the same kind of things. Folks gathered each evening on the office porch for Happy Hour, or just to chat, and commiserate about the work and its progress. Nights were cool, requiring a blanket on the bed for the first time in almost three years. The nip in the air felt refreshing. We had missed the changing seasons, so enjoyed once again having something akin to winter. But during the day it got into the upper eighties, so it seemed we were forever changing clothes. It was strange to hear the noise of the birds in the middle of winter. Also the cows. Their mooing often sounded as if they were right next to the boat. They were fenced out of the yard, but when going for a run, we had to shoo them out of our way. One big bull intimidated me, but he just continued munching his grass. The calves were a delight, as they kicked up their feet romping after their mothers. Watching the cows and counting the many huge trucks going by piled high with oranges, provided our "F.E." (Florida experience) entertainment in this isolated spot. It was at least unique, if not very exciting.

"You had an emergency call last night. They said they'd call back at 8:30 this morning," said the office lady.

Oh no. Not again. But it wasn't the moms this time. Page called to say that Dawn was in the hospital in New York after an injury to her hand. It had developed into a systemic infection. She would need four or five days of IV antibiotics. My "Mama Bear" instincts were on full alert, and I was ready to go, especially after hearing that she had spent the night on a stretcher in the hallway since there were no beds available. After talking with Dawn on the phone, I realized there was nothing I could do, and resigned myself to fretting. Thankfully, Fred kept a level head.

"I thought that once we got back in the States, we'd be accessible to communication and transportation and all the amenities. But here we are stuck out in the boonies. I feel like we're in a foreign country. And she sounded *terrible.*"

Page kept an eye on the situation over several days, and they had a plan for Dawn to recuperate at Page's house when she left the hospital. I guess they could handle things without me, but it was sure hard not to be there. *What are we doing out here?*

Fred had been working for four days to get the pin out of the lifting keel, in order to change the Kevlar ropes. Nothing seemed to work and to say that he was frustrated, was an understatement. A number of other folks had tried to help him get the job done, but with no success.

"I think I may have found something that will help you get that pin out," said Cliff, one of our neighbors, when he climbed up our ladder one afternoon.

Unknown to us, he had bought a tool he thought might help when he was in Fort Myers the day before. Sure enough. In a short time the job was done. What a Sweetie. Coming into Florida, we had worried that we would lose the "cruising community" feeling on the East Coast. But here in the yard, we experienced plenty of it. People who had a car and were going to town would ask if we needed something; many came aboard to help troubleshoot when we got stuck on a difficult project; others offered to loan us equipment. Cliff and Lucille were likely fifteen years older than we, while the English couple on the boat next to us were probably fifteen years younger. Age wasn't a factor in our friendships.

I continued to wash and wax the deck and hull, and we both worked to fill, scrape, sand and ready the bottom and rudder for new paint. There were so many steps in the preparation—remove the rust, take off the anti-mold agent, remove the "no sanding" stuff. Each step had a different product. Painting the bottom, the final step, was easy. All that physical labor had body parts screaming, and the ship's supply of Advil depleted. It wasn't a lot of fun, and our concern about Dawn continued.

"Oh me. Dawn finally got home from the hospital, but she had to go by herself in a taxi, to an empty apartment. Her roommates were all flying. But she finally had a shower—her first in six days." How I wished that I had been there.

"Still nothing," Fred said coming back from checking the mail at the office.

"Why don't you call England and see if they have sent it?" I suggested.

We needed one tiny screw for the furling apparatus on our head-sail. Because the boat was built in the UK, it was a metric size screw. Despite searching through *dozens* of boat chandleries, we had found no replacement. Frustrated, we finally had asked the builder in England to send us one. We couldn't believe the time and effort we had put into finding just one little 25 cents screw. Finally it came.

"Hooray—here's the envelope from Northshore," I said with delight.

"Not so fast. There's nothing in it! Look at this hole. The screw must have punctured the envelope and fallen out. Can you believe that?"

Back to "Square One." Another call to England and a second screw was sent in a padded envelope, only this one turned out to be the wrong size. This time the mistake came from our side of "the pond." We had asked for the wrong one! And in the process of obtaining a similar screw, we had raised the jib partway, only to get it stuck in such a way that we couldn't move it either up or down. It was one of the few times I have seen Fred get truly grumpy. Well, I guess he was entitled—it only happens once every ten years. Finally we got the sail down, but we knew we couldn't use the headsail without that miserable screw.

"Well, there won't be any opportunity for sailing while we

cross the Okeechobee, except for the lake. Perhaps we can find a replacement in Fort Lauderdale—it's known as the 'Yachting Capital of the World.'" Hope springs eternal.

After two full and backbreaking weeks, we were ready to get the boat back in the water. We took a quick shower, not knowing when we'd get another. Our water tanks were very low. We could have filled them up at the boatyard, but the water was brown colored, smelled like sulfur and tasted terrible. It had been very cold the previous two nights; down to 35 degrees. Much too cold for a sun shower. We had been using jackets and mittens in the early morning and at night, and knew it would feel even colder once we were on the water. One final celebration dinner with our new friends and we were launched. Seeing *Grace* float gracefully in the river brought tears to my eyes, and we could hardly wait to be underway.

"On the road again," we both sang in high spirits under a cloudless sky, with sunlight sparkling off the water, and a gentle breeze ruffling our hair. Being midweek, there were few other boats on the waterway, and we motored along the calm channel, feeling like we were the only two people left on the planet. At first it looked like we were in a narrow river, but as we approached the big shallow Lake Okeechobee, the vegetation changed. It appeared much like what we had seen in movies of the Florida Everglades and swampland, or some southern bayou. There were lots of palm trees, but many live oaks were also tightly packed along the shoreline and dripping with huge growths of Spanish moss. It was everywhere, giving the impression of an ancient, sub-tropical and untouched forest. Sometimes there was a faint mist floating above the ground, adding an eerie, mystical ambiance to the thick vegetation. There were herons, egrets and birds we'd not seen before flying over the water and calling from the treetops. And yes, there were alligators— big ugly ones at that. One especially large one lazed along the shoreline, partly hidden by the grasses and hanging moss, which hung almost to the level of the water. It eyed us closely and gave me the chills. It felt like I was on a Disneyland jungle ride, only those big monsters were *real*.

We're definitely not in Kansas anymore.

But civilization appeared often in the form of bridges. These we either had to go under or have opened in order to proceed eastward. One bridge, however, was a fixed bridge. It did not open, and it was only 49 feet high. Our mast extended 55 feet from the water. This created a problem. We had heard of a service to "list" or lean sailboats through the bridge, and had called them while we were still in Cartagena to confirm that this was possible. Yet as we approached, our anxiety was climbing. If we couldn't get under this one, we had to go back and sail all the way around the peninsula of Florida in order to reach the eastern coast.

"Nothin' to it," a large sized man told us. He had come to the boat with his friend—also a "super size" fellow. "We put these 50 gallon drums on the deck over on one side, pump them full of river water, push the boom out as far as it goes, and then we hang on to the end of it while you motor through."

Really? This will really work? My mouth was dry as cotton as I incredulously watched them prepare the drums and boom. We pumped up our keel so that it would be easier to "list" the boat. We braced ourselves with one foot against the side of the cockpit as the boat gradually tilted way over to the starboard side.

"Be sure to take some pictures as we go under," he laughed.

I grabbed the camera, and Fred started to slowly motor toward that imposing rigid steel span that crossed the river and blocked our way.

"Listen to that," I squealed. It was the VHF antenna twanging as it hit the underside of the bridge structure when we slid just beneath it. "That's cutting it close!" Always an adventure.

One of the men that had helped us, owned a marina just beyond the bridge. He said they were having a potluck barbeque that night, and a big Super Bowl party the following day. The price was good by Florida standards, so we decided to pull in. And fun it was. About 50 people came to the potluck and we enjoyed visiting with many of them. We stayed on for the weekend and walked a mile into town to go to church on Sunday.

"That was a nice service, and it felt good to worship in *English*," Fred said when walking back to the boat.

"I'll say, but I almost giggled when the pastor welcomed us as a 'couple from the far corner of our country—Oregon.' And I learned that if I say we are from the 'West Coast,' people here automatically think we mean the west coast of Florida."

"Right. And they just assume we had the boat trucked across the country. Everyone is surprised to hear that we actually sailed here."

After a fun afternoon watching the Super Bowl, we continued on our way the next morning. Shortly after leaving, it began to rain in earnest. How we loved staying warm and dry in our inside-steering station, only going outside to line through a lock or through some of the bridges that had to be opened. As we neared the eastern coast we were astounded by the huge, opulent mansions we saw along the shore. We had definitely left the backwoods and remote country of inland Florida.

When we reached the Atlantic Ocean, we turned southward on the Intracoastal Waterway, or ICW. This popular route is a mixture of natural channels, bays, rivers and manmade passageways that extended far north along the Atlantic seaboard, and down around the Florida peninsula into the Gulf of Mexico all the way to Texas. Much of the waterway is protected from the ocean waters, so it is often used by small craft and recreational boats. The dredged channel was, however, very narrow in spots, and although these were usually well marked, it required constant attention to avoid going aground. The VHF radio often had calls for a "Mariner's assist" to help get a boat back into deeper water after it had strayed from the channel.

When we got to Lake Worth, we found an anchorage—one of the few in this area. Most places in southern Florida prohibit anchoring, not wanting live-aboard folks to stay for long periods of time. We set up the dinghy and went ashore, tying it up to a chain link fence with other dinghies. As we climbed the hill to get to the sidewalk, we laughed at what we must have looked like.

"I feel like I'm one of the homeless or a vagrant," Fred said, lugging a bag of garbage.

"Yeah. I think I now have the distinction between *yachties*, and *cruisers. Yachties* stay in big fancy marinas with all the amenities, and travel short or protected distances, usually in big cities. Cruisers do all of the opposite. For the most part they are self-contained, travel as much as possible and look for different places and experiences. There are times I'd definitely like to be a *yachtie,* but for the long haul, I love what we are able to see and do by cruising. Our trip would surely be much shorter if we had to pay for a marina every night."

We checked out a number or boating stores looking for our tiny metric screw, but "no joy." (Radio jargon for "no contact.") We did, however, get a lot of exercise.

Traveling the ICW meant going through or under many bridges. Some had a schedule for openings, which often meant throwing out an anchor and waiting for significant periods of time. One day, while waiting for a bridge to open, we got bunched up with four Canadian boats on the way south. We were able to form a little flotilla, which was great. It saved each of us from having to radio ahead to each bridge to request an opening. The leader made the contact for all of us.

When underway, there was always a good deal of boat traffic in both directions. In the Okeechobee waterway, the large power vessels slowed when they passed us so we weren't thrown around by their big wakes. Many of the boaters on the ICW were not so courteous. Since in many places the shores of the channel were lined with cement walls, a powerful wake continued to reverberate back and forth, causing a lot of turbulence and concern. For some, it seemed an "everybody for themself" mentality, which was a real change from our previous experiences.

As we neared Fort Lauderdale, we saw a protected little bay with a couple of anchored boats. Since it was late in the afternoon, and a storm was predicted, we were relieved to drop the hook. The next day we called one of the other boats to find out where we could leave the dinghy to go into town. Their directions took us under a bridge that had seven feet clearance at low water. But we were at high water and barely had two feet clearance.

"We're going to go under *that*? We'll never make it," I said.

"Just lie down, and watch your head," Fred said.

I was afraid to look up when we went underneath, knowing for certain there would be dozens of spiders and other yucky things about to jump on my head.

We entered a huge marina that moored the largest sail and motor yachts I think we had ever seen. We gasped in wonder at the sight. Some even had pads for helicopters to land, and swimming pools, and "garages" for multiple additional vessels onboard, including jet boats, speed boats, sailing craft—all the toys imaginable. Uniformed crew members could be seen moving about the many level decks. We felt dwarfed as we passed alongside these marine behemoths and our necks hurt from looking up at them towering many stories above us.

"Wow. These boats are incredible. They look like floating hotels or resorts. And there's so many of them."

"Think of what they must cost, and how many people it would take to operate them. It's staggering. Simply unbelievable."

The marina manager said we could leave our dinghy and showed us where to put it.

We walked the streets for *hours*, looking in five or six marine stores for the illusive screw, again without success. Finally we called a store quite some distance from us. A tiny strand of hope—at least he had heard of our system, and after hearing our tale of woe, said he'd come pick us up. *Wow—how nice.* He did just that, and took us back to his store where he searched for about an hour for the screw replacement.

"O.K." he announced. "I found one on a German sewing machine, but it's too long for you." We groaned in dismay. "But I'll go next door to the machine shop and grind it down to the right length."

What a Sweetheart. And then he drove us back to our dinghy, and said, "No charge." We were stunned, and very touched. Besides our effusive thanks, we wrote a little note to the store owner to express our appreciation.

"You know, these kinds of experiences continue to awe me and restore my faith in people, especially when there's so much pain and sadness and thoughtlessness all around us."

"Yeah. And it makes me want to pass on the kindness—'do unto others...' What a world it would be if we all passed it on all the time." *Gracias a Dios.*

We rowed back to the boat to install that illusive little bugger in its rightful place. Using the winches, I hauled Fred up the forestay in the bosun's chair, and an hour later, the job was done. Finally, we could cross "replace the jib furling screw" off the "to do" list.

A big storm came in the following day creating wind, rain and cold. We stayed on the boat, marveling in the realization that Florida really did experience winter. The following morning, we were getting ready to go to shore, when we were visited by the Fort Lauderdale police boat.

"There's no anchoring allowed within the city," the officer said politely. "You need to move your boat."

When I mentioned the storm that was forecasted to continue, and that we'd traveled over 10,000 miles in fourteen countries and never had been told to leave a place, he replied that we could stay for 24 hours.

"You really know how to 'sweet talk' the police," Fred laughed later.

"Well, maybe that comes from growing up with a dad that was a policeman. At least we can say we've been kicked out of some of the country's best places—first, the Pebble Beach Golf Course, and now Fort Lauderdale's waters."

One of the joys of our dream was sharing it with the kids, and now that Dawn could fly for free, she came to visit us. It was fun to be a tourist; spending a few days going to the malls, taking in some beach and sunbathing time, and checking out Happy Hours that had free food.

One day we went to a popular place right on the ICW. Although it was cold at night, it was definitely hot during the day and we savored the warm sunshine as we sat on the deck overlooking the water, sipping a cool drink and watching all the pleasure boats coming in to the dock for a special event. Observing docking procedures was often amusing, and had even been labeled "marina theater" and we were enjoying the show. Skippers often faced a challenging maneuver as they dealt with changing winds, currents, tidal flows, and different types of docking requirements. Added to the mix were varying levels of seamanship skills, and sometimes alcohol use, along with "performance anxiety" created when many others were watching—it all combined to make a sometimes humorous (as long as it wasn't happening to us) and often exciting event. It was verbally colorful and sometimes chaotic with lots of shouting and dashing about. Up in the overlooking restaurant there was loud, infectious and upbeat music blaring. It was a real party atmosphere.

"There. See that? That's the kind of boat you should get," Dawn said and pointed to a huge power vessel. "Wouldn't that be cool? Or how about that one?" Another impressive motor yacht. After all these years, we still were not going to make a sailor out of her.

She was not anxious to return to snowy New York, but going back to work was softened by plans to fly to Italy with us in a few weeks, using those wonderful parent passes.

We talked with Page and Steve to find that they also had three inches of snow in Oregon. They also told us that the renters' check had bounced and they were again behind in payment. *Would we have to fly home to get new renters?* It wasn't a pleasant thought.

Now that we were back in the States, getting around in cities was often a challenge without the use of a car. Our transportation usually involved taking buses. We quickly found that the U.S. systems were not as frequent nor as easy to use as those in many of the Latin countries. There were lots of challenges in navigating around a city in a bus. Sometimes a driver would say he'd tell us when to get off, and then forget to do so. One driver got out of the bus, saying he needed his relief driver, and then disappeared. No replacement ever showed up. Getting to a church or a particular marine store often involved transfers and complex routes, as well as *lots* of walking.

Along major highways, we often found that there were no sidewalks and crossing the motorway meant going across eight or ten lanes of traffic that had no pedestrian signals. It felt rather death-defying. When we asked someone for directions, they were always given in terms of driving time, and people would be incredulous when we said we were walking. Sometimes our "dogs" were killing us. We'd stop to get groceries, and by the time we'd get back to the boat with all our bundles, not only our feet, but also our arms were aching. One day we carried 25 letters around with us all day looking for a mailbox.

But there was one perk in riding the buses—it was an up close and personal look at life in that city. It also was great for "people watching" and I could imagine a story about almost everybody we would see. Some of them were real corkers. I enjoyed that activity more than Fred who was more interested in reaching our destination.

After one very long day of traveling around Fort Lauderdale by bus, we returned to *Grace* dead tired and aching all over.

"Do you think that maybe we are getting too old to be doing this?"

"Well, I'm sure glad we didn't wait any longer to try it." *Oh the joys of cruising.*

As we traveled southward, we found more rural areas, less traffic and less speedboats, which was a welcome relief. That all changed when we arrived in Miami—another metropolis of boaters. The Miami Boat Show, the largest of its kind, was in full swing and it was quite an event. We had known boaters that flew from Cartagena to Miami just to attend it. It was huge and had three different venues with a shuttle bus to travel between them. It was a great place to get our questions answered about products we already had, or pick up smaller needed items. After looking at many displays we wearily stopped at a bench in the shade along the ICW to eat the picnic lunch we carried with us. It even included a glass of wine, packed in a glass jar—so many ways to save money. I often thought how nice it would be to eat out, or buy off the street. But if we included all the "extras" we wouldn't be able to afford to do all we were doing. So for now, we'd continue traveling on our "shoestring," be grateful that we're able to realize the dream, and hope that our house renters paid up soon.

"It's great to see all this stuff, but it sure doesn't have the allure and excitement of those great weekends we used to have at the Seattle Boat Show when the dream lay ahead of us."

"That's for sure. Those were really special times. Hey, look. It says in the brochure that Northshore has a booth here. Let's go find it."

What fun it was to find the exhibit of the company in England that had built our boat. We talked with Alan, whom we had met when we were at the boatyard taking possession of *Grace*. He was tickled to see us. It was like "old home week." There were only a few Southerlys in the U.S. at the time, but the plan was to develop a market here. It was good to see so many other types of sailboats and know that we were very pleased with what we had chosen. Of course, there were times when it would have been nice to have a little more space. I think all boaters, regardless of the size of their boat, end up saying that.

We moved on down the ICW, stopping to anchor in Biscayne Bay. The docking procedure in the previous marina had been harrowing. A strong wind in the wrong direction had made it almost impossible to get stern lines around large pilings, and there had been no one around to help.

"It feels *so* good to be away from a dock and on the water again."

"Sure does. Why don't you get out your guitar for a while?"

Fred knew that music tended to "soothe the savage beast" or at least provided a good outlet for me. It was also one of those ways we had devised to provide "private" space in cramped quarters. Another good form of therapy for me was to write in our daily logue. It was a good way to get out the grumpy feelings or complaints, without having to carry them around inside.

"We'd better get out of here before you strain yourself from all that 'rubbernecking,'" I said with feigned irritation.

"Hey, I'm just 'people watching,'" Fred laughed. "You always say *you* enjoy it."

"But I'm not focused on just the twenty year old *topless* beauties."

We had gone to the famous (or was it the *infamous?*) South Beach. Walking the streets of that art deco suburb of Miami was like walking in a Humphrey Bogart movie set—a step back in time to the 1930's. It was so different from the proliferation of large, sleek, modern hotels on other beaches in the area. Along the boardwalk were throngs of young folks, even in midweek. Many were roller-skating and wearing crazy "get-ups." And of course, there was the beach itself—the notorious topless sunbathing beach. I pulled Fred along to the shopping area, but I must admit that I'd never before seen so many beautiful women in one place.

Finally, there was a day of great sailing in brisk winds. By late afternoon we had found a small island and got our anchor down just as torrential rains began. Fortunately, the island afforded us some protection from the 35 knot winds. Three other boats came into the bay and anchored, but fearful of dragging, each one had someone out in the cockpit to control their vessel with their engine. We were feeling pretty good with our choice of location and our all-chain rode as we observed the others out in the rain. That was to change a few hours later.

"Aarrgh. Should have known better than to start feeling smug," Fred groaned.

The wind had changed from the forecasted direction, we lost our protection and we bounced up and down in the waves the wind created. I think the Sea Gods must like to keep folks humble. I was mad. It was the principle of the thing. We planned carefully, listened intently to many weather reports and picked our positions accordingly. But still the forecasters so often got it wrong.

"Hey—there's no guarantees," Fred said calmly. "That's cruising."

We lay down on the main cabin settees that evening, expecting a long uncomfortable night with frequent anchor watches. Thankfully, the wind died down about nine and we were able to go to bed for a calm night and good sleep. Although grateful for the reprieve, I was still feeling irritated.

When we came near to Key Largo we decided to go into a marina that had a long, winding, narrow channel approach through very shallow water. I doubt we'd have tried it without our lifting keel. It was a small "mom and pop" operation with friendly people, old but stable appearing docks, and a woods-like setting.

"We don't get many transient boats in here," the woman said. "Welcome! What can we do to help you?"

Wow. I think I like it here. It was inexpensive too, so we thought that if we could get from here to the airport, it would be a good place to leave the boat to go to Rome with Dawn. We still didn't know, however, if she was going to be able to arrange for time off work.

Following the owner's suggestion, we rented a car from a "Rent-a-Wreck" place in Key Largo. We packaged up some equipment that needed to be sent in for repair, and took the boxes along with our life raft, which needed to be serviced in Miami. We had finally made the decision to eventually head north up the eastern seaboard this year, and possibly go on to Europe the following year, but we would still need the life raft recertified for going to The Bahamas and travel in the Atlantic. Hopefully, our other equipment would be sent back to us by the time we returned from Rome.

A woman we had met at the restaurant by the marina gave us a ride into Key Largo. Our car was indeed a wreck, but the old station wagon functioned. We were tickled to have "wheels" and be independent and went first to the life raft service store in south Miami. We had been warned that it was located in a very rough part of town. While we were there, the owner opened and inflated the raft, showed us all of the emergency gear inside, and explained how to use it.

"That was cool to see what the raft contained," I said, "but I sure hope we never have occasion to see it again."

We were also grateful that it could be serviced and repacked while we waited, rather than having to come back for it. It was a thoughtful, extra effort on the owner's part.

Another less delightful part of the morning, was when we learned that we had become victims of the infamous "Miami Tourist Special." After leaving the raft shop, we went to the West Marine store in order to obtain repairs for our hand-held VHF radio. I had put it in the backseat when we left the boat, but after thorough searching, we could not find it. Then I discovered that our lunch cooler was open, and a can of beer was missing.

"We've been robbed," I cried.

"You're right. They must have come in through the back hatch while we were inside the life raft store."

"But look. They didn't take any of our other equipment that was in the boxes. Just the radio. They must have been in a hurry."

"Thank goodness for that. Obviously, they didn't know what was in the packages. Those things are worth thousands of dollars."

"And 'Ha' on them! The radio wasn't even working. But I'm really ticked that they took our beer. Its creepy to think of them pawing through our stuff."

The West Marine manager was sympathetic when hearing our story and said he'd sell us another radio at wholesale cost. It was still an unexpected hit on the cruising budget, but it could have been so much worse.

Trying to find the UPS store, we got hopelessly lost several times. Each time we'd ask someone for directions and end up in a different, but wrong place. Since I was the navigator, I was totally frustrated and finally had had it.

"It's just not been a very good day," I sniffled as I wiped my tears. "We had planned to do the Okeechobee Waterway so we could skip this whole area of Florida, and here we are—right in the middle of it, spending a good deal of time in our least favorite place. And we're not even sure we'll get to go to Rome after all this waiting. We could have gone on to The Bahamas."

Fred was consoling and supportive as usual, but I wasn't done with my pity party.

"And we might have to go back to get new renters, they owe us a ton of money, and we're stuck in the boonies again."

"You're right. Let's quit, sell the boat and go home," said Fred with a straight face. "Why would *anyone* want to do this? It's crazy. Absolutely crazy."

That made us both laugh and I realized it was time to stop "crying in my beer." I felt better for having done it, however. Certainly the perks of this lifestyle more than compensated for the struggles and inconveniences. I guess a little rain must fall in every dream. We were still truly grateful for the opportunity and the experiences—well, most of them.

We decided it was time for a *fun* day with no boat stuff. We traded our wreck for one with a trunk so that we could lock things more securely in the car, and left the following day for Key West. Driving down the Overseas Highway with the Atlantic Ocean on the left and the Gulf of Mexico or Florida bay waters on the right was eerie. So much water—as far as one could see. One bridge was seven miles long. It felt like we were going to drop off the edge of the world.

The Keys definitely exhibited a "laid-back" lifestyle compared to the hustle and bustle of Miami and we enjoyed the contrast. Key West was all we had heard—quaint, charming "gingerbread" houses with a lacey old fashioned, "story-book" architecture, lined the narrow residential streets like rows of colorful flowers. Each home was surrounded by a small yard with lush, green tropical gardens and a white picket or stone fence with arched gates. I almost expected to see a lady walking down the sidewalk with a big fancy plumed hat, long bustled skirts and parasol. Colorful little shops crowded the funky downtown area with all the usual tourist entrapments. It was a little like a miniature San Francisco. There was evidence of a large gay population, as well as a rowdy "anything goes" kind of atmosphere. Many "adult" bookstores were interspersed with dive shops, bars, restaurants and beach gear. And it was hot. Finally finding a little shade, we sat on a curb by the large cruise ship dock to eat our picnic lunch after exploring the streets baking in the full blazing sun. We debated about spending the night in order to see the big daily sunset celebration, but opted to wait to spend our nickel in Rome—still hoping we'd be able to go. Driving back, the power steering went out and the fan worked only intermittently, but we stopped for a cold beer and enjoyed some good music. All in all, a fun and different kind of day.

"Hooray. She's got the time off and the tickets. We're going to Rome."

Back at the marina, we had twice walked the half-mile to the pay phone in the dark in order to contact Dawn. One time, I had almost stepped on a snake. Yuk! I shivered even at the thought of it. And the no-see-ums had returned to plague us now that the hotter weather had returned. Yesterday it was 90 degrees and muggy. But it should be nice in *Italy*.

We had to wait almost a week before the trip, and plans to go out on the hook were thwarted by one of those notorious "northers" that shot down the coastline from Canada. So we paid for the marina with the monthly rate and returned to repair/maintenance projects. The leak in the bow had again returned when we had been under sail. How frustrating. We didn't know where else to look for the water's entry point.

It was Sunday morning. We were packed and ready to go. On Monday we'd get up at three in the morning to try for a six o'clock standby flight to New York, as all the other later flights were full. Flying standby was always anxiety producing, as we never knew until the last minute if any seats would be available. The plan was to meet Dawn at JFK airport, where she would be returning from an earlier flight that day.

I decided to take my blood pressure, something I hadn't done in months, as I had some blurry vision in one eye. *Whoa*—the pressure was all right, but my heart rhythm was very irregular. I listened to my heartbeat several different times with the same results.

"It's foolish not to get it checked out," Fred said. "I'm going to see if that guy who lives here will drive us to a hospital."

Harry was quite willing to drive us the 30 miles to the ER at Florida City Hospital. I was quickly put on a cardiac monitor, and given a number of blood tests, an EKG and X-ray. After five hours of observation, the doc said they weren't sure what was causing the irregular pattern, but it had converted back to a normal rhythm, and I should see a cardiologist. Knowing that we were planning a trip the following morning, she somewhat reluctantly said it would be OK to go. What an exhausting day. We had bounced around from feeling the whole situation was unreal, to being scared and anxious, and eventually concerned, perplexed, relieved and grateful. Harry had patiently waited all that time, assured us that it was no problem for him, and even took us to the airport the next morning at four. Another angel unaware. How they blessed the world. Those prayers of loved ones continued to surround us with grace. *Gracias a Dios.*

"*Arrivederchi, Roma!*" we all cried as we flew over that marvelous Italian city after spending a wonderful week there. Dawn had worked hard to put together a great vacation for the three of us using her flight attendant privileges, which included a nice Holiday Inn hotel for half price. We walked the streets until we were ready to drop, and savored the history, art and architecture of one of the most beautiful cities in the world. And oh yes—the wine! A favorite pastime for all of us, was sitting in the sun at a sidewalk café, or sharing a bottle of wine while sitting on the steps of one of the many beautiful squares adorned with ornate sculptured fountains. Dawn had never been much of a sightseer, but even she was impressed with all there was to see and do, and we paced ourselves as we took in one incredible sight after another. She was great fun to be with—a real character in fact, but kind and thoughtful in so many ways. She certainly was the object of a good deal of attention from the Italian men. After talking for some time with one nice young man at the Trevi Fountain, we stood up and said we had to go.

"But can *she* stay?" he said as he smiled at Dawn.

One night I ate from an antipasto buffet bar, and unfortunately got food poisoning. But I was better by the following morning and we made our third trip to St. Peter's to see the pope wave to the crowd in the immense plaza. It was a nice way to spend our final day in Rome. We kept the party spirit alive as we soaked up the luxury of the Business Class cabin while flying home, and arrived back in Florida tired but happy.

"O.K. The time-crunch is on. We've got just ten days to get to The Bahamas and pick up Page and Steve in Nassau."

"Oh me. We're doing it *again*. Another schedule to keep, and a rough body of water to cross. That Gulf Stream is definitely not to be messed with in lousy weather."

We took the boat back up the ICW about ten miles, turned into a winding creek that led to the outer channel next to the ocean, and sailed about eighteen miles south to a small cay. Three other boats were waiting there for favorable conditions to cross to The Bahamas. We set our alarm for two the next morning, but we were up checking the forecasts at eleven, one, two and four before finally deciding it was a "no go."

"It's really disappointing, but I think we made the right decision," I said. We had just listened to the latest weather report.

"It's that big front that's moving down from the north, that I'm worried about," said Fred. "If that arrives, it will be at least three or four more days before we can get out."

When wind from the north hits the strong current of the Gulf Stream coming from the south, big violent seas are set up. One does not want to cross that body of water with any kind of north wind, and that came often in the winter and early spring. Again, we set our alarm for the following morning. Bob, a fellow we had talked to on the radio from one of the other boats, wanted to come with us if we decided to go. He was single-handing and wanted the company. We were up an hour before the alarm went off. We needed to leave very early in the morning in order to enter onto The Bahamas' banks while there was still daylight.

"Hooray—a 24 hour weather window to make the crossing. Its light wind, and coming from the right direction. Let's go."

We worked our way across the Florida coastline reef and headed northeast. Soon, the Gulf Stream caught us and gave us a push of two to four additional knots, which made for a fast passage. Although the wind was light at first, it freshened and we had a great sail until we came close to the narrow entry channel leading onto The Bahamas' banks in the late afternoon. We took down the sails and started the engine. We were in very shallow water when a thunderstorm went by, with lots of rain, wind, limited visibility and lightning. As if there wasn't enough to think about, the radio weather reports always referred to the "deadly" lightning. The squall passed. We lined up on range markers and began to wind our way through the tricky entrance. The wind was blowing hard on the beam, threatening to push us out of the channel and we rolled from side to side with the gusts, all within yards of threatening rocks. Once inside, we breathed a sigh of relief, motored a short ways and threw out the anchor in calm water.

"Well, this is a first," Fred said. "We've gone from water that was virtually miles deep, to water depth that's ten to fourteen feet in less than a mile."

"I guess that's what 'banks' means. And it will be about the same depth almost the entire hundred miles over to Nassau," I added.

Bob, who had closely followed us over from the mainland, had anchored nearby. Immediately after doing so, we were slammed with another thunderstorm directly over us.

"Sure glad this wasn't fifteen minutes earlier. We'd have been

Kay Koudele

right in that twisting channel and wouldn't have been able to see a thing."

"It's not coincidence, you know. No such thing as coincidence. We were just plain *blucky!*"

We had planned to wait a day before going on to Nassau, but the wind the next morning was from the west—a great direction for us, so we and Bob left about six. It was a good downwind sail with strong wind, but by afternoon we knew we'd not make it to the next anchorage by dark, so we fired up the engine. About six, just before we lost daylight, we arrived at an anchorage protected from the north wind.

"Come on," Bob was saying on the radio the next morning. "It's only 36 miles to Nassau, and the wind is good. Let's 'git while the gittin's good.'"

We had never met this man face to face, although we knew that he liked to talk, and we had talked dozens of times on the radio over the last few days. The pressure was now off for keeping the schedule to meet the kids. We had planned to check into the country at this stop, and were really ready for a day of rest. But Bob was charged up and raring to go on. He had also become a cruising "buddy," so we reluctantly agreed to make the final leg with him. As we got things together for another day on the water, I remembered my mom saying, "no rest for the weary."

We had only been underway for a couple of hours when the wind shifted from north to east. *Of course*—right where we were going. We could still sail, but it was close into the wind, not nearly as comfortable, and we had a strong current flowing against us. Our speed slowed significantly. It took us twice as long as we had anticipated before finally arriving in Nassau. By the time we entered the harbor just before dark, we were exhausted and wearily looked for a place to drop the hook in the crowded anchorage. Just then, we heard a call on the radio.

"*Amazing Grace, Amazing Grace,*" a voice said.

We answered, wondering who was calling and why.

"You don't know us. We are here for a week visiting friends, but

142

we've read every one of your "Awesome Adventures" newsletters! We love them."

In a quick conversation, we realized that we had mutual friends that had shared our letters that we had sent to our church family. What a small world! But there was no time to talk further. We hurried to find a place to anchor before dark.

"Wow. There are hundreds of boats in here," I said. "Look at them all."

"Well, if we clear in to customs now there'll be overtime charges. Let's just throw out the hook and hope the authorities won't care if we wait until tomorrow to check in."

Due to the large number of boats and strong tidal current in the harbor, everyone used a Bahamian Moor—which required setting an anchor from both bow and stern. This limited the boat's swing. It wasn't going well when we attempted it the first time. After getting one line fouled and eventually both anchors set, it was dark. We raised our yellow quarantine flag, and almost fell into the cabin.

"I remember what it is about making a passage that I like so well."

"What's that?"

"It's ever so *sweet* when it's over."

We laughed as we savored our ritual "Miller Time" and toasted our arrival in *The Bahamas.*

Eight
The Magical Bahamas

We had known that marinas in this country would be expensive, so we were pleased to find one that had no amenities, but a good price. We hadn't needed to worry about clearing in late, as we found the officials friendly and helpful, not even asking when we had entered the country or the harbor. We quickly cleaned up the boat as items became scattered all over during a passage, and then went to meet Bob for lunch and explore our new surroundings.

"Can you believe there are 400 banks in this place? Look. There's several in every block and on every corner. That's a lot of money flowing through this country."

"Yeah, but most of the locals seem to have only a modest income. But there's certainly a higher economic standard than Central America. And they sure are friendly."

"I'll say. Well, tourism's their number one industry. It looks like everybody sees themself as a personal representative of the Chamber of Commerce. I love those 'Hi, Mon' greetings."

Downtown Nassau was a bustle of activity. Traffic and pedestrians crowded the streets in the early afternoon. The buildings had a special charm of an earlier era, but there were many modern street level shops with all the latest in fashion and necessities. Small sidewalk stalls with colorful displays sold local produce and tourist souvenirs. Most prices were high by the U.S. standards. Whenever we were about to cross a street, someone would quickly caution us when we looked the wrong way for oncoming cars. Traffic here, flowed in the "wrong" (for us Yanks) direction—evidence of the British influence.

Back on the dock, we enjoyed talking with many of the other boaters. Most were from Florida, with some from the U.S. east coast, having come south via the ICW. It was an annual migration for the winter months, much like the RV "Snowbirds" on land.

"When we say that it's our first time in The Bahamas, everyone assumes we are new to sailing and starts telling us how to do things. It was amusing at first, but it's happened so much it's starting to be irritating. Many act like they know it all."

"Well, the 'local knowledge' stuff about the area is good to have. Maybe you should just tell them that we've come 10,000 miles in the last three years. That usually gets their attention," Fred laughed.

From our marina it was an easy walk over to Paradise Island, the epicenter of the tourism trade. Huge, modern hotels lined the beautiful white sand beaches, which were full of bikini-clad sunbathers. The graceful palm trees and stunning turquoise waters truly made this place look like a tropical paradise in the glittering sunlight. But one's attention was abruptly jarred from the serenity of the picturesque scene by the invasion of many "Banana" boats, jet skis, para-sailing boats, and all kinds of tourist vendors. Everyone wanted a piece of the tourist action. The spectacular Atlantis Hotel was a favorite place to explore. It had lush tropical gardens and an aquarium with a tunnel where we could walk under the water and watch the fish swim overhead. They charged thirty dollars a day for the use of their pool and grounds, although a guard said we could come on their beach without charge.

There was no end of tourist and recreational pleasures offered along the busy streets. And of course, there were the time-share presentation sales pitches. We actually signed up for one, as it gave us "free" money to use at the big casino. We checked out the

Radisson Hotel on our way back to the boat, and after asking, found that we could swim in their pool just for patronage of their bar or restaurant. We were glad we had inquired. We had lots of things on the "to do" list for when the kids arrived.

Being from the Pacific West Coast, our image of The Bahamas held a sort of magical allure. Not many from that distant location came here for vacations. Perhaps those from the East Coast felt the same way about Hawaii. As a result, all of our kids wanted to come and visit us while we were here. We had originally hoped to see a lot of the islands, but with kids flying into Nassau on three different occasions, we likely would not get too far away from this home base. The thrill of having them with us, however, made up for the disappointment of not seeing more of the island chain. Page and Steve were the first to arrive. We had cleaned up the boat, prepared some special foods, cleared out and made up two berths in the bow cabin. We excitedly went to the airport to greet them. We had not been able to reach them to confirm our arrival with the boat, so I was anxious that they saw us as they stepped off the plane in the bright morning sunlight.

"I can't see for sure without my glasses," Page had said, "but that woman over there has got to be my mom."

"Who else would be jumping up and down, and waving their arms like that," Steve had laughed.

Poor things. They had flown all night. A long trip and a tiring way to travel. But, oh how good it was to see them. There was so much to catch up on as we enjoyed some relaxing poolside time. Hopefully the late afternoon sunshine wouldn't burn their "winter white" skin. Page had received her first choice for a residency program in Internal Medicine, and would be staying in Portland. Yippee. Steve was also busy with his studies in the College of Oriental Medicine. They were both ready for a vacation.

We soon put some of that medical knowledge to use as Page listened to my erratic heart rhythm.

"Gee, Mom. I really think you should have a cardiologist evaluate that," she said. "Is there one here?"

The dock-master told us of a doctor trained in the U.S., whose office was within walking distance. When we called, they arranged for us to be seen the following day. Page was there to listen and interpret all the tests I was given. I appreciated her company. The result was that it was a non-life threatening problem, but that I should probably take medication to help control it. How nice to have our own personal physician make "boat-calls." We began to call her D.D.D.D.—Darling Daughter, Doctor Dardis.

"Once again, we were in the right place at the right time for this to happen," I said to Fred as we lay in bed. "I don't like being reminded that I'm not immortal, and that the ol' bod' is starting to break down. But can you imagine how hard it would have been to get medical care in some of the places we have been in? *Blucky, blucky.*"

"And yes, yes, I know," Fred replied with a smile as he squeezed my hand. "It was no *coincidence.*" *Gracias a Dios.*

On Sunday morning, while Page and Steve slept in, Fred and I went to the nearby Church of England—the oldest church on the island. It definitely exuded a British flair. While we were two of only a half dozen Caucasian folks in attendance, it was perhaps the warmest, friendliest, and most joyous church we had ever visited.

"Can you believe that service lasted over two hours?" Fred marveled. "And even more amazing—I didn't want it to end."

"Me either. What a treat. That processional must have had 75 people in it. And the music and singing—they sang with their whole body and soul. I can't wait to go back."

It was a fun nine days. We enjoyed time at the beach, pools, and casino before spending three days in the outer islands. Only a short distance from the Nassau harbor was the little island used for the opening camera shots of the television series, "Gilligan's Island." The "Koudele tour boat" took a detour to see that familiar landmark while the crew serenaded the passengers with the show's theme song. Page and Steve joined in, and we sounded pretty good. We anchored at a neighboring island for some snorkeling and spent the night. The anchorage was pretty roll-y, however, and Steve resorted to taking some Dramamine in the afternoon. That put him to sleep until the next morning. He woke up hungry. As always, they were good sports and never complained. Steve loved to play, especially in the casino, and had a great sense of humor that often had us all laughing.

Many of the islands had a windward side, where the shoreline was covered with rough black volcanic rock. Its jagged edges made walking difficult. On the other or leeward side, there were lovely little white sand beaches, ideal for anchoring. Crystal clear water allowed us to view the ocean bottom while sitting in the boat, just as if we were snorkeling. The colors of the water were absolutely breathtaking. Never had I seen such vibrant, sometimes illuminant turquoise in so many different shades. But the winds were fickle and strong, particularly at this time of year, and often changed directions so that what appeared to be a protected anchorage when we arrived, sometimes became "Rock and Roll City" during the night. Sleep was especially challenging on such occasions. At other times, four people on a boat became a little snug, so it was good to be somewhere where the kids could get out on their own for a time. Sometimes they swam in for a walk on the soft sand beach.

On Page and Steve's final night, we walked about a mile to a nice recommended restaurant. We had been cautioned about walking after dark as Nassau had its share of big-city problems, one of which was theft.

"Oh, you'll be all right," our waitress had said. "They leave the tourists alone. You are our 'bread and butter.'"

All the locals wanted to take care of us, so that our stay in the islands was enjoyable. Their efforts all felt genuine. Tourism was also Hawaii's leading industry, but we hadn't felt that same sense of caring from the people when we had been there on several occasions.

On Sunday morning we loaded the kids into a taxi for the airport and said our goodbyes, then hurried off to be with our *other* family—the wonderful Church of England. It was just as good as before.

"Oh no. I just broke off the whole side of my tooth," I cried. "What next? I really am falling apart."

Fortunately, there was a dentist's office right across the street from our dock. When I went to talk to them, they had me wait a short time, and then put on a temporary crown.

"Man, I've never heard of this kind of immediate service. Incredible."

We were very impressed with not only the level of medical and dental care, but also the manner and timeliness in which it was delivered. They really catered to the tourist. But we needed no more examples, thank you very much.

We left the following morning to see the Exuma Islands before we needed to return to Nassau for the next family visit. After about two hours of sailing, the winds became very strong, and the seas uncomfortable. We decided to turn in at Rose Island. Because the north side was so roll-y when we were there with the kids, we anchored on the south side.

"Ha. The north side was *nothing* compared to what we had here last night," Fred said the next morning. "If I tried to lie on my side, my whole body flipped back and forth like a sausage in a frying pan. I don't think I slept at all."

"I know. I tried to get up one time, and laughed out loud when the boat made a timely roll just as I was leaving the bed. It propelled my out of there like a rocket launcher."

It was too rough to go ashore, so Fred put out another anchor and we tried to nap and read. By afternoon the bouncing had diminished some after the passing of a big squall. A French boat came in, and they came over to ask about marinas further north. They spoke very little English. We couldn't answer all their questions so we called our friendly dock-master and relayed his information back to them, for which they were very grateful. It felt good to help someone else, after being on the receiving end so much.

That night we were slammed with another storm. *Where was that lovely spring weather? It surely wasn't here.* Fred decided to stay up to keep an eye on the anchors. I was almost asleep when immense blinding lightning flashed directly over us, along with the simultaneous crashing roar of thunder that shook the boat and reverberated in our ears. The solar panel lights immediately started blinking.

"Were we hit?" I cried and jumped out of bed.

"I'm not sure," Fred yelled. "Let's get this gear away from the nav station."

We ran around the boat moving electronic equipment and looking for any sign of damage. Fred checked the bilge to see if we were taking on any water. I took our two GPS units and put them in the pressure cooker and closed the seal.

"Does that protect them?" Fred asked.

"I don't know. Somewhere I read that. Doesn't hurt to try."

We couldn't find anything amiss, so finally I went back to bed, with Fred coming a little later. The wind had changed direction *again*, things calmed down completely, and we had a good nights sleep. Ah...we needed that. *Oh, the joys of cruising.*

I had gotten up early, and sat in the cockpit to watch a beautiful sunrise unfolding over the clear horizon. Its gentle colors turned the sky from gradually lightening grey to soft pink, and eventually the golden orange and brilliant rose that heralded a beautiful day— God's paintbrush at its best. The coolness of the air and the stillness of the water wrapped around me like a favorite velvety shawl, and filled me with a sense of peace and wonder. I was flooded with thoughts of the bountiful grace and blessings that had sustained us these past three years on the water, and speculated about what lay ahead. Recently, we had talked more about this dream of cruising, wondering if we were beginning to approach the end of it. While the idea of going on to Europe next year was not entirely gone, it certainly had dimmed. *Was it time to begin another chapter in our lives?* It was a bittersweet thought. I smiled to myself as I remembered what my mom had written in my autograph book when I was in the fifth grade:

We cannot change yesterday, that is clear,
Or start tomorrow before it is here.
So all that is left for you and for me,
Is to make today as sweet as can be.

From October, 1913 Farm Journal

I was sure it was going to be a very sweet day.

We had stopped at another uninhabited little island and gone ashore.

"Not too close around the ears," Fred chuckled.

"You'll get what you paid for," I retorted with feigned irritation.

Fred was sitting on a rock on the beach while I gave him a haircut. I liked not having to sweep up the hair falling on the floor or deck. Afterwards, we spent some well-deserved (we told ourselves) lazy time sitting in the shade of some palm trees and reading our books. When going for a walk on the beach, we saw a "party boat" from one of the big cruise ships that regularly came to Nassau. They had brought a load of people to the island for a barbeque lunch and time to play in the sand and water.

"Let's go over there and see if they'll sell us a meal," I suggested.

We found the staff very accommodating, and they gave us lunch without charge, asking only that we didn't spread the news to other cruisers. When I asked, the cooks were quite willing to share a traditional Bahamian recipe—peas and rice. It was really delicious, and I didn't even like peas. Island music filled the air, adding to the party spirit. We saw that one of the steel drum players was a woman. We had only seen men playing these unique drums, and she seemed to enjoy our attention and questions about her skills and the memorable, mellow music of this typical Caribbean instrument. When we got back to *Grace* about five o'clock, the wind had begun to freshen and turn to the northeast.

"Oh, oh," Fred said. "This doesn't look good for tonight. Let's go."

We quickly hauled up the anchor, sped around to the opposite side of the island, and had both anchors down by six-thirty, just as it got dark. We exchanged high fives as we saw the wind increase substantially but noted that *Grace* lay calmly behind the protection of the island. We finally had figured out the pattern of this island wind and felt a little smug, although we tried to hide that fact from those cantankerous Sea Gods. We also knew that the pattern could change tomorrow, or even in an instant.

East Bay Marina was starting to feel like a second home, as we came back for family member number two. Although we dozed on the settee until four in the morning, Dawn had apparently not made the standby flights and we reluctantly went to bed. The next morning, there she was. We took her on our now routine tourist highlights trip, including the Straw Market downtown. The many informal small cubicles were packed with local crafts, products and souvenir specialties. The interaction with the fun loving stall owners was the best part. Then the Koudele Tour Boat made its trek to Gilligan's Island once again. We talked Dawn into snorkeling, although she wasn't keen on "swimming with all those fish." Once she got in the water, she loved it. Despite all of our efforts to warn her, she had refused to wear a T-shirt to protect her back from sunburn.

For Easter Sunday, we returned to the harbor and took her to the now familiar old church. Such pageantry and song. It raised the rafters. The service lasted two and a half hours, and while Dawn got a little fidgety, we loved it. Near the end, they asked for those celebrating special occasions to come up front for a blessing. A number of people started forward. The people sitting beside us knew it was our anniversary, and urged us to go.

"Go for it," Dawn said and pushed us out of the pew.

We were at the end of the line, and the only white folks when the priest came to us. He asked, "an anniversary?" When we told him, he said to the congregation with gusto, "32 years." Everyone clapped and yelled a warm approval. We were home!

A little relaxing around the pool, some good food, and it was too quickly time for Dawn to return to Portland, where she was now based. We so enjoyed her company and always seemed to have so much to say to each other. As we put her in a taxi for the airport we could only laugh as she nonchalantly said, "tell Lance and Tanya to wear a T-shirt when they go snorkeling." Her badly burnt back was bright red and peeling.

While it always felt a little lonely after the kids left, there was also something mighty nice about the peace and quiet, the calmer activity level, and not having to do so much cooking. We washed the sheets so that we were ready for our next round of family guests, and then took off for Allen Cay.

"Holy cow. Look at the size of that one up in the bushes," Fred shouted. "He must be five feet long."

"The beach is crawling with them," I replied, "although most of them must be three feet long or smaller. Look at those pointed crowns on some of them. There are dozens of these ugly guys."

We had anchored off the shore of a long white beach on Allen Cay, an uninhabited island famous for its many iguanas. They scampered out of the bushes and ran towards the water when they saw or heard approaching boats. Watching them watch us gave us the feeling we were back in prehistoric times, with miniature dinosaurs, complete with spiked backbones, forked tongues and thick, leathery reptilian body armor. They were advancing towards us, preparing for an assault. In reality, these unique creatures were vegetarian, but as we brought the dinghy close to shore and they came to within three or four feet of us, that fact brought us little comfort.

"Do we *really* want to go ashore?" I questioned. We both stood in shallow water ready to jump back in the dinghy.

We giggled with nervous anticipation as we walked further up onto the beach, but relaxed as the ferocious looking creatures turned their long pointed tails, and ran for the bushes. They never let us get truly close. That was O.K. with me.

Iguanas on Allan Cay in The Bahamas.

We had heard from other boaters about a reef off the island that provided good snorkeling, and checked it out.

"I'm sure glad we put on these short water-ski suits," I said when we climbed back into the dinghy. "That water is pretty cool when you're in it for more than a few minutes."

"Well, I didn't want to stay in very long anyway. The reef was all right, but didn't compare to some of those we've seen."

We moved on down the island chain to another small island. It had an inner harbor, which we explored with the dinghy. The water in the shallow bay was eight feet deep, and in the middle, halfway submerged, was an old rust covered propeller airplane.

"Goodness. I wonder what the story was here."

"And how long has it been here? From the looks of it, it could be World War II vintage."

Looking underwater from the dinghy, we could see a number of big coral heads that often made for good snorkeling, but we couldn't get very excited about making the effort to go in. The sight of a six-foot barracuda reinforced our reluctance and we headed back to *Grace.* In a conversation earlier in the day with cruising friends on the ham radio, they had expressed the same feelings we were now experiencing about cruising in this area. There was a general sense of disappointment after having known the tight "family" feeling with cruisers when far away from the U.S. mainland. We'd met some terrific people here, but there was something missing. It was more like cruising the San Juan Islands of Washington State, or the Canadian Gulf islands. Perhaps it was us, and we were just becoming saturated with sun and sand, snorkeling, boating adventure and life aboard a boat. It was something to think about.

We pulled up our anchor (well... Fred pulled while I directed) and moved on to another cay. There we found a luxurious 100-foot yacht. I guessed we could share a beach with the rich and famous. Later that afternoon, we talked with a couple of European women from that vessel while walking on the beach. Upon our leaving, we noted that they removed their swimsuit tops in the European sunbathing style. Fred was hastily reconsidering our departure, but I pushed him on to find the island ruins described in the guidebook. We climbed over rocks and scrubby vegetation looking for the trail. This entire area was nothing like the lush green of Central America, but more like the arid desert of northern Mexico. We finally found the old rock walls, but were generally unimpressed. And it was hot. We were anxious to get back to the boat and cool off in the water, when we met another couple that *loved* to talk. They wanted to anchor where we were located, but couldn't get their boat in due to the shallow water. Perhaps they were missing contact with other folks, but their talking was non-stop.

"I'm sure glad I have you to talk to," I said to Fred when we got back to the boat. "Of course you don't always listen, but at least I can talk as much as I want."

One night we were in the cockpit when we were intrigued by seeing strange lights in the sky. The following morning we heard on the radio that there had been a rocket launch at Cape Canaveral. We had seen the rocket jettison from the capsule, but didn't know what it was at the time. We were excited about the possibility of seeing another launch before going north.

We ventured into several small anchorages with very shallow water in these abundant islands, often with the help of "local knowledge." How delighted we were again and again with our wonderful lifting keel. On trying to find the "pond" on one island, we could not identify the landmarks that were supposed to indicate the entrance. The outside water was rough, but we put out an anchor. Fred got in the dinghy and motored in to check out the depths, while I stayed on the boat with the engine running, ready to control our position should the anchor not hold. I was glad that Fred was back shortly, as I had not relished the wild rock and roll time. We slowly and successfully inched our way into a completely landlocked body of water and anchored in deep (twelve feet) water before finally sharing a sigh of relief. The wind howled in the rigging that night, but we remained calm and quiet, bobbing in the pond. Let it blow.

"What is it today?" Fred asked as I finished checking my blood pressure and heartbeat.

"It's finally coming down. I think doing the meditation exercise and listening to the *SeaWellness* tape has helped the medication do its job."

We knew that stressful times in high anxiety situations made my irregular heartbeat much more prominent, and were hoping that it could be controlled successfully through a variety of efforts. So far, so good. Negotiating the waters in these islands was often anything but stress-free. Weather fronts also continued to roll down from the north. This surprised us as it was late April. Severe weather could certainly get the heart pumping and was always a factor to be reckoned with when cruising. Come to think of it, we seldom had that peaceful idyllic time of sailing off into the sunset that was such a big part of the dream. *Hmmm...*

We were beginning to get excited about our return to Oregon for

Page's graduation from medical school, Fred's reunion in Nebraska and our summer "vacation." Since we had heard the renters would be moving out shortly, we knew we could stay in our house, and hoped it would not take too much work to get it ready for new renters. If only we could find some who would consistently pay the rent.

Finally there came a day of good rain. We needed it to wash off all the salt that had accumulated on the decks and windows. Spending the day in the cabin, I began to write down some of our boating adventure stories with the word processor. The daily logues provided abundant memories of our cruising experiences.

"You know, this is really fun," I said. "I really like doing this. I think I could get hooked on writing. I don't say much of any importance, but seem to have lots to tell. Maybe it's something we will someday want to share with our grandkids, should we ever be so *blucky* to have any."

"Ouch! That *hurts.* Oh, *baby.* Did we hurt you?"

With the keel down, we had bumped hard for what seemed an eternity, coming in to a pass from the deeper, rougher waters of the sound.

"That wasn't sand we were hitting," I said. "That had to be coral or rock. The chart guide said we could enter there. Now I don't know if we can trust it."

"Let's just hope it didn't do any damage," Fred said.

After pumping up the keel, we backed out of the area to try a different approach. Finally we were snuggly hooked up to a mooring buoy and he dove under the keel to examine it.

"Looks good. I think we dodged the bullet that time," he said as he came up the swim ladder.

We dinghied to shore and watched a local fisherman clean conch. We took three of the large beautiful, twisting pink shells wishing we had room to store more. Of course, they smelled of fish until they were thoroughly dry and clean, so we left them on the deck. Walking down the beach, we met a lady who had caught nine dolphin or mahi-mahi fish. She gave us one after it was cleaned. What a treat. We had missed not eating as much fresh fish as we had done in the Pacific. After dinner we took apart the dinghy as part of our getting ready to cross the banks to return to Nassau. After our encounter with the coral, we decided to take the long way around rather than attempt the tricky, shallow shortcut route.

Once back in the marina, which now felt like a second home, we prepared for Lance and Tanya's visit. I baked some cookies and a cake when it rained, and decided to also make Lance's favorite dish—lasagna.

"Kick me if I ever get the idea to do that again on the boat," I told Fred. "It takes so much longer to prepare anything and lasagna has too many parts. I never have enough counter space for everything when I'm making it. He'd better enjoy it."

Since Lance had spent two and a half months sailing with us in the Pacific, as well as a couple of weeks onboard in Honduras, he was well acquainted with the boat and loved playing with all the "toys and whistles." It was fun watching him show and tell Tanya what everything was used for. He was anxious to see the islands, so after a little of the Nassau tourist tour we once again sailed for Rose Island. On the way, we tried some fishing.

"Well, no fish for dinner, but we caught a fourteen foot fishing boat with four men inside," Fred said with a chuckle.

We all shared a good laugh, although when their boat had run over our line we weren't laughing. We had all anxiously shouted and waved, trying to explain that they had hooked our line. Not being able to understand, they simply smiled and waved back. Finally they got the message and were able to release our line.

After lunch we went snorkeling. It was a first for Tanya. She was so athletically fit, that she took to it right away and we were happy to find some amazing fish and coral. After hearing Dawn's tale of woe, they took her advice and wore T-shirts. Lance was just like a big kid in the water. He'd dive down to inspect something on the bottom, turn somersaults, and tease the rest of us unrelentingly.

We spent a couple of nights at the islands, which allowed the kids to get off the boat and go ashore by themselves, even taking the lawn chairs with them so they could sit in the shade. They were getting more than enough sun. When we returned to Nassau we enjoyed the fun of the big casino, and sent the two of them off to the disco, declining their invitation to come along. We showed them the Atlantis resort, had a drink and a swim at Pirate Cove, went body surfing, and sent them on a tour of downtown in a horse-drawn surrey. One evening while eating dinner ashore, the power went off. The waiters were used to the inconvenience, and we finished our meal by candlelight.

"Hey, Mon. It's the *island* way," Lance was fond of saying.

Their five days and nights with us went by all too quickly. Lance planned to be in Portland for Page's graduation, so when saying goodbye we knew we'd see him then and that made their leaving easier for me.

"Whew. This having the kids aboard is great fun, but I think we need a bigger boat."

"Let's just get a little one, put them in it, and tow them along behind."

Not a bad idea.

Our "work" here in The Bahamas was done, so we set about readying everything for our passage back across the banks to enter the Gulf Stream. We planned to use it to zing farther north before returning back to the States.

"I'm really looking forward to riding that current again. I hope we'll make some good progress with its push. Maybe we can get all the way up to North Carolina," Fred said when we were finally underway.

"It's great getting that extra speed. Just as long as we don't get any north wind," I replied. "Everyone has horror stories to tell about conditions in those situations."

We continued sailing and motor sailing on into the night, finally anchoring at the edge of the banks about two in the morning.

Anchoring in the dark in a new place was a first for us, but all went well. A little sleep and we were up checking the weather reports the next morning before deciding if we'd make "the jump." Weather and wind in our current position was not indicative of what we'd find once we left the banks.

"O.K. It's calling for east winds, changing to southeast, which would be even better. Let's go."

After filling up with fuel, we ventured forth through a channel that was much more straightforward than the one we had used coming onto the banks. Still, it took a watchful eye on the depths until we were well clear of land. We also carefully watched the wind direction indicator. To my dismay, the wind was still coming from the *northeast*, and that was anxiety producing. But all the reports had it turning to come from the east, so into the current we plunged. *It surely will be turning east soon.*

"Yahoo. Look at that. Eleven knots! This is unbelievable. We are *flying*," Fred yelled.

Indeed, it was amazing. But the wind was getting stronger, and with it came the rougher seas from the waves hitting the opposing current. *When was that wind going to turn east?* That became the predominant thought of the day. I could feel my heartbeat start its "samba" thing and took a second dose of medication about five in the evening. We could handle these seas—we'd been in worse before. *When was that wind going to turn east?*

By midnight, we were really being thrown about. The wind had become stronger yet, and had actually turned more north than east. In order to sail with a little more comfort, we had altered our course to go more westerly. White caps on the waves were beginning to look more like snow-covered mountaintops. Spray was flying off the tops of them and over the deck. Rather than bucking into the waves, we were taking most of them on the side of the boat, causing it to roll a good deal. I think I preferred the up and down motion to that of side to side. The dark night added to the sinister and threatening feel of the ocean, now provoked by wind and current. I took a third dose of medicine as the first two didn't seem to help the erratic rhythm that was pounding in my chest. With each huge, loud and sudden slam on the side of the hull, the boat would shudder a little, things not tied down would fly to the other side of the cabin, and both boat and crew would groan in the process. I tried not to look at the seas when I was off watch, and lay on the settee to calm myself and practice some meditation. It wasn't helping. Despite my growing anxiety, I was really getting angry. I was just plain *mad.*

"Can you believe it? They're *still* calling for east winds. Where in the heck are these people located anyway? They surely can't be sending those reports from around here. If they're government employees, I want to fire them."

I knew that Fred was concerned about me, and that made me feel worse. This wasn't fair to him. He rarely slept on these passages anyway. He surely wouldn't now. We talked about what our choices were, and finally decided to give up the fast ride north, exit the Gulf Stream as soon as possible, and altered our course to aim for Cape Canaveral, Florida.

"This is a *huge* disappointment," I said. "I know how much you were enjoying that eleven knot speed. And here we are, still in Florida."

"Hey—it was the only wise thing for us to do. If I really wanted speed, I'd have bought a power boat."

That's my man!

It seemed to take forever to approach land. Of course, once we left the Gulf Stream, our speed dropped back down to the familiar five knots over ground. As we wound our way into Port Canaveral, we were fascinated to observe the missile launch sites, and even a rocket that we could see standing off in the sand dunes. We struggled to tie up at a small marina due to the winds that had by now increased to a small gale. Another couple helped us in the task, and in talking with them afterwards, we learned that they were now calling a halt to their intermittent cruising of the last five or six years. *Was that the direction we were going? Would offshore sailing work for me medically anymore?* So many questions—so few answers. Later, we heard from another boater who had just come in to the marina, that conditions were "really nasty out there" and we were just happy to be where we were. So much for weather reports.

Nine

Living It Up on the ICW

"Boy, there's nothing like 'local knowledge' to make life easier," I laughed.

"I'll say. Those folks really gave us a ton of information that'll be useful. This ICW stuff is different than what we've encountered before. I'm not sure I'm going to like having all these bridges opened."

Bridges were indeed something to be reckoned with when traveling on the ICW. They were frequent, had standard opening times in many places, and were closed completely during vehicle rush hour traffic. If you arrived late for an opening, you had to wait. If you arrived early, you had to wait. That often meant throwing out an anchor several times a day. Fred began to think we should have invested in an electric windlass. With the threat of frequent anchoring in mind, timing our travel became important. And because the dredged channel that provided the depth we needed for passage was often narrow, it required constant attention to ascertain and maintain our position. There would be no naps, reading books or autopilot use in these parts. One of us would be hand steering most of the time. That made for long days.

After our discussion of the ICW with some boaters who also took us to the store for some fresh food, we set off. The scenery as we moved northward was certainly a change from offshore cruising where we saw mainly water. While I had previously visualized Florida as being densely populated, along the ICW there were many long stretches of rural land without any signs of housing or people. We didn't encounter much boat traffic either. Bird life was abundant however, and there were many nature preserves. The countryside changed from winding tributaries flowing through acres upon acres of low lying swamp grass waving in the breeze, to defined banks of various sized rivers lined with large live oak trees, all heavily laden with hanging Spanish moss that draped from each limb.

While radio reports told of strong winds *outside* (in the ocean) it was very pleasant motoring along in the channel, although by afternoon it became very hot with the light wind. By late afternoon, we realized we would have to hurry to make the opening of the last planned bridge of the day. The charts didn't show any good spots to anchor on the south side of the bridge.

"I've got the engine at full throttle, but we're still not going fast enough." Fred said. "We're not going to make it."

"Let's pull out the jib and see if it will give us a boost."

It did, and we made it just by "the skin of our teeth." We celebrated with high fives, found a quiet spot to anchor and I fixed a good dinner. We were satisfied with our day's adventures on this ICW, and we both enjoyed being away from a dock and underway again.

About noon the following day, we began hearing radio reports from the Coast Guard of approaching "severe thunderstorms." The messages were frequent and ominous sounding and warned people to take cover "indoors." A really big storm was hitting about twenty miles out to sea, and we were once again glad to be on the *inside*. But we soon found that there was plenty to deal with right where we were. We could see the big, rolling, dark black, threatening clouds approaching. When the wind and rain hit we scurried to get hatches closed, outside sun curtains off the windows, and scramble below. It was as much "indoors" as we could get.

"I'm not even sure where we are in the river," I yelled over the sound of the rain and thunder. "It's raining so hard; I can't see anything through the windshield."

"That lightning is *close!* I'm putting on the rubber fishing gloves to steer. I don't like holding onto this metal wheel. We'd better disconnect and move the electronics too."

The earsplitting, cracking sound of the thunder and simultaneous flashes of lightning had us frequently flinching and ducking, as if we could somehow avoid a hit by being a bit shorter. Knowing we had to stay in the deeper water of the channel or run aground, yet nearly blinded by the heavy rain, we inched our way along for about an hour before the storm passed. Breathing a sigh of relief, we pulled ourselves together and continued on our way. It was only a short time later before we could see more dark clouds approaching. This time we pulled out of the channel just before they hit and threw out an anchor. It lasted more than an hour, but it felt more comfortable than when we were underway and we didn't have to worry about where we were going.

"Well, I guess all the excitement isn't just on the *outside,*" Fred laughed.

"And at least here there are support services all around if a person gets in trouble. You could practically *shout* for help."

"Plus the fact that it's so shallow you could probably *walk* to shore if you needed to. I guess the ICW has its advantages."

"Looks like your bruise is finally starting to heal," Fred said as we got ready for bed.

My *war wound* was a six by four inch circle of black and yellow on my upper thigh. I had been crossing the lifelines to step from the boat onto the dock when my foot slipped and I had fallen hard onto the lifelines.

"You were really lucky you didn't end up in the water that time. It's a wonder that one of us hasn't taken the plunge before now."

"Yeah. It pays to watch where you're going and not be in a hurry," I replied. "But it was *blucky*, not lucky."

165

It was late afternoon and we were waiting for the bridge to make its last opening before rush hour closure in the charming town of St. Augustine when we saw the blackest cloud we'd ever seen approaching. By now, this afternoon thunderstorm thing was becoming routine, and we had heard the warnings on the radio, but this was the biggest, ugliest, and scariest looking system we could possibly imagine.

"We'd better pull over and anchor," Fred said after seeing it.

"But then we won't get through the bridge today. We can make it. There's an anchorage right on the other side of the bridge," I pleaded.

Despite his better judgment, we anxiously waited and willed the bridge to open. As we finally slid through its raised spans, gunning the engine to full throttle, the bridge tender yelled out to warn us about the severe thunderstorm coming. We went about 50 yards to the first place possible, threw out our anchor and set it just as the storm hit with a fury. Wind and rain, thunder and lightning. It felt like we were in the middle of Hell. Fred yelled at me to get inside, while he finished up with the anchor. As I watched him from below, I knew that if anything happened to him out there it would be my fault for wanting to get through the bridge before anchoring. Fortunately, he ducked inside a minute later. I vowed to be less impulsive and more cautious next time. *Could a leopard change its spots?*

St. Augustine is the oldest European settlement in our country. Its delightful waterfront, appealing Spanish architecture, and the old castle of San Marcos could be seen from the boat. We were anxious to go ashore and explore the area, but we were also wanting to get farther north before our return to Oregon, so decided to wait until coming back this way in the fall. In the morning we called on the radio to be certain that the next bridge would be open on time, as it was a Saturday. The schedules sometimes changed on the weekends. Sure enough, it would open, so off we went.

Just as we were about to proceed through the opened bridge, we heard another report that the next bridge, thirteen miles up the channel, was to be closed until Monday. *Oh my. What to do?* The only other way north was to go out in the ocean. With more than a little concern about the weather, we decided to go for it. As Fred turned the boat around and headed for the ocean entrance channel at St. Augustine, I furtively began putting in waypoints and a route on the GPS, which would allow us to navigate up on the outside. And we had just started to enjoy being on the *inside.*

"Hey—did we come out into a different ocean?" I laughed. "It's like glass out here."

"It is. And boy, does that wind feel good. Not so hot," Fred replied. "It's an unexpected and very pleasant change."

The weather remained stable throughout the day and we arrived at the next port entrance. We were so enjoying being in the ocean again, that upon hearing reports for continued stable weather we decided to go on to Savannah, Georgia before returning to the ICW.

"At least we can use the autopilot out here, and read a book or go to the bathroom. And we don't have to constantly be watching for those markers and other boats."

"Yeah. This is really nice. Just as long as we can avoid those nasty 'severe thunderstorms.'"

While the forecast was for southerly winds, they were still coming from the northeast. But our movement through the water was fine as we were no longer in the strong current of the Gulf Stream. We laughed when we realized that the longer we cruised, the more anxious we had become about ocean passages. Maybe in the beginning we were more naïve—and lucky. But it sure felt good to sail again, turn off the engine, and relax a little. This was about as good as it gets. Blue skies, warm sun, light winds, calm seas, happy crew, beautiful amazing boat. *Sure hope it lasts.*

The moonlight was so intense for a time that night that it blocked out most of the stars. I could almost read a book by it. But later, we carefully watched the clouds developing south of us, hoping they didn't bring more storms. By morning, we were approaching the entrance to Savannah Harbor. It was Mother's Day, so we were tickled to reach a port where we could phone the moms. The big fancy marina was full, and likely would have busted the cruising budget, so we traveled ten miles up the ICW to a small marina and RV resort. It was nicely set up with a pool, restaurant, green grass, trees full of that lovely Spanish moss, and colorful flower gardens. But there were also lots of bugs and several folks warned us to use our screens. Too late. They had already found me, as the welts on my skin could attest.

"I feel like a kid in a candy store," I said. We had quickly put on our swimsuits and hurried to the pool after tying up.

"The pool is great, but I'm beginning to get a picture of what summer must be like around here. Hot, hotter, and humid."

After a time on the boat, small pleasures made for good living. It was a treat to do some laundry, get some fresh bread and milk, and have a nice dinner in the restaurant. And the frequent pool dips felt heavenly. We spent most of the day there. A sudden "unusual" wind storm that night, had us again thinking about the need to find a safe place to leave the boat for our trip home. The plan was to leave it in a small marina that we should arrive at in about a week. We had heard good reports about the Stono Marina on the outskirts of Charleston and had made a reservation there, but had yet to see it. We stayed as long as possible the next day in order to use the pool one more time before moving on.

We saw few recreational boats in the waterway and decided that most had already gone north for the summer. The scenery along the channel continued to impress us with the many trees, marshes, birds, small towns and charming houses that we passed. It all provided glimpses into the old southern, traditional and the seemingly slower pace lifestyle. Homes almost always had a porch, and often people were seen gathered there to visit. Perhaps it was also the heat that influenced many of the things we saw.

After another afternoon and evening of thunderstorms while at anchor, we found ourselves longing for some of the good old

Pacific Northwest gentle rain. But we were making good time in our progress northward so we didn't complain. We found that hitting the right tide made a big push in our speed. With some moderate wind coming from the south, sometimes we were even able to put up the jib. That helped our speed significantly, but the channel curved around so much in the winding creeks, that it meant we constantly had to be adjusting the sail. The last two bridges of one day had no electric power to open the gates, so we practiced patience (or tried to do so) as we waited almost two hours for each of them to open.

Finally we arrived at Stono Marina. Docking was tricky in the brisk winds and strong tidal currents created by seven to eight foot tidal changes, but we received a helping hand from some willing folks on shore. The marina was again some distance from the city, but we hoped that there would be bus transportation into Charleston. Dawn had sent our airline tickets to the office, and friendly folks were anxious to chat and offered us rides into a nearby small town. Everyone we met expressed interest when hearing that we had sailed from Oregon, and wanted to learn about our trip. And of course, we always loved telling the stories.

"Look at these gorgeous old mansions. Can't you just see Scarlet O'Hara flouncing down those steps with a frilly parasol and her beautiful gown billowing all around her?"

Fred didn't quite seem to be getting the picture. I think he was more impressed with all the brick architecture and coachman rings of the stately old homes that lined the sea-walk of downtown Charleston.

We had met a charming older fellow at the marina who had brought his boat around from San Diego many years ago. He was tickled to talk with anyone from the Pacific coast, and offered to give us a ride to the bus stop so that we were able to come to the city for the day. Buying a self-guided walking tour book, we had immersed ourselves in exploring. We were charmed by this lovely old city with all of its significant history. There was a large local market and modern, *air-conditioned* tourist center that attracted us as well. The historical implications of Fort Sumter sitting out in the harbor interested us both, and seeing it had made history lessons fascinating. But walking the streets, we soon began to wilt from the heat and humidity of late May and sought out a place to stop for a cold drink.

"I feel rather like Dawn did in Rome," Fred said. "I just can't quite get into this sightseeing stuff."

"I know. And I think we've lost our 'walking legs.' I rather suspect that right now our hearts are already in Oregon, but the bodies are still here in South Carolina."

We vowed to do more exploring when we returned to the boat after our trip home, and found the bus to return to the marina.

We needed to move the boat from the transient dock to a slip that was further inland and more protected. Our plan was to wait for slack tide to minimize navigating in that strong tidal current, but a single-hander we had met suggested we help him move his boat, and he'd help us. We were glad to assist, although thought that likely we hadn't needed any help. But extra hands on a dock were almost always a plus (unless those hands didn't know what they were doing).

Securely tied up in our new slip, we set about the routine of readying the boat for our absence. Fresh food was used up, linens and clothes were washed, refrigeration turned off, lockers opened for ventilation, all equipment stored below decks, extra mooring lines added and chafing gear applied to lines. Sails were tied off, sea cocks closed, and instructions, keys and contact information given to the marina office. We were packed and ready to go. Just as we left the boat, we opened packets of "Mil-du-gas" that were supposed to retard the formation of mildew on sealed up boats in storage. *Oregon and Nebraska, here we come.*

It was early September before we returned to *Grace*. The summer months in Oregon had gone by quickly, but we managed to include a trip to Nebraska to see Fred's mom during that time. The renters had moved out of our house (owing a substantial debt for past rent) so again we had moved in and "camped" with only survival supplies, a mattress on the floor and virtually no furniture. But we didn't mind a bit. We were just so glad to be able to spend the time in our own home. *And* we didn't have to get up and check to see if the anchor was dragging at night. There was, however, a lot of work to be done. Once again, we completely cleaned the inside and did a huge amount of yard work to get it all in shape in order to advertise for new renters. The endless list of projects also included replacing the carpets in the great-room area. *Doesn't anyone train their pets to be housebroken anymore?*

While at home, we continued to hear frequent weather reports of hurricanes on the east coast of the U.S., along with periods of considerable heat and humidity. Such news allowed us to relish the wonderful summertime weather of the Pacific Northwest while we waited for milder conditions before returning to the boat.

We so enjoyed being with all the family without feeling hurried or having a limited amount of time. The moms were doing well and continued to wish us well on our travels, although they preferred that we "stay put in that beautiful home." We were able to give Page a fun celebration when she graduated from medical school, and made a raucous cheer as she received her diploma in an otherwise solemn and formal event. Dawn was in and out with her flying schedule with Delta, and had found the man she was "going to marry." But we'd heard that statement many times before, so we didn't get too excited. Most of the men only lasted for a couple of dates, and then it was on to someone else. Lance spent some time with us at the house since he was between jobs at the ski resorts. It was satisfying to catch up on all the small things going on in our adult children's lives. We realized again, that while we were gaining much from the last three years' adventures, we were also missing much. It was the most difficult part of cruising for us, compounded by the difficulty of long distance communication.

When at last our house was ready, we found a family wanting to rent it. We were sure that this time they had enough financial stability that we would not always be concerned about whether the rent check was "in the mail." It was with ambivalent feelings that we returned to *Grace*.

"I don't remember what Phil looks like. Do you?"

"No. It's been three months since we left. But he told us he'd pick us up at the airport when we returned, and he sounded eager when we talked to him on the phone in Portland."

We managed to find Phil, and as we drove back to the marina we confessed that we had been a little worried as we hadn't been able to remember what he looked like.

"That's good to hear. I was thinking the same thing about you," he said and we all laughed.

Grace looked wonderful. How strange to feel at *home* in two places. The mildew gas product had worked well in the cabin, and other than a little dust, everything was fine. Our outboard gas can had developed a leak, leaving a little mess on the transom, but it was easily cleaned off. It took some time to stow our gear, check all the electronics for "bugs" due to the constant humidity, run the engine, get a stuck through-hull valve open, and generally get the boat ready for living again. We had been instantly aware of the humidity when we stepped out of the airport terminal, and adjusting to the heat again took its toll. And oh yes, the *mosquitoes* were out in mass to welcome us home.

As soon as we had achieved some sense of order below, I began cleaning the outer deck. Fred was working at installing bonding wire as additional lightning protection, and we kept a close watch on the reports of the location of Hurricane Luiz. Our bodies were soon aching with all the bending and stooping, and some of the worst was yet to come for me. In order to install a lightning diffuser at the top of the mast, Fred climbed to the spreaders using the folding mast steps. But to reach the top of the mast, he had to sit in the bosun's chair while I winched him up the rest of the way. This took all the strength I could muster. Unfortunately, it took two trips to get the job done, as a thunderstorm with lightning came up the first afternoon while he was swinging at the masthead.

"Get down here," I yelled. He didn't need a second invitation.

Fred in bosun's chair on his way to top of the mast.

Fred also tackled the yucky job of going in the water to clean the hull. Since we couldn't get the engine started on our Hooka system, he free-dove under the hull rather than using his scuba gear. Due to the strong tidal current, he would have used up all his energy just trying to stay in place in the water, so we tied a rope around his middle, which I controlled from up on the deck. This allowed him to do the job without being swept out to sea.

"Sure glad there's no alligators in *these* waters," I said when he came up for air. "Even so, I'm definitely delighted that this is a *blue* job."

"Just as long as I get to watch the Nebraska football game when I'm finished. You'd better have a cold drink ready."

Thoughtful boat neighbors offered to take me to the store for groceries. I loaded up, but then had trouble finding places on the boat to stow all of them, particularly the refrigerated or frozen things. Our little converted English icebox didn't hold a lot, which made it good for a minimal electric draw, but it took careful planning in order for it to contain all the necessary items. A "tried and true" observation of the ship's galley, was that *whatever* was needed from the 'fridge, was *always* found at the bottom and least most accessible place. Unable to find room for a pot roast, I decided to cook it, and ended up serving it three nights in a row.

"Hey—I could eat pot roast seven nights a week," Fred kept assuring me.

I wondered what his saturation level would be, as this pot roast reminded me of the biblical account of the five loaves and two fishes. The more I served it, the more left-overs we seemed to have.

Finally we had finished enough projects that it was time to push off, with a goal of meeting Page in Baltimore for her week of vacation. Yes, we'd done it *again*. We'd broken the cardinal cruiser's rule by having another schedule to keep. *Did we never learn?* Although there were a lot of miles to cover in order to get there, we also had a good deal of time, so we weren't worried. Little did we know!

"The pager's going off," Fred said. "It's from Page and Steve. It says 09 next to their number. What's that mean?"

"Oh, fun. That's sending 'warm fuzzies.' We don't need to call them back. They're just calling to say that they are thinking of us."

Cell phones were still not readily available, but a paging unit was. We had purchased one before leaving Oregon. If anyone needed to reach us, they could notify us to call them by using the pager. We had devised a code to mean different levels of urgency, or just to send "warm fuzzies." It was fun to use, but I kept forgetting if "01" meant call right away, or call anytime it was convenient.

As we entered Charleston Harbor, the water was very choppy due to strong winds opposing the strong tidal flow. We had trouble finding the ICW buoy markers initially, and then slow going as we fought a strong ebb tide when leaving the opposite side of the harbor. We hadn't covered many miles when we decided to anchor in a little creek that was surrounded by swamp grass.

"I understand why they call this the 'Low Country,'" Fred said when looking around. "There's miles and miles of mostly grass, and only an occasional tree. And it's all flat."

"I bet there's thousands of these little grassy islands. But there sure is no other boat traffic. I feel like we are alone on the planet."

At times, the ICW must have been crowded with pleasure boats making their annual migration south, and later north, but there surely weren't many at that time of year. The following day was cloudy and mercifully cooler. No complaints from this crew. We chased hundreds of pretty butterflies as we motored northward. We had not seen so many of these delicate and colorful creatures since leaving Costa Rica. As we had been warned, our hull began sprouting a brown "mustache." The high level of tannins in the water of this area created a stain that looked just like tea along the waterline. Most boaters considered it a nuisance as it was often difficult to remove.

Many unfamiliar Native American names identified the dozens

of creeks that flowed into the wide river we were traveling. We took a side trip down one that we were told "should not be missed."

"This looks like the Multnomah Channel near Portland," Fred said. "Nothing very special."

"You're right. Other than we don't have all that Spanish moss hanging from those big old trees. It's funny how we take the scenery at home so much for granted. Really, the Pacific Northwest is loaded with gorgeous scenic places. I think folks around here would be blown away if they saw it."

"Ah. Do I hear some 'hometown' bias?" Fred said with a laugh.

One day, after we had called on the VHF radio to request a bridge opening, we were surprised to receive a call from *Wind Eagle*, a boat that we had met in *Isla Providencia* and Honduras. They were in a nearby yacht club, had heard our call to the bridge and suggested we join them. What a delight to talk with them, and share a glass of wine in celebration of their purchase of a new powerboat. That made the sixth cruising couple that we knew to make the switch from sail to power after returning home. We weren't ready for that yet.

Another "09" pager call came from Page and Steve, and since we were at a dock, we called them back. It was always fun to hear their voices. Amongst other things, we learned that our "grand-dog" was doing well, and Dawn was in love. Wow—that guy had been hanging in there for some time. Maybe he really was "the one." We wished we had met him before we left Oregon.

We got a push from a favorable tide the next day, and were making good time when we approached a huge body of water—the mouth of the Cape Fear River.

"What a name," I said. "It just fills me with comfort. There surely must be some stories about this place."

"I know we planned to go up and cross the river tomorrow, but I think we'll have time to do it today. Let's go."

It was early afternoon as we began winding our way up the wide river with its strong currents and tidal flow, carefully watching for the ICW markers. At one point, we had to cross a large expanse of water by staying in a narrow dredged channel that was surrounded by water that charts showed as only two feet deep. It had been cloudy all day, and the clouds appeared to be darkening the further we progressed.

"That's the wrong marker number," I said when passing a buoy. "I can't figure out where we are on this chart. We should be starting to cross pretty soon, but we'd better be in that channel or we'll really be in trouble."

It had started to rain, and the wind had increased significantly. Soon it was a downpour and we struggled to control the boat with the wind gusts. It was difficult to see the markers, and when we finally found them, they were all the "wrong" numbers. *Where were we?* I tried to find our position on the GPS, but it wasn't working correctly. *What's happening?* The radar wasn't any help as the rain was so heavy, that the total screen just reflected a mass of green. As navigator, I was greatly anxious about our need to stay in the channel and further baffled by the confusing charts. To complicate things further, we were soon in a thunderstorm. Visibility was extremely limited. Not only was I anxious, but I was now *mad*. We had expected charts to be inaccurate out of the country, but not in the States. *Could things get any worse?*

"Ouch! What bit me? Ouch! That *hurts*."

"It's these damn horse flies. They came with the rain and they're *huge*. They're all over the boat and that bite is vicious."

All our actions in controlling the boat were interrupted by frequent slaps on our bodies, as we tried to fight back at the painful invasion. We weren't winning. We were hopping around soaking wet and trying to maintain our headway in a storm, unsure of which way to go. What a day! Not only were we lost in the Cape Fear River with no usable charts or GPS, and right in the middle of a thunderstorm, but we were now being eaten alive by those humongous flies!

Somehow we made it across, the buoy numbers again matched the chart, and we threaded our way into a nice little anchorage. But I was "spittin' nails" and even Fred was irritated—a rare occurrence. *Ah yes—another boring day in the cruising life.* (Later, we learned that new charts had replaced our outdated ones, and the GPS had suffered "operator error.")

We went to bed so early after our busy and tiring day that we were up and ready to go at five-thirty the next morning—but it was still dark. Nudging our way out of the anchorage we went aground, gave thanks for that swing keel, pumped it up, and slowly went on until it was light. We were now in an area that showed many more signs of civilization, and we enjoyed looking at all the styles of homes along the shore. We liked to talk about ideas for improvements to our home that we might do when the cruising life was over. When we had initially left, we were not sure where we would want to live after we had completed our journey. We could have gone anywhere. Now, we were certain that we wanted to remain in Oregon, and rebuild our original house.

As we talked, we laughed too, at the small irritations of boating that we had forgotten about but with which we were becoming intimately reacquainted. Like the annoying feeling of the cockpit floor grate on bare feet after being in the cockpit for long periods. Or the sore bottom after sitting on the hard teak seats of the cockpit, even when using a cushion. Or the burning eyes after being in the wind all day. Sometimes it felt like we were "gluttons for punishment." Then again, such things really were a small price to pay for the freedom and adventures we gained.

"Look. That's the place we saw on the TV coverage of Hurricanes Luis and Marilyn."

We had carefully watched the hurricane weather reports of North and South Carolina. Thankfully, *Grace* as well as the communities we passed, were spared from the incredible destruction that such storms can create. The ocean waters had huge waves created by the passing hurricanes, but we were in protected waters, and only experienced strong winds. *Gracias a Dios.*

One night we anchored on a U.S. Marine Corp base. There was no firing going on, but Fred watched some exercises involving a huge helicopter while I cooked dinner.

"Come out here and look at this," he said. "There's a helicopter flying with five men dangling on a cable below it."

"Sure enough. That's certainly not a way I prefer to travel."

During several rainy days we were again grateful for the inside steering station of our boat. Surely this Southerly had been the right choice for us. We could seldom sail as we traveled along the ICW, so we plugged along motoring and it was nice to be inside, out of the rain. It was mid-September and we began to see lots of pleasure boats going south for the winter. It seemed we were always going the "wrong" way.

When we reached Beaufort, North Carolina, we decided to go into a marina, even though it was expensive and required tying onto four pilings, with the bow into the dock. While this set-up was common on the East Coast, it surely wasn't as easy to get into or get ashore as the side-tie docks of the West Coast. After a short walk in town, we returned. Fred said he was feeling stiff and sore. I took his temperature and it was 102. Darn. He obviously had picked up a bug somewhere. Although he was willing to go out for dinner after resting all afternoon, I knew he wouldn't enjoy it, so we settled in for the night and I made him chicken soup.

The following morning he still was not feeling well, and had a slightly elevated temperature. While he rested, I attended a Sunday worship given by the "Waterways Ministry." It took place in a nearby park right on the waterfront and I met some nice people. There were lots of boaters in attendance. They were all concerned when hearing about Fred and offered help should we need any. By afternoon Fred's temp was again over 102, and I continued to load him with aspirin and fluids. I was becoming increasingly concerned. I was grateful for my Registered Nurse background and was trying to implement as many actions as possible to help him heal. While he rested, I walked about town by myself. The people of this community had made the waterfront into a very nice place with quaint shops, a museum and lovely park. But it wasn't much fun seeing it without my hubby.

By Monday, Fred's temp was 103 at seven in the morning and

he had a frequent deep cough. His skin felt like a furnace. With the help of the dock-master, we arranged an appointment at a doctor's office and took a taxi there, although I knew we could have asked folks we had met for a ride. We were seen by a Physician's Assistant and told it was a viral infection and that he would need to "tough it out." We were given a prescription for antibiotics, but told to use it only if he began coughing up "green stuff." It was back to the boat for rest and liquids.

Since we'd likely be in the marina for a few more days as Fred recovered, I loaded up the headsail in our little red cart and took it into a loft for some repairs. I also used the cart to take the propane tank in to be filled. It was good to have something useful to do and marine facilities were handy in this very boat-oriented community.

Although Fred did a lot of coughing at night, he felt better each morning, so one day at noon we decided to go a short distance and anchor out. I picked up our sail from the loft, but put it below rather than try to hank it on the forestay while at the dock. We had only been gone a short ways when we hit some strong wind and choppy seas.

"Daggone. That darn jib furling attachment is bouncing all over in these winds without the sail being attached," I said. "You stay put. I don't want you using up any more energy than is absolutely necessary. I'm going up to the bow to tie it off."

By the time I had crawled to the bow in 30 knot gusting winds with the boat rocking and rolling, corralled the furling mechanism from far up the forestay, tied it off, and returned to the cockpit, I was drenched and cold.

"I want you to get better for sure," I laughed. "These *blue* jobs aren't fun."

As soon as we could find a protected area we dropped the hook.

"I'm not sure this idea to move on was wise," I said. "There are some big open sounds ahead and that northeast wind makes for uncomfortable conditions."

"It'll be fine. I feel lots better. You worry too much."

But he wasn't fine. During the day he was in good spirits and humor, and didn't act sick, but he coughed all night, and I had insisted he start taking the antibiotics. Neither of us was sleeping much. I had started sleeping on the settee so I could build up his bed with pillows to elevate his head and chest, which seemed to help a little. My mind worked overtime at night. The PA had mentioned the possibility of viral pneumonia. Antibiotics don't help with viruses. People used to *die* of pneumonia before antibiotics were available. Fred kept reassuring me that he was OK, and I was aware of my own denial as well as his. We both wanted him to be well. We were feeling the push to get to Baltimore in time to meet Page, and this being sick wasn't a part of the planned schedule.

"A shrimp boat just came into the dock upstream," said a boater who was anchored nearby and had come to our boat in his dinghy. "You can go up there and buy shrimp and fish at a really great price."

Sounded tempting, but I didn't want to set up the dinghy. A short time later, he returned to say he'd take me up if I wanted to go. How nice. It was good eating that day and I was encouraged to see Fred have a good appetite. His temp was down to 100, but he was coughing up green stuff. I was glad for those antibiotics that must have been helping.

"No way! I can bring up the chain, and you can help me with the anchor," I said over Fred's protestations. He didn't like my bossiness, but I refused to let him drain his energy.

We had decided to go on, and hauling up the anchor was a challenge. The luxury of an electric windlass was something that never got to the top of the equipment purchase list. Fortunately, I got the job done with minimal help from Fred.

Despite the fact that neither of us was sleeping due to the constant night coughing, we had a good day with a great sail across some open water. Even though it was late September, it was warm enough that evening for a cockpit shower in a secluded anchorage, and that raised our spirits.

"I'd forgotten how good it feels to shower outdoors," Fred said.

"Me too. I actually prefer it. *And* we don't have to clean up the head afterwards."

Again that night, we were up and down many time as I helped Fred take aspirin, drink water, use cough syrup, and sponged off his fiery body. I couldn't take this worry any longer.

"We're going back," I insisted the next morning. "I read that there's a hospital in that little town eight miles back, and we're *going*."

Fred wasn't happy, but I was determined. Up until then we had used an "always go on, never go back" strategy. But it was at least three more days of travel to reach Norfolk, Virginia. It was the next populated place and getting there was through some very remote areas. When I couldn't sleep at night, I had imagined scenes of a Coast Guard emergency helicopter air-lifting Fred off the boat in some isolated place. I didn't want any part of that. We turned around and went back.

"How long are you going to be here?" said the dock-master when we arrived at a marina in Belhaven, North Carolina about eight in the morning.

"Just a couple of hours," Fred said.

When I explained the situation, the man was so kind and encouraged us to go straight to the hospital, just a few blocks down the street. We could fill out the paperwork when we got back. He even offered to let us drive one of the marina's golf carts in order to get there.

The Emergency Room doctor immediately diagnosed "bacteriologic pneumonia" after he had listened to Fred's lungs and ordered X-rays.

"Wow! Look at that," he said upon examining the completed X-rays. "That's one huge infection."

Even I could see the massive white areas that filled *both* lungs. Fred was one "sick cookie." Almost immediately there were a dozen people taking blood, starting IV fluids, administering medications, doing an EKG, and recording vital signs, history and assorted paperwork. The ER room was filled with activity and I stepped away, not able to hold back the tears any longer. It was such a relief to know what the problem was, have someone take over and do something to get him well, that I just crumbled. My nursing efforts had been intense, but they were not what were needed to do the job.

"Oh Honey," said a large black ER nurse in her slow, southern drawl. "I'm taking you home with me, Sweetie." She had come over and put her arms around me. When I felt her compassion and caring, it made me cry even more.

"Maybe you'd better call Page to see if she's already purchased her ticket for Baltimore," Fred suggested in all the pandemonium. "Looks like I might be tied up for a few days."

He was quite relaxed and a little embarrassed about all the fuss, joking with all the personnel, and trying to make light of the situation. I went out into the hall to find a phone and compose myself. When I called Page's number, I heard the answer machine and started to leave a message, but found that once again I succumbed to tears and sobs. It was quite difficult to talk but I did manage to leave the name and phone number of the hospital and told her not to buy her plane ticket as we might not be able to make it to Baltimore as planned.

It wasn't long before Fred found himself in a lovely private room, with a large window overlooking the waterway, color television, air-conditioning, and a menu with anything he wanted to eat.

"Hey, this is just like being in a fancy hotel," he said with a grin. "I think I'm going to like this."

I again tried to call Page, and caught her just as she was coming in the door after working an overnight shift at the hospital. After much reassurance about Fred's condition, I gave her his room number and the name of the hospital, and she agreed to hold off buying her ticket to Baltimore.

It was only a few blocks back to the marina. Returning there felt so strange and lonely without Fred. Being on *Grace,* meant being with Fred. After all this cruising time together on a 24/7 basis, we sometimes had joked about being "joined at the hip." Now, it seemed I was walking with only one leg.

I completed the paperwork with the friendly and sympathetic staff, and did a few odd jobs before going to the marina restroom to take a shower. As luck would have it, when I tried to leave the shower stall, I found myself locked inside with no way of getting out. I hollered. I screamed. I pounded on the door and walls until I had cut my hand. Fearing that the staff had gone home, I envisioned spending the night in the cramped cubicle. Finally, another blast on the door in frustration released the lock and it popped open. This certainly hadn't been my best day. When I told the staff about the incident later, they acknowledged that they had similar problems in the past.

That night at the hospital, Page called to talk with her dad. Later, she talked with me.

"Oh, Mom. I'm *so* glad I had talked to you before I heard the message on the phone recorder. It was so hard to understand what you were saying. I'd have been frantic, thinking Dad had died! You sounded *awful.*"

Fred's temperature was still up the following day and I was disappointed. I had been hoping for an instant cure. It looked like he might be in the hospital longer than we had first anticipated. But it was football season, and lots of games to watch so he was a happy camper with his reclining bed and color TV, despite the frequent severe coughing.

I remembered that cruising friends on *Yankee Rogue* lived in North Carolina, and saw on a map that they were only about twenty miles away. I called them and learned that other cruising friends on *Lamorna* were there with them. They were excited to hear that we were so close and said they'd all be up to see us.

"And whom are you here to see?" said the hospital receptionist when they arrived.

"Fred...hmmm...Fred...?"

They all looked at each other. Cruisers knew each other only by first names, and the name of the boat that folks were on.

"You know," they laughed. "Fred from *Amazing Grace*."

Fortunately, it was a small hospital and town, and everybody had heard about "the poor sailor who became ill on his vacation." We all enjoyed reconnecting and remembering our shared experiences in foreign places. Fred tired easily, so I joined our friends for dinner before going back to the boat. The weather had turned cold, and rain covered the dark streets. I shivered and pulled out my "long johns" before getting into bed. I sure missed my friendly foot warmer.

I showered and dressed up a little the following morning, planning to go to church after seeing Fred.

"Kay, you sure clean up good," Fred said with a grin when he saw me. He was trying to imitate a slow Texan drawl and thought he was being so funny. You had to love the guy.

I found an old, quaint looking Methodist church a few blocks from the hospital and was blessed by the service. When I saw that the lesson was on the "Balm of Gilead" and God's healing touch, I had a hard time holding back the tears. Later that evening, the pastor came to see Fred at the hospital, for which we were very grateful. It sure helped to have *family* around. Our spirits were also lifted when a huge balloon bouquet arrived from the kids. Getting to talk with them frequently on the phone was also a great perk.

It was five days of continuous IV antibiotics before the doctor felt Fred could leave the hospital, and then only because we agreed to stay at the marina for two more days. He reminded us that Fred was healing from "a very bad pneumonia in both lungs" and he would need much more time for full recovery. How *blucky* that we had come back to this little town and had the fine care available. It was frightening to think of what might have occurred had we gone on. *Gracias a Dios!*

"We should get a picture of this," I said. "You're really coming home in style."

"Got to admit it's a first," Fred laughed.

We were driving from the hospital to the marina in a golf cart, decorated with balloons dancing about in the breeze. I had taken some of the balloons to the room of a five year old before we left. All the nurses had given us a good send-off and I was relishing getting the skipper back aboard *Grace.*

We spent the next two days driving about the area in our little golf cart, admiring the grand old southern homes, and taking short walks so Fred could rebuild his strength. There were only 2600 people in the little community of Belhaven, and they certainly exuded that "ol' southern hospitality." Everywhere we went, folks would wave and call out greetings. It was a definite warm fuzzy. I did lots of chart work for our travel to the Chesapeake, while Fred took lots of naps. He still had little appetite, but was sleeping well with the aid of strong cough medicine. We took the golf cart to the supermarket up on the highway to load up on groceries before we left the marina for Baltimore. Although the date had been postponed, we still planned to meet Page there for her vacation.

"Wouldn't you know it?" I complained. "A week ago we had a nice wind out of the south, and now it's coming from the northeast—just where we want to go."

"But we've got a good push from the tide going our way," Fred added. "Could be worse."

I was still concerned about Fred doing too much, and monitored his condition continually. While he coughed much of the time, he kept assuring me he was OK. I remained hyper-vigilant. We surely didn't want a relapse in his recovery.

As we moved northward, we saw many other recreational boats, all going southward to warmer climes. They looked inquisitively at us as we passed, rather like they were wondering if we were lost.

"Crossing this Albemarle Sound might be tricky. The seas sound pretty choppy but the weather forecast is looking even worse for the next three days. A big nasty system is coming in."

We had planned to anchor for the night and cross the sound the following day. When we approached it about four in the afternoon, with the poor weather forecast for upcoming days, we decided to proceed. We hoped we'd be able to get across it before it became dark. We said a little prayer and entered the large sound.

"Who would have guessed? It's really rather lovely out here. We can even sail with the jib and the main. We should make it across easily before we lose daylight."

"But there are those darn crab traps *everywhere*. We really have to keep a sharp lookout for the little suckers."

"For sure. And we'll have to steer by hand in order to avoid them. As the sun lowers, they get harder to see."

Crab traps had a small float on the water, with a line descending to the metal trap basket on the sea floor. While some of the floats were bright pink, most of them were black or a dirty white that made them very difficult to spot in the water. If the line of the trap came into contact with a boat's propeller, it wrapped tightly around the shaft and disabled the engine. It was not something you wanted to add to your day. Dodging around the ubiquitous traps, we made our way across the Albemarle to the North River and quickly looked for a place to anchor just as the sun was setting. We felt quite pleased with ourselves and our 75-mile passage day.

"I think this is a *two* Miller time," I said.

"Roger. But let's get those bug screens up. The flying force is coming out—big time."

We enjoyed our days of winding up the rivers and Intracoastal Waterway now that some of the more difficult parts were behind us. We heard many "May Day" radio calls coming from the Albemarle Sound the day after we crossed and were glad for the decision we had made. We continued to see many folks fishing and crabbing along the shores, so we decided to buy a crab trap after giving away the one we had on the Pacific Coast. At our next anchorage, Fred went up to the bow deck to try out the new trap.

"Shoot. There's nothing in this place but these little things," Fred said, throwing a number of small crabs from the trap back into the water. "Where are the big ones?" We were disappointed with our efforts.

We had been trying to buy a cruising guide to the Chesapeake Bay, but so far had been unsuccessful. There was so much information needed that wasn't on navigational charts. Cruising guidebooks and local information made our travel in strange places so much easier.

After going through a swing bridge and a small lock, we entered the waters around Norfolk, Virginia.

"Look at all these Navy ships," I said. "They're *everywhere*. It's awesome."

"Certainly is impressive, as are the shipyards."

Norfolk was the biggest port we had seen from the water. Besides the myriads of huge Navy ships, there were hundreds of commercial vessels and pleasure craft. The military ships intrigued us the most. The waterway was lined with the typical dull grey colored vessels of varying size, moored to numerous docks. It felt rather intimidating to be moving closely alongside so many warships. It was almost like we were in some kind of combat zone, and it was such a contrast to so many of the remote, primitive waterway scenes we had encountered in so much of our travel. As we left the city and the Navy ships, we were moving up a creek in a stiff wind toward a charted anchorage. The skipper of an outgoing sailboat yelled to us, cautioning us about where we were going, so we altered our course for a more protected anchorage on the Lafayette River. We appreciated the tip. Boaters looking after boaters.

Neither of us slept well that night. With the weather unsettled we were both a little anxious about entering the big, open expanse of the Chesapeake Bay. A large part of our passage across the mouth of that bay was exposed to the Atlantic Ocean. Had we known what we would encounter, we likely would not have started out the following day.

"This is terrible," I said. "It's the 'washing machine' seas all over again."

Short, steep waves came at us from virtually every direction, and the wind was brisk and as usual, "on the nose" as we attempted to round the corner and make our way up into the huge bay. We needed to cross to be able to enter the more protected waterway that continued northward on the opposite side of the bay. The large open area of water allowed the waves of the Atlantic to build to considerable height, and there was almost no interval or "down" time between them. *Grace* plowed on through the mess, and we went along with her. For about three hours we held on and gritted our teeth while we were thrown about. Eventually we got a push from a favorable tide, the seas flattened out somewhat, and we were able to make easier progress.

"Look at those folks in that boat," I said. "They only have on a T-shirt, and here we are in jacket, cap and mittens—and I'm still cold."

"But they're going the other way with the wind at their back. It makes a huge difference in temperature—especially when the wind comes across big open areas of water like this. We should get some relief when we turn the corner."

Finally, we turned into a lovely small tributary called Jackson Creek and anchored. We were sitting in the cockpit studying the charts for the following day's journey, when we heard someone call out.

"*Amazing . Grace*," yelled a fellow in a small day-sailboat approaching us, "welcome to Virginia." He held up two cans of beer and handed them to us with a big smile before moving on. He denied working for the Chamber of Commerce, and wouldn't stop to come aboard. He told us that he just wanted to say "enjoy."

"Wow. We were just reading about how friendly the folks are along this creek, and 'lo and behold.' I think I'm going to like this Chesapeake Bay."

"I'm touched. Things like this help me to continue to have faith in the goodness of people, despite the evening news."

Another boat came in and anchored and we chatted with them for a time. That felt good. We had been so busy putting on the miles to get to Baltimore that we really weren't taking any time to discover places and people. We were missing a big part of the joy of cruising. We vowed we'd amble our way back south on our return trip.

Now that we were in more protected waters, our progress was more enjoyable. We would get up early, quickly dress and pull up the anchor, and then eat our breakfast underway. One morning we watched in awe as the sun came up while we motored along with a light breeze on still water. The big glowing red globe slowly ascended on the eastern horizon, shining through the early morning haze and promised a day of untold beauty and adventure. Few boats were on the waterway, and we felt a sense of calm and peace. It was such a contrast to the morning we entered the bay. By evening, we had found a nice anchorage with a small restaurant nearby, and decided to go have a crab dinner, for which the area was famous.

"Would you like one dozen crabs, or two?" the waitress said.

"*A dozen!* A *dozen* crabs?" we both asked incredulously.

"We usually serve a dozen per person in a bucket," she said.

Obviously this was not like the Dungeness crabs we were used to in the Pacific Northwest where one crab could easily feed two people. Such was our introduction to the East Coast Blue crab.

"Well, it tastes pretty good," I said as we, complete with hammer, bib and washcloth, worked our way through the bucket.

"But it's sure a lot of work to pick through these little things. I guess some people eat the shell and all when it's soft. Be a lot easier."

"And think of all those crabs from the trap that you threw back in the water, thinking they were too small," I laughed. "Little did we know."

Another evening, we anchored in a small bay. We were delighted to see *Dawn,* another cruising boat we had been with in Guanaja, Honduras. As we chatted with our friends until late that night, we reflected on the shared longing so many of us felt—to see cruising friends and continue that bond established in other countries, other lifetimes. It was almost like an affirmation that, yes, we really had done all those things and been all those places that now, back in the U.S., seemed almost unreal.

But unfortunately similar in *any* place on the water, were the surprises and often uncomfortable twists that weather changes so often created. After a tiring day of motoring with virtually no wind, we carefully selected and anchored in a place that was protected from every direction but the south. We felt certain we'd have a quiet night. But by evening a strong wind was evident and coming from our only exposed direction—the south. By bedtime we were really rocking and rolling; so much that I thought we'd get no sleep that night.

"Hey, this isn't as bad as some of those anchorages in the Pacific," Fred said.

By early morning the wind had died and we finally managed to get a little sleep before pushing on. The weather had definitely changed to being cooler, cloudier and windier. But at last the wind was *behind* us and gave us a push. That was good, but Fred had been coughing more and generally not feeling well.

"Let's stop in Annapolis and have a doctor check you out. It's what they told us to do in North Carolina," I implored Fred. He was adamant in his refusal.

"We're only a couple of days from Baltimore. I'll do it then."

Stubborn man.

As we approached Baltimore, we both were feeling excited. History was beckoning us. Passing the Francis Scott Key Bridge, and realizing that this was the place where back in 1812 he had written what would become our national anthem, was especially significant.

"Oh look. That buoy there is red, white and blue. How cool. That marks the place where they could still see our flag waving after a night of attack from the British. That gives me 'goose bumps.' And you can see the forts along the shore."

"How about that Tall Ship about to pass us? It's from Hawaii. I bet it's here for that big race. Maybe we can watch it."

As we entered the inner harbor, we decided to splurge and go to the marina rather than anchor, as the rates were now off-season. Besides meeting Page in three days, we also would be seeing Fred's brother and sister-in-law, Ed and Shirley, who were coming here to meet us. Being in the marina would be much more convenient than being at anchor.

"Boy am I loving being in a nice modern facility," I laughed. "And look at those skyscrapers all around us. It feels a bit like being in Cartagena."

"We're definitely in the downtown area. And Federal Hill and a park are right next door."

We felt a little like kids in a candy store and not knowing what to try first. We quickly put on our tennis shoes and walked about the harbor.

"Hey, there's a public health van. I bet we could get someone there to listen to your lungs."

The medical folks in the van were very accommodating when they heard our story, checked Fred out well, and said they could detect no problems but encouraged him to continue taking the antibiotics. Such good news. Perhaps we just worried too much. We found a place that had free Happy Hour food and cold beer and giggled like school kids at our good fortune. *Ah, the joys of civilization.*

Morning brought with it rain—*torrential* rain. It was the tail end of Hurricane Opal, now just a tropical storm in intensity, but with plenty of water in its punch. It felt good to be tucked into the relative safety of the marina. While Fred napped, I was busy making frequent trips out to the cockpit to lift up the center of the bimini and spray cover in order to drain the rainwater that had pooled on top. I could have washed clothes in all the runoff.

By afternoon the rain had diminished and we took a city bus to see the Museum of Art. We quickly became aware that the bus and bus stops were filled almost entirely with African Americans. Normally, we'd have thought nothing of this. But recent events were keenly on our minds. When we had been out of the country, we had received little news of what was happening in the U.S. But since our return, we had heard plenty of news about the O.J. Simpson trial with all its intricacies and issues around racism.

"How sad. We've ridden buses being the only white persons on board many times in many countries and never felt this kind of tension," I said to Fred as we entered the museum. "We've never given much thought to the color of our skin, or of anyone else's. But after all the media blitz, today felt different. I was really uncomfortable."

"It was really almost palpable, wasn't it? This whole trial thing has set the country back 50 years in interracial relations. Sure hope some good eventually comes of the whole mess."

Perhaps as a stress reducing mechanism, we got the giggles while viewing some of the displays in the modern art section of the museum and hurried outside.

"That's enough culture for today," I laughed. "Let's go to the Sheraton Hotel to get a newspaper and try their free Happy Hour food."

After another day of preparing the boat for Page we were ready for her visit. We usually stored a good deal of gear in the forward cabin, but now needed to find other places to stow it so that she'd have room to sleep and keep her luggage. We were so looking forward to seeing her. We walked up to the taxi stand by the marina where we were to meet. After no taxis for several minutes we began to worry.

"Mom...Dad," we heard her call from behind us. She had gotten off the airport van three blocks early and was lugging her bags down the street. What sweet medicine she was. It was all worth the saga to get here. We returned to *Grace* to let her settle in.

"There's lots of things going on this week. The Pope is visiting and there are some fun festivals going on right here in the harbor. We'll have plenty to keep us busy."

"And your uncle and aunt arrive tomorrow as well."

We walked to one of the festivals, going through a secluded, dark industrial area to get there. It was not a good place to be walking alone, and we hurried to the park. But the festival was fun, and we stopped to eat at a Mexican restaurant, taking a table outdoors that had a great view of the harbor. Just when we sat down, a large fireworks display started out over the water.

"It's in honor of your visit, Page. Well...also the Pope's visit and the Columbus Day celebration," I had to admit.

"Let's take a taxi back," suggested Fred after dinner, to which Page and I quickly agreed.

There was a Lutheran church a couple of blocks from the marina, so we attended the next morning. Sitting with Page between us in that big, beautiful sanctuary, we listened as the wonderful majestic and calming music of the choir and organ swept over us. It brought tears to the eyes of both Fred and me. We looked at each other and shared a smile; an unspoken mutual acknowledgement of how very *blucky* we were.

"There he is," Fred yelled.

It was the Pope in his Popemobile riding down the street in a parade in his honor. The crowds on the street were enthusiastic and loud as he neared. There were *tons* of security people and police surrounding him as he passed, smiling and waving. With his kind eyes, snow white hair and stooped posture, he looked like he carried the weight of the world on his aging shoulders.

Then came the annual Columbus Day parade with marching units from each of the city's ethnic groups. It was interesting to watch, as I recalled no such celebration in the Northwest, but the parade continued on and on, with no end in sight. Finally we decided to head to a museum that had free admission that day in honor of the Pope's visit. Later we stopped for ice cream and watched some musical groups performing down by the marina.

Ed and Shirley showed up the following day and we all enjoyed seeing more of the historical sites of the city and area. It was nice to have the use of a car. Shirley also enjoyed viewing the history of the area through the antique stores.

"If you know what it is you're looking at, it's rather interesting," Fred said. "But most of it looks like junk to me." Page and I nodded in agreement.

Picking up some fresh shrimp, we returned to the boat and fixed cruiser's pina coladas. (Coconut rum and pineapple juice.) We also prepared and enjoyed the local seafood dinner aboard *Grace*. It gave Ed and Shirley a sample of what living on a boat was like before they returned to their nearby motel.

The week passed quickly as we soaked up the history lessons and enjoyed the sites of the Baltimore area. The city tourist trolley was great for getting from one place to another. At one museum we dressed up in old-fashioned clothes for picture taking, and marveled at the skills demonstrated in cooking over an open fire. That made us all hungry and we walked to a sandwich shop by going through a rather rough area of town that had several of the "projects" housing structures.

"These buildings look more like a huge jail than a housing complex. There's no plants or yards; it's all dirty cement. Look at the graffiti and wire grates over those windows. How bleak for kids growing up here."

"Take a look there. That ambulance crew is caring for someone, and he's in handcuffs. Nobody seems to think it's a big deal—like it's something they see all too often."

"Big inner cities certainly have diverse cultures and economic groups," Fred agreed. "It's certainly foreign to what we all experienced." It gave us much to ponder.

A delight for all of us was going to Annapolis, particularly in seeing the Naval Academy.

"I'm glad we got to watch the noon muster of the midshipmen. They all looked so sharp in their uniforms and nobody missed a step in the drill," said Page.

"These young people are some of the 'cream of the crop'," Fred said.

"Too much discipline for me," said Ed.

Ed was so easy going, much like Fred. Page and I thought that maybe there's something in the genes—so much patience. The two guys and Shirley decided to spend a day in Hershey, Pennsylvania while Page and I planned to stay home and go shopping. It was really just an excuse to spend some unhurried and fun time together for the two of us. Christmas would be here in only two months, and there were lots of unique things in the shops and stores for gift ideas.

On Page's last night, we enjoyed going to a nice Italian restaurant for a good "send off" dinner. We had gussied up and were ready to leave boat and water behind, and immerse ourselves in an evening of culture. Following dinner we took a taxi to the Meyerhoff Symphony Hall.

"A *taxi,* no less," said Page. "No city bus?"

She knew us too well.

It was a wonderful concert with a variety of groups and artists. Page then treated us to a late night glass of wine and some great jazz music at a small harbor hotel. She was wonderful company. She never complained, appreciated everything, and would try almost anything. We loved hearing stories of her medical school experiences, and family pets. After all, we were their dog's first nanny when she was just a wee puppy. We affectionately called Hana our "grand-dog."

"What a fun evening," I said to Fred when getting ready for bed. "My feet hurt like the devil from having to wear heels, but it sure was fun to dress up for a couple of nights."

When Page left to return to Portland, Fred gave her a big chocolate bar from the Hershey factory.

"This is for Steve," he said. "It's a gift for him as a way of saying thanks for his sharing you with us this week."

As if the heavens were sad in her leaving, the sky opened up and it poured. We walked back from the airport shuttle stand to the boat using our umbrellas, but still managed to get soaked. The weather had been sunny and warm for our whole week in Baltimore, but fall was definitely in the air, the wind had come up, and it was becoming cool at night. We pulled out our winter clothes that had been in storage for almost three years, washed and put away many of our summer things, and prepared to get underway again in the morning if the wind was not too strong.

Ten

Southbound Once Again

Baltimore, Maryland was as far north as we would travel on the eastern coast of the U.S. We had earlier hoped to make it up to Maine, but there simply wasn't time for that. It had become cold in late October, and it was time to begin the return to Charleston, where our plan was to leave the boat and fly home for the holidays.

"I almost get giddy when I think of being with the family for Christmas," I said. "It's sure nice to know we have those free flight passes from our Delta Dawn."

"But we've got lots of places yet to see here in the Chesapeake," Fred replied. "We may not get back up here again, so let's get moving."

"On the road again...," we sang once more as we left Baltimore via the Patapsco River. We were pleased to find a following wind and the opportunity to sail. It was invigorating to turn off the engine, see the sails fill with the wind, and slide quietly down the river. The autumn landscape punctuated the shore with brilliant maroon, red, yellow and orange leaves. After the previous day's rain, sunlight danced on the water and cheered our spirits. Gentle clouds drifted overhead. It was invigorating.

"Look. It's fall! We have so missed the changing seasons. For three and a half years it has been eternal summer. And here we are in the midst of autumn. Look at that man raking the leaves in his yard."

"We'd likely be doing the same thing back at home. Makes you a little homesick, doesn't it?"

It was Dawn's birthday and we had tried unsuccessfully to reach her before leaving the dock. She was on a trip to San Francisco. I had so wanted to get the latest update on her most recent boyfriend.

"I'm getting mighty curious about this 'Jeff' guy," I said. "He's certainly hung in there longer than the others. Maybe he's the one she's been waiting for."

We crossed the Chesapeake, zinging along about seven knots, dodging all those infernal crab pots. With the sun in our eyes, they were really hard to spot. Safely across, we entered the Chester River. It quickly narrowed and we could then see the large, beautiful old farms and mansions along the shore. Many had huge rolling lawns so much like the old plantation scenes in the movies. I was into a "Scarlet O'Hara" reverie, when I heard Fred's angry voice.

"Darn. That depth sounder isn't working again. We should have had it fixed in Baltimore. This is not a good place to be without it. Some of this water gets really shallow."

We nervously proceeded and finally anchored off of the small and very old community of Chestertown, Maryland. It was late afternoon and very windy, so we decided to wait until the following day before setting up the dinghy and going ashore. I lit our oil lamp in the main salon to take the chill off the air, turned some music on the radio and fixed a nice dinner. I also put a blanket on the bed, when it seemed that only a week ago all we needed was a sheet, and then we got hot and kicked it off. It was the first time we'd used a blanket on the boat since our travels in the Pacific Ocean. This change of seasons felt snug, cozy and comfortable when we were tucked away in the cabin of *Grace*.

"You know," Fred said. "This newspaper I bought a few days ago in Baltimore? It gets more interesting every time I read it. Since the news really doesn't change that much, maybe I'll save some money and just buy one paper a week and keep rereading it."

The following morning did not start well. After setting up the dinghy and attaching the outboard engine, Fred was unable to start it. Finally, we hauled the motor back onto the boat and took out the oars. We knew they weren't a great alternative as the city dock was some distance away across the river. Once again we were in the dinghy and ready to leave. Fred took one big pull on the oars as we started out when we heard a sharp "pop" sound. The oarlock had broken.

"Quick! Grab ahold of the boat," Fred yelled.

I was closest to reach out for something to hold onto to stop our drifting away downstream. We scrambled for a few moments and finally got the dinghy tied back up to *Grace*. Had we drifted out into the river current, we'd have been in a real pickle. There wasn't any nearby activity on the river to turn to for help. More things to fix.

"Oh my, this is just like stepping back in history. I love it."

We had finally made it into town and were walking down the quaint and charming streets of Chestertown, lined by shops and houses all in the architecture of the 1700's. A self-guided walking tour booklet provided us with lots of information about the original buildings and that led to wonderful imagined scenes of life in colonial times.

"Look at these old brick sidewalks," Fred said. "They must be the original ones. They undulate up and down, in and out. You sure have to be careful where you step."

It was a wonderful day of learning and enjoying a part of our own country and its history, and we savored it all, including a great "all you can eat" shrimp dinner. We hurried back to our dinghy just as dusk was descending. We needed to get back to the boat before it became dark as we had no running lights on the dinghy. A nearby Coast Guard boat started up just as we left shore, and we watched it nervously, but fortunately it went elsewhere. In so many of the places we had been cruising, there were no "rules" to follow, nor any enforcement. It was different in the U.S.

"Look at those geese flying south. They're sure noisy fellas with all that honking."

"They're smart. It's getting cold. We'll need to be following them very soon."

We had talked with many marine folks about our problems with the depth sounder and the outboard engine. Many said that we needed to go to Annapolis for repair resources, but that first, we should check to see that the transducer on the hull was not fouled. That meant diving in some *very* cold water. Thank goodness it was a *blue* job. If it had been up to me, I'd have hired someone to do it.

Anticipating the task at hand, we traveled down the river for a couple of hours while waiting for the sun to rise higher in the sky and provide better visibility in the water. After anchoring out of the current, Fred put on a Lycra suit, a shorty waterski suit, a diving hood, and aqua socks. It was the best we could do to "jury-rig" a wet suit. He jumped right in the river, dove under the boat and got out as quickly as possible.

"Bless your heart," I said when he was done and went directly for a hot shower. "You never even complained."

"Oh I did, you just didn't hear me. My voice was probably so high it was out of your hearing range."

Sadly, his efforts had not fixed the problem. We entered a marina and he scrambled to find places for repairs—a huge and time-consuming hassle. Finally, I went for a shower, but couldn't get the hot water to work. *Oh, the joys of cruising.*

After arriving in Annapolis, we made our way to a West Marine store for needed items. While shopping there, we heard a call for "Norm" on the loud speaker.

"You don't suppose that's the Norm we worked with at the West Marine store in Portland, do you?"

"Let's go find out."

Sure enough, the manager was the same guy. He had been so helpful as we outfitted our boat, and we had worked with him on so many things that he felt like a personal friend. Finding someone we knew from home when we were all the way across the country was a celebration. Small world.

"Wow. Look at these prices. These are terrific bargains."

"Why don't they have these places on the West Coast? This place is a *mecca* for shopping. To heck with Christmas gifts. Let's get some things for ourselves. It's been almost four years since we've bought any clothes and our cruising wardrobe isn't cutting it anymore."

We had discovered the joy of Factory Outlet shopping, and the prolific opportunities for bargain shopping. Fred was even getting in the swing of it. It was a welcome diversion from the frustration of the depth sounder. We'd walk in one of the many stores in an outlet mall, head for the clearance rack, and just as quickly leave if we didn't find any good "buys."

"I feel like a kid in a toy store," I exclaimed. "Where shall we go next?"

"Well, it's certainly different from looking for boat parts," Fred agreed.

But the saga of repairs continued. It appeared we would have to buy a new transducer, and have the boat hauled out to install it. *Ouch.* That would be a heavy hit on the budget. We needed to do one more test while underway, so on a stormy day that was better suited for reading a book by a fireplace, we reluctantly took the boat out into the harbor.

"Oh great. Now it's working. But it probably will stop again two miles down the river."

"But at least it shows that we don't need to buy a new transducer and haul out. So now what?"

After many hours and efforts in additional trouble-shooting together, we finally found the problem. A boat owner in the marina, who was also an electrician said we could get a part at Radio Shack that would fix it, although we'd still need a repair to our alternator.

Terrific. *Now, how to get to Radio Shack?* Another friendly boat owner offered to have his wife drive us there and back. The world is full of wonderful people.

"I'm not sure either one of us would have been able to figure out the problem on our own," Fred said. "It was the 'brainstorming' together that did it."

"I agree. Two heads are better than one. Got to admit—we make a pretty good team," I added with a wink.

The following day we left Annapolis for Saint Michael's on the other side of the Chesapeake. The eastern shore of the bay was much quieter and more laid-back than the highly populated and fast paced society of the western shore. It was a beautiful warm, sunny, fall day and we spent several hours touring the grounds and buildings of the Maritime Museum there. A number of volunteers were available to give information about what we were seeing.

"You know, I think I'd enjoy volunteering for some organization when we go back home," I said. "Maybe using some of the knowledge we've gained through this experience."

"Well, since we seem to encounter a disaster on almost a daily basis, maybe we could volunteer for the American Red Cross in responding to disasters," Fred chuckled. "Plus, its interesting how more and more our talk turns to *after* our full-time cruising," Fred added. "Maybe it's getting close to that time." It was a bittersweet thought.

We had lots of opportunities to shop for Christmas gifts as we explored the area. It also was a fun way of anticipating flying home for the holidays. The people were all so friendly, and it was always a conversation maker when we said we were on a sailboat from Oregon. In one place, after talking for some time with the shopkeeper, she insisted we go on a gala Halloween dinner cruise that night. It included music and dancing and sounded like fun, but it was expensive.

"Oh, but you've got to come," she said. "I'll give you a $20 discount." How could we refuse?

It really was great fun, with good food and enjoyable music. They even had karaoke, and I just *had* to try it.

"Hey, the crowd really cheered for me," I said when I had finished singing.

Fred kindly did not point out that they had cheered for *everyone* who was silly enough to try it.

It was a windy day when we worked our way over to Kent Narrows through a narrow cut. Still not realizing that our charts were outdated, we were confused by the mismatched buoy numbers. Frustration. As we turned into the Choptank River, a fresh wind was on the bow, and steep choppy seas had us bouncing around, feeling miserable, and getting soaking wet in the process.

"It's funny," I said. "It used to be that I'd take this stuff as a part of cruising. Now I'm thinking—'been here, done this.' Don't need anymore. Time to go home."

We struggled to tie up at a small restaurant-marina in Oxford. With the strong wind, getting four dock lines around four different pilings was difficult, and there was no one available to help. It didn't improve my disposition. But it was a quaint and sleepy little town that was not as tourist-oriented as other places. Fortunately, we were planning to meet Dick and Lynn, our friends on *Dawn*. Unfortunately, we discovered that we'd needed to go to a neighboring town eight miles away for our marine needs, and there was no bus service or car rentals available on "the shore."

Docking in the rain.

"I don't like this. That wind is really picking up. Look at those skinny little dock lines on that boat in the slip upwind of us. If one of them breaks, it will be blown right on top of us."

"And that rain and lightning are fierce. Maybe we'd better get out our foul weather gear in case we need to go on deck or go ashore."

We had gone to bed early but had gotten up again when the wind and rain had risen to the point that it almost required shouting in order to be heard. Because the wind came across our beam, and we were tied in the slip, the boat was prevented from turning into the wind as she would have done at anchor. This caused *Grace* to heel way over at a frightening angle. It made walking about in the cabin very difficult. The adrenalin was really flowing when we saw the wind gauge hit 59 knots. Not knowing what the storm might develop into, we considered that we may need to get off the boat, or possibly add additional lines. With great difficulty we put on our foul weather gear, only to realize that there was simply *no way* we could get off the boat even if we wanted to. Due to the severe lean of the boat, the little finger dock that led to the main dock was a considerable distance from our boat's deck. We were stuck where we were.

The waves in the river were huge, and it was alarming to see them slam into the restaurant pier. The air felt strange, and our ears were popping. *What was happening?* Fortunately, the whole affair lasted only about 30 minutes, but after the storm was over it was almost impossible to try to relax and go to sleep. We had been wired for *survival* mode.

"It had to be a small tornado," the restaurant owner said the following morning. "It created a vacuum and sucked the garbage right out of the cans. We couldn't open the front door either. Never saw anything like it."

As we talked with him about the strange event, Fred asked if there was any transport service to the neighboring town. The owner immediately offered us the use of his car. And it was a Mercedes.

"Oh boy. This really is our day. We got to the repair shop with only 30 minutes to spare, and got the alternator fixed the on the spot. And it just cost eighteen dollars. Think of what it would have cost if we had been hauled out."

"And in that other shop the guy was able to fix the Hooka in only a few minutes as well. We are indeed *blucky*."

Watching the Nebraska football game that afternoon while we enjoyed steamed blue crab, and taking in a play at the community theater with Dick and Lynn that evening rounded out a wonderful day. Things were looking up.

"I must put 'being in a play or musical' on my 'to do' list," I mumbled as we fell asleep that night thinking about all the things for which we were grateful.

Our experiences in the Chesapeake were definitely more educational than nautical, but as we turned south in the bay after leaving the Choptank River, we were able to turn off the engine and have a wonderful sail with a strong beam wind. Of course, we had to keep a sharp watch for those pesky crab traps. It's the one we *didn't* see that would be our undoing. The weather was definitely colder. It was nice when the sun was out, but got chilly quickly as it set or when it was cloudy.

"I'm sure glad I bought this wool sweater at that used clothing store. I certainly have gotten my two dollars and fifty cents worth of value from it."

"We look a little like 'Pillsbury Doughboys,'" Fred laughed. "We have so many layers of clothing on that it's hard to move."

When we turned to go up the Potomac River to Washington, D.C., we were excited to get the push of a favorable tide. It was a three-day trip up the river to the nation's capital, and we wanted to make good headway.

"This is beautiful," I exclaimed. "The fall colors and rolling hills are spectacular."

"But we're the only boat on the water. What does that tell us?"

The second day we woke up to thick fog—not a pleasant experience in unknown waters. Thank goodness for our radar. Again we had a good push from the tide.

"We should be close to Mount Vernon. Get ready to ring our bell," I said from the nav station. "There. There it is. Ring it!"

We could barely see through the fog, but spotted the outline of the stately old mansion high up on the shoreline. We followed nautical tradition and gleefully rang the ship's bell as we passed, feeling like we shared a bond with the real mariners of old. Hopefully we could see it better and stop there on our return trip.

We had met an English couple shortly before we entered the Potomac, also headed for Washington, D.C. We talked several times on the radio, and had them over for a glass of wine after we anchored in a little creek near a swing bridge that we had to pass through. It would only open for sailboats between midnight and 5 am. We got ready for a 4:30 am departure from the creek, hoping that when leaving in the dark there would be less fog than when we entered.

"Those English folks have been cruising for eight years. Amazing."

"But they don't have any children. There's nothing for them that pulls them back home."

As the holidays approached, we were definitely feeling the pull of family.

Neither of us slept well that night, fearing that our alarm would not ring and we would miss our chance to get through the bridge. By 3:30 am we were up and slowly edged our way in the darkness out into the main river to be ready for the requested opening. The fog was lighter, which gratefully made it easier to see the navigational lights. As we worked our way upriver after passing through the bridge, we were startled to see a faint light glowing in the black sky straight ahead of us. It appeared to be hovering above the city off in the distance. It was still very dark, but the glow continued to brighten as we got closer. Our curiosity was peaked.

"Here, take a look through the binoculars," Fred said with a grin.

"Oh my gosh. It's the capital building! Oh, it's beautiful the way it rises above the city lights. And there's the Washington Monument. It gives me *goose-bumps*."

We moved slowly as we approached the marina, as we had not wanted to enter until it was light. No one was around and the office wasn't open when we found an open slip and tied up, so we took a little nap. The marina was right downtown, and only a fifteen-minute walk from the National Mall. There were so many things to see there, and almost everything was free—courtesy of the U.S. government and the Smithsonian museums. *What to see first?*

Business before pleasure, so we went to a medical clinic for Fred's chest X-ray and flu shots; then off to the Mall. When we approached that vast park space framed by Washington's Monument at one end and the Capital Building at the other, our first view was breathtaking. This was the center of our government. We were awed and inspired. We first went to look for our congressmen's offices to request tickets for a White House tour, then on to the myriads of sights and attractions that beckoned us.

"It says here that it would take 80 years just to view everything that is in the Smithsonian museums alone," I exclaimed. "And on top of that there are all the governmental facilities. This is going to take some time."

"Let's go to the Voice of America building," Fred suggested. "We really enjoyed listening to that when we were in Central America."

The choices were endless. For almost a week we walked, toured, gawked and giggled our way through one impressive museum or federal edifice after another. Typical was when we thought we'd spend a few minutes in the Library of Congress building, but instead spent a whole afternoon there. Each day we'd pack some sandwiches and find a place to sit for lunch while resting the weary "dogs."

"My dad would love seeing us do this," I said. "When we were here as a family, I always wanted to eat out, but we seldom did. It's amazing how much I remember from that trip and all the historical places we saw. It surely must have impressed my ten year old mind."

One day we were in the Capital building itself. It was cold and raining outside but it was time for lunch and we were hungry. We searched around until we found the end of a hallway that had a small bench and very little traffic. Sitting down, we tried to keep our sandwiches hidden when slyly taking each bite.

"Stop eating when someone comes by," I giggled. "We don't want to be obvious about this."

"But I bet the security men are having a good laugh while watching us on their hidden cameras," Fred responded. It was difficult to laugh and chew at the same time.

After going to church on Sunday, we took our first Metro ride to find a restaurant that advertised a "two for one" champagne brunch. It was the first time we had spent any money since arriving in the capital. Later, because it was the weekend, the mall area was crowded with tourists and we joined the throng. Finally tiring, we aimed for the marina, stopping at the Holocaust Museum on the way.

"How incredibly sad and grim to see such reminders of what people are capable of doing."

"And with the assassination of Israel's Rabin yesterday, some of those things are still going on."

Because it was Sunday, the many huge federal office buildings were all empty and we walked along deserted streets on our way back to *Grace*.

"This really feels eerie. I've never seen so many huge vacant buildings. It feels like we are alone on the planet."

"Think of what it must cost the taxpayer to build, maintain and staff all these places. I wonder if they're all necessary."

One day we took the "Tourmobile" to see some area attractions that were beyond our walking capability. All the memorial buildings were impressive, but the Viet Nam Memorial had me in tears. I had known some of those whose names were on the wall. We were fortunate at Arlington National Cemetery to be in time to see the changing of the guard at the Tomb of the Unknown Soldier. But such reminders of war and its terrible losses left us with both feelings of sadness as well as appreciation of our freedom and its cost.

Another day was raining and nasty, but there was "no rest for the weary" as we had tickets to tour the White House. It was interesting, but it felt like we were herded around like a bunch of sheep. In the Capital building we watched Newt Gingrich open the House of Representatives, but wondered about the sanity of it all as no one listened to anybody else. And a final splurge was going to the Kennedy Center for Performing Arts to see Andrew Lloyd Weber's "Music of the Night" for my birthday celebration.

"It was wonderful. Thank you so much," I said to Fred. "And taking a taxi—wow. Now I'm really looking forward to our holiday tradition—going to the Nutcracker with the kids when we get home."

"Well, first we better get further south and quickly. Those were 30 knot winds today, and it's forecast for 25 degrees tonight. That's too cold for living on a boat."

"Are you O.K?" I shouted in alarm.

"Yeah, but don't try to get off. The dock is like an ice rink, and the lines are frozen solid."

Fred had stepped off the boat and fallen on the slippery frosted dock as he tried to untie our dock lines. It was in the low twenties, ten o'clock at night, and we were getting ready to head down the river.

"This is insanity," I yelled.

"Well, it's the only way we're going to get through that swing bridge and get out of here."

At least it wasn't foggy. We carefully made our way in the dark, with the help of dozens of navigational lights, to the infamous bridge, waiting only 30 minutes for it to open. The little creek anchorage on the other side was a welcome stop and we huddled under the bed covers after setting the anchor. No "Miller Time" that night. It was too cold—definitely time to go south.

About noon on the following day we were making good progress on a rough river when we listened to the weather reports.

"Oh great. Now there are Small Craft Warnings," I said.

"I think we should go back to that protected anchorage we

just passed, and wait for that storm to pass. It sounds like a wicked one."

"Oh but it's so early. I really wanted to put some miles under the keel today, and we have a good tidal push." Seeing Fred's set face, I succumbed. "But it's a long ways to the next good anchorage. Darn. I suppose you're right."

We reluctantly anchored in that small creek, putting out lots of chain for the potential big blow. But the storm did not materialize as predicted. However, it was still forecasted, but not until the following day.

"Daggone it. Now we need to wait *another* day."

"Well, let's take apart the dinghy and stow it. That'll help our speed when we do get going."

About five in the evening the storm hit. We put on all our foul weather gear *just in case*. The wind meter hit 50 knots, but since we were at anchor we were pointed into the wind. The boat bounced up and down but rode pretty well. We were glad that the dinghy was stowed. About eight, the boat started swinging and in a very short time we had turned 180 degrees to face the opposite direction. Still the anchor held well. About ten, the front had passed and the temperature dropped. We were thankful for the cabin diesel heater. It was cold.

Pulling up the anchor the next morning was tough. It had dug deep into the mud of the creek in the heavy winds, and it took endless buckets of water to wash off all that sticky mud before stowing the chain. Poor Fred. His hands were red and numb by the time we got going.

"What was *that*? Did you feel that? The whole boat shuddered and vibrated."

"And we've lost power. Something's definitely wrong with the engine." *Oh no.*

We turned back into the creek to find out what was wrong. After having gone only a short distance, everything sounded and felt normal again. Relief flooded over us as we considered the possibility that we might have had a crab trap line around the propeller, but that it slipped off when we turned around. Once again we entered the Potomac. *Oh for a day without drama.*

It was with great disappointment that we gave up our hope of stopping at Mount Vernon and Alexandria. We needed to get to warmer climes. But we rang our bell in passing once again. Over and over on our way back through the Chesapeake, we marveled at the joy of our inside steering station. It would have been just miserable to have been outside all the time, or hiding behind a dodger in such weather.

On my birthday, we turned into a creek and tied up in a small marina. Fred had the cabin decorated with balloons, and we had looked forward to going out for dinner in a cozy, warm restaurant to celebrate.

"Good grief. There's *nothing* here. No stores, no restaurants, no transportation. There isn't even TV reception. The manager said they were at the 'end of the earth' and I believe it."

"There's some showers, but there's no heat in them and the windows don't close. Not pretty."

We were again disappointed. I knew I had to make the best of it, but I wanted to pout. The following day brought more storm forecasts, which meant staying put. Fortunately, the skipper of a moored research vessel next to us came to the dock to check on his boat. He offered to drive us out to see the quaint community.

"Oh, these houses are fantastic," I said. "They look like ornate doll houses of the eighteenth century. They've been beautifully restored with all the gingerbread trims and multi-color designs."

"There were many millionaires here at one time, but the fish packing plant folded, and most folks left," said our new friend.

He took us to a roadside café and then to a grocery store before returning us to the boat. How touched we have been by the kindness of so many people. *Gracias a Dios.*

On this leg of our travel, our "Long Johns" became our new best friends. We wore them 24/7.

"How long do you think we can wear them before they'll stand up by themselves?" we mused.

Each time we stopped for the day we'd go through our cold weather routine. Quickly after anchoring or tying up, we'd take off the doors to the engine room to let the heat of the engine warm the cabin. We'd also light the gas lamp and start to cook something on the stove to create more heat. We'd put up all the inside curtains on the big pilot-house windows, and later in the evening we'd turn on the forced air diesel heater. But all that warmth inside the cabin when it was very cold outside, created a good deal of condensation on the windows. This meant that we routinely ran around wiping off the water before it dripped. It was a definite inconvenience and sometimes a *learning* experience.

"Oh, *ick*," I yelled from the head one night.

"What's the matter?"

"When I sat down, I discovered there's even condensation on the toilet seat!"

Leaving the Chesapeake Bay and crossing the waters open to the Atlantic Ocean was much less traumatic than when we had traveled north, and we once again found ourselves in the hustle and bustle of the huge and exciting port of Norfolk, Virginia. We even saw a helicopter pulling some type of large structure through the water. Perhaps it was a target, as we had read that the Navy often engaged in target practice in the nearby waters. We soon were tied up at the Norfolk Yacht and Country Club. Several folks had told us not to miss it. It was a beautiful facility, and after a good shower and change of clothes, we reveled in the luxury of just sitting in the lounge amongst the elegant surroundings.

"How we have come to appreciate the simple pleasures," I said.

"This place hardly qualifies as simple," Fred teased. "But yes, I know what you mean."

"When we go home, how long do you think it will be before we take them for granted again?" Before he could answer I added, "It's a rhetorical question."

We arranged for a rental car for three days and took off for an inland trip, feeling like two kids playing hooky. Our first day was spent in Williamsburg, Virginia and we soaked up the lessons of history that were told in such a unique and marvelous way. Our country's beginnings as an independent nation, and the way of life prior to the Revolutionary War became alive right before out eyes. The many costumed people on the streets and in the shops, doing things just as the colonial folks had done, all made the history of this time period meaningful. It was fascinating watching the blacksmith shoe the horses, the women cook over the open fire, the merchant making ladies hats. We also gained new respect and appreciation for the early patriots, and a greater understanding of the strife created in the decision to separate from England. By late afternoon, our brains were saturated, and our bodies tired. We drove back to the yacht club and boat. We had just gone to sleep when our pager beeped.

"It's from Vail. It must be from Lance, but he put a one after the number. That's the code that means there is an urgent need for us to call," I said. *Oh dear.*

We quickly got up, dressed and went to the clubhouse to make a phone call. It was just about time for them to close for the night. We were worried. Occasionally the girls paged us just to let us know that they were thinking of us, but the code for that was the number nine following their number. No one had ever paged using the number one code.

"No answer," I said after returning his call. "Maybe we can reach him at work."

Still no answer, but not sure we had the right work number we ran back to the boat to get it, then ran back again to the clubhouse. The receptionist had said she'd wait for us before closing up. By now our anxiety was soaring, and my "Mama Bear" reactions had taken over.

We tried his home number again. On the second ring, Lance answered. He had been asleep when we called before. I was so relieved, until I heard him say he was just thinking of me and wanted to send belated "warm fuzzies" for my birthday.

"Can you believe that?" I sighed when finally back in bed. "He got the code *backward*. I could have wrung his neck, but I was so thankful that everything was alright, that all I could do was laugh."

Our next day's history lesson started in Yorktown and the Victory Monument, where the Revolutionary War ended. The Visitor Center and replicated war camp were fascinating, but we couldn't go on the battlefield.

"The U.S. government is playing games and shut down federal services as the budget was not passed," Fred said. "What a fiasco."

"Well, this day is certainly not a high point in our nation's history, nor in my esteem of our legislators," I agreed. "At least it didn't happen when we were in Washington, D.C. That would really have made me mad."

Going on, we visited Jamestown Settlement, where life for the first European settlers in this land was depicted. We explored the replicas of the settlement, the three ships that brought the pilgrims from England, and a Native American village. This all took place 150 years before the Revolutionary War, so everything was less refined, but designed mostly for survival.

"Goodness. Life was really hard back then. It made our living on a boat look like 'a piece of cake.'"

Again, by afternoon our brains were no longer taking in new data, so we drove on to Annapolis to pick up our repaired outboard engine—a major reason for the car rental and road trip. The bill was a heavy hit for the cruising budget, but it was cheaper than it would have been to buy a new engine, and cheaper to rent a car than having the engine shipped to us. On our way back to the boat we stopped again at some of the many outlet malls to do some real Christmas shopping. It was great fun, but exhausting. Finally, we took our treasures, returned to our amazing *Grace* and collapsed. It was a side trip to remember.

"Good news. UPS delivered our repaired wind vane, so we can take off," Fred said as he climbed aboard.

"Terrific. Let's go."

Just as when traveling northward, we had hurried along with

a goal of reaching Page in Baltimore, now our goal in sailing southward was to quickly reach Charleston, thaw out and get ready to fly home. Thanksgiving would arrive in less than a week, and I had purchased a smoked turkey breast in case we had to celebrate the holiday at anchor somewhere. We were pleased that we often had the wind behind us, helping our speed through the water, but again experienced the irritations of traveling "the ditch." Due to the often narrow channel of the ICW surrounded by shallow water, cross currents and shifting shoals, it meant being outside in the cockpit more frequently for safer navigation.

"I counted. I have six layers on top, and four on the bottom."

"Cruising's definitely more fun in warm countries."

At one stop, I winched Fred up the mast so that he could replace our repaired wind vane. This time, it was much more difficult for me. Unlike in the tropics, he could not assist in hauling his weight by using his bare legs and reef runner shoes to grip the mast.

"I don't know whether to cry or scream," I hollered up at Fred. "If someone offered me a nickel for the boat about now, I think I'd take it."

On another stop we were able to contact one of Fred's friends from high school, and have her over to the boat. It had been many years since they were in touch, and they enjoyed reminiscing and catching up.

"Do you think we'll be able to make it in time?" I asked.

"It certainly doesn't help that we missed this bridge opening by only *four* minutes. Now we have to wait 30 minutes for the next opening. I had already begun to smell that turkey and taste that dressing."

It was Thanksgiving Day, and we had so hoped to celebrate with dinner at a special restaurant in Belhaven, North Carolina. Now we weren't sure that we'd arrive before they closed. But a favorable wind and tidal current managed to push us along, and we arrived just three hours before the restaurant's closing time. It was located in an elegant, stately old southern mansion close to the waterway. We hurried up the cobblestone circular carriageway that was surrounded by huge live oak trees dripping with Spanish moss, and observed the tall, formal white columns guarding the front entrance. Inside, the rich antique furnishings of a gentle yesteryear, transported us to a time of elegance and luxury in the charming old southern style. Although we so missed the family, we were keenly aware of our blessings, and savored the day, the food, the wine, the relaxation, and yes, the warmth.

We had another reason for stretching the budget and staying at the marina in Belhaven. It had cable T.V., and the following day was *the* big game—Nebraska versus Oklahoma. Before it started, we walked the half-hour to town for a little exercise. I looked for a craft project while Fred went to the hardware store. It was good to spend a little time by myself—I missed that private space I needed occasionally. The rest of the day's activities revolved around the game. Since Nebraska won by over 30 points, Fred did less of his usual pacing during the game, which was a good thing. It's difficult to pace on a sailboat. Also good was the win. A happy hubby always made for a good week.

Moving on, we stopped to see the friends that had come to visit Fred when he was in the hospital. Seeing their home, reminded us of our own, and an awareness of a growing yearning. We would have enjoyed accepting their invitation to stay with them for a while, but that slippery dock coated with frost was a reminder of our desire to get south.

After many attempts to find a place to anchor one evening, and going aground in the process, we finally decided to try another area listed as "poor holding." Because of that, we set out two anchors, and as the weather report was benign, hoped we'd be O.K. The tidal currents had become increasingly stronger as we made our way southward, and when they changed from an incoming tide to an outgoing one, the boat would swing 180 degrees. Fred would often get up in the night when that happened to make sure that the anchor still held. Such was the case that night. But when we went to pull up both anchors in the morning, we found that they had become twisted around each other. It was a terrible mess and took a good deal of time and effort to get all the chain and anchors aboard. It was a "we" effort, but fortunately I had drawn the long straw and only had to maneuver the boat from the helm. A good "pink" job.

Another delay occurred when we missed a bridge opening by only five minutes.

"Darn. Now we have to wait for a whole *hour*."

"We'll never make the anchorage before dark now. That means paying for that expensive marina in Wrightsville."

"With all the water around here you'd think there'd be *someplace* to anchor, but so much of it's only two feet deep."

We delayed our departure the following day in order to use a favorable tide in the Cape Fear River. We had no pesky thunderstorms this time when we crossed, but a strained miscommunication between us regarding an approaching freighter made for some discomfort and more grey hairs. Later, at a dock, I became frustrated after repeated unsuccessful attempts to make a phone call. Even here in the states, pay phones would often cut us off, not work correctly, or we'd make errors in punching in the myriads of numbers needed to use a credit card. So many of these things we had endured many times before and we could usually laugh about them, but now they were becoming increasingly irritating. We didn't want to focus on the inconveniences, rather than the blessings, but sometimes we realized we were doing just that.

"Here, let me try it," said Fred when I slammed down the phone and was almost in tears.

He took over, but soon was walking away mumbling about quitting this cruising stuff. *Oh dear.* We mustn't both get "down" at the same time—it was bad enough when it was just one of us grumbling, although admittedly, it was usually me.

"Another 'outlet mall mecca,'" Fred said. "These places are all over."

"But this one is a free stop. There's no charge for staying at the dock."

"With all the restaurants and shopping, this hardly qualifies as a 'free' stop," he laughed. "I think I've spent more time *shopping* in the last few weeks, than I have in my whole life."

We had tied up at the free dock for a couple of days. It allowed us to get off the boat and get some walking exercise, which helped to reduce my blood pressure. Our plan was to leave *Grace* in the same Charleston marina we had used before for our trip home. We expected to be gone for two to three months. But we didn't want to arrive at the marina too soon. It had good security and was priced reasonably, but it was quite some distance from town, had nothing around it and no transportation available. The roads in that area were narrow with no shoulders, and had a good deal of truck traffic. They were definitely not safe for walking.

In a phone call to Dawn, we heard again that the relationship with Jeff was a serious one. *Wonders never cease.* We were excited to meet him. They did have a little "tiff" but she wasn't worried about it.

"She said she thought they just had been together too much," I told Fred.

"Well, we certainly know about that, don't we?" he laughed.

We packed up all the Christmas gifts we had purchased, and decided what clothes we would need both for home, and then for going on to Portugal and Spain. How exciting it was to think of doing some air travel with those Delta parent passes. But for now, we began doing the things necessary to prepare the boat for long-term moorage. I also spent a good deal of time writing our monthly newsletter, "The Awesome Adventures of Amazing Grace," on our computer. When I attempted to print it for mailing, the printer would not work. More fix-it projects. I also took time for getting a haircut and permanent—something I desperately needed. The following morning, when I awoke and stumbled out of the aft cabin, Fred gasped and pointed to my hair, which was flying *everywhere*.

"How in the world are you going to tame *that*?"

Admittedly, it wasn't what I had pictured for my new "do" but I sprayed it with water and got it somewhat under control. Some projects just didn't turn out as expected.

As we moved closer to Charleston, we were struck by how different the scene was from what we saw on our trip northward. The trees had all lost their leaves, leaving dead-appearing sticks surrounded by acres of dry grasses. All looked so very grey and dull. We anchored in a small creek close to a bridge that we needed to have opened the next morning. The tidal currents in the creek and in Charleston harbor were very strong, so our plan was to use a slack tide in getting up to a downtown marina the following day. To do that we needed to leave early in the morning before it was light as the bridge would not have boat openings from seven to nine o'clock. Our cruising guide said that due to the submerged stumps in the creek where we now were, we should use a buoy marker on our anchor. Fred was concerned about that. He was afraid that it would trip the anchor when the tide changed, and also about how it would affect our leaving in the dark. But we did as the guide recommended and then went below. It was always good to go into our cabin after anchoring. We would turn on the heat, listen to PBR on the radio, have a glass of wine and a meal, and do a little reading or handwork. The cozy surroundings felt a little like a "cocoon" and it was peaceful and comforting. About nine that night, Fred went out again to check on the anchor. He hurried back.

"Blast it, I knew this was going to happen. Hurry! The tide turned and we are drifting right into another boat."

The adrenalin quickly started flowing. We rushed out, started the engine, and while I maneuvered the boat to avoid hitting our neighbor who was *way* too close and rapidly getting closer, Fred went forward to pull up the chain and reset the anchor. It wasn't an easy task in the dark, and we ended up closer to the main channel than we'd wanted to be, but we finally returned to the cabin. It had been a close call.

"How can you *do* that?" Fred exclaimed as he watched me pick up my sewing handwork.

"Do what? It's just my needlework."

"Good grief, we almost ran into that boat, and here you are calmly stitching away."

"But we got the job done, didn't we? It's O.K. now, right?"

I was ready to move on, but apparently Fred needed some time to decompress. Maybe he should try some handwork to relieve stress.

"*Another* close call. With our antenna, I figure we're 55 feet tall, and that bridge had just that amount of clearance at high tide."

We had made our way out of the creek in the dark, and past the first swing bridge when it had started to become light. The fixed bridge was closer to Charleston Harbor, which was much more easily navigated on the slack tidal current, and we arrived at a lovely marina close to downtown while still early in the morning.

"I feel incredibly grubby. It's been eight days since I've had a real shower."

We quickly used the facilities to clean up, made some phone calls to find a place to fix the computer, and started into town. The day that followed was simply unbelievable—a true comedy of errors. But we weren't laughing. Suffice it to say that getting the computer repaired required almost ten hours, five bus rides, and two taxis. And after all that, we discovered that all it needed was a new mouse. We had to go to several shops and so far away from the downtown area that we thought we surely must have been in another state. We waited for buses that never showed, got on and off the wrong buses, made bus transfers, crossed eight lane highways that had no pedestrian crossings, ran three blocks to catch the final bus of the day back into the city, and froze from the lack of a coat. (It had been warm at ten in the morning when we started.) And the only sightseeing we accomplished was that of the city slums from the windows of the buses. It was dark when we limped back to the boat.

"We have to laugh. I'm so mad that we'd probably get arrested if we started screaming in the streets."

"You got that right. Let's go to bed. I'm too tired to do laundry tonight."

"Laundromat laundry sucks," I complained.

"Its better than doing it by hand," Mr. Sunshine replied.

Actually, we were very glad to be able to wash everything we could find in preparation for our trip. Stono Marina, where we stayed before and would be staying again, had no facilities for laundry. Clean things left on the boat were less likely to develop mildew. And even though we liked the idea of turning the tables on the kids by bringing all of *our* dirty laundry to *their* houses, we preferred to pack something clean. We had an early start on the job, and were able to finish up and go into town to explore the main marketplace. It was colorful, chaotic, lively with music and full of activity. There were many tourist-oriented stalls and shops—all a welcome diversion from boating. We got back to the boat in time for the slack tide, and were quickly on our way. Passing through a bridge and very narrow channel with relative ease, we arrived at Stono Marina only an hour later. There were several folks on the dock ready to help us tie up, and everyone said how glad they were to see us again. How nice! It felt familiar and hospitable. Our friend, Phil, said he'd be glad to take us to the airport for our flight. It was good to be back. And it was good to connect once again with several of the folks who lived aboard their boats in the marina, especially George and Kay, who lived on an unfinished steel boat.

"Do you think they'll ever finish rebuilding that big old boat?" I asked one evening.

"I seriously doubt it, but who cares? They are enjoying the project and the dream of one day 'sailing off into the sunset.' That's enough for some folks."

They were one of the couples that had befriended us before, loaning us their car, taking us for groceries, and generally looked out for us. We had just had them over for tea. They were so pleasant, and made our stay so much more enjoyable, but their boat had a *long* way to go before being ready for cruising. It reminded us that there were many ways to realize "the dream."

Since we had a few days before we hoped to leave, we were able to get the boat ready without being pressed for time. Dawn had sent our tickets, and though it was an exercise in frustration to use the pay phone to check the loads on the flights, it looked as if there would be available seats. It was always an adventure to fly "standby." Although they were free, those parent pass benefits were not without stress.

Fred doubled and tripled our dock lines, changed the oil, winterized the engines, and filled the tanks in preparation to leave the boat. I cleaned out all traces of food to discourage bugs, defrosted the refrigerator, washed the sheets at a neighboring marina, and packed. We had taken all we could off the deck and stowed it below, disconnected the battery, and left all our contact information with the office.

"Let's go home," Fred said with a grin.

I was more than ready!

It was eight weeks before we were to return to our beautiful *Amazing Grace*. During that time we made six different flights across the country. In addition to the delight of being with the kids and moms for four weeks during the holidays, we spent a week with Dawn in Puerto Vallarta, Mexico, a week with Lance in Vail, Colorado, and more than two weeks in Portugal and Spain. We were certainly appreciating those parent travel passes. We were thrilled to get Business Class seats for the international flights, and felt spoiled and pampered by the extra "perks," roomy seats and great food.

"Here's to our Delta Dawn," we giggled as we raised our glass of champagne and toasted our daughter for the "umpteenth" time.

Once we arrived in Europe or Mexico, we definitely were on a "shoe-string" budget and tried to live as the locals did. We often laughed at the contrast.

"You know, I think the best meal of the trip was the one we had on the plane."

It hadn't always been easy, as there were long waits in airports, and always the uncertainty about getting a seat on a flight. We had even spent two successive nights in the air, but it was all worth it.

Renting a car and driving in Portugal and Spain was an adventure in itself. Huge potholes, roads without any signs, narrow twisting streets, and not speaking the language made many stressful moments. For example, when we were ready to leave Seville, we had walked two blocks to the garage from our hotel to retrieve our rental car, as we had not driven it in the large, busy city. But our simple plan for getting back to the hotel to pick up our luggage became a disaster when our return route was blocked by a truck that was stalled in a narrow one-way street. We thought we could just go around the block, but there was no way to do that. As we wound our way through the endless serpentine and one-way streets that took us further and further away from the central city, we became hopelessly lost. And of course, our city maps had been left with our luggage at the hotel. After all, it was only supposed to have been a two-block trip. Skies were cloudy, so we couldn't even tell what direction we were going. Forty-five minutes later we were feeling desperate until I finally spotted a familiar place.

"Turn left here," I shouted to Fred, ignoring the prominently displayed "no turn" sign.

As luck would have it, we were immediately whistled to stop by a not-so-friendly policeman. I leaned across Fred to the open driver's window and hurried to frantically explain in my limited Spanish with many accompanying hand and body gestures, that we had been lost, our hotel was just down the street, and we didn't speak the language. Appearing somewhat incredulous and shaking his head with resignation at this obviously crazy tourist woman, he stepped back and reluctantly waved us through the intersection. *Whew!*

Although we had loved the opportunities experienced, the sights encountered, and the knowledge we had gained from our inland travel abroad, we loved being back on the boat even more.

"It's so good to be back *home*," I laughed. "It's crazy to be at home in two places."

"It's so good to have a place of our *own*, and not have to lug everything around living out of a suitcase. She really does look good."

We were pleased that there was no mold, mildew, break-ins or damages. Since our bodies were still on European time, we took a relaxed pace as we settled back into living aboard. One thing that made that task immensely easier, was that while we were gone, George and Kay had bought a second car, and simply gave us the keys to it.

"Just use it as you wish until you have to leave," they had said.

What Sweethearts! We could hardly wait to get to the local Piggly Wiggly for some real coffee. Drinking European coffee had spoiled us. Now we couldn't stand the instant stuff we had previously used on the boat.

When Page and Steve paged us and we returned their call, we learned that our renter's husband had just died.

"Poor Laura. What a year it's been for her. First she loses her job, and now her husband."

"She wants to remain in the house to finish the school year before moving her daughter, but she can only pay half the rent now."

We agreed to accept that. It seemed the least we could do. Fortunately, there was also good news from the home front that day. Dawn had called to say that she and Jeff were looking at rings and planning a wedding! What fun. We had enjoyed getting to know him when we were in Oregon, and liked him very much. Dawn sounded so happy. I wanted to know *all* the details and could talk of little else that evening. They had not yet chosen a date, but I knew that we wanted to be home for all the preparation and anticipation of this special time in their lives. Yet here we were, three thousand miles away.

When checking the engine, Fred noticed something that did not look right on the drive shaft and had a mechanic out to assess it. He confirmed that we needed to replace the part, and we began the hunt to find what was needed. Unable to find it after considerable effort, we finally called the boatyard in England.

"Oh great. Only the U.K. has it," Fred said. "I asked them to ship it today, but the 'post' had already been collected, so now they'll have to wait until Monday to get it out."

"Well, we're in a good spot for waiting. Besides, there are several more of those big storm fronts forecast. So many folks say that this is the coldest spring they can remember."

Although it was early March, and often warm during the day, the nights were still very cold. We even wiped off a little ice from the *inside* of the front hatch one morning. The warm days also brought out the bugs—and they were hungry. As usual, I was their feast of choice.

"This east coast weather is crazy. It goes from temperatures in the teens to the eighties in just one day. And those thunderstorms continue every few days."

We were to receive more tragic news about cruising friends. We had just learned that our dear friends, Cindy and Reed, had lost their boat, *Yobo.* They had been anchored in the San Blas islands of Panama when a storm had drug their boat onto a reef and it had capsized.

"How awful! Thank goodness they are both O.K."

"But they lost almost *everything.* They only were able to save what they could carry out on the dinghy that night in the storm. When they went back the next day, the boat had been stripped clean by the natives."

We were stunned and saddened. It was every cruiser's fear— losing your boat. We sat in silence for many minutes as we tried to absorb the impact of such devastation.

"Well, that seals the deal for me," I said eventually. "We've been agonizing about whether to sail on to Europe, or to end the full-time cruising. With all the things we've been talking about, the wedding coming up, and now after hearing about *Yobo,* I know what I want to do."

"Me too. There are just too many indicators that the time has come to end this chapter in our lives. We've had the dream fulfilled, but there are lots of other dreams out there too. It's time to end this one and head for home."

We decided that for at least a few years, we'd leave the boat in a safe boatyard in Florida, and hopefully come back for two or three months each year to cruise in the Bahamas in late winter and early spring. With the renter wanting to stay in the house until June, we knew we had some time to get to Florida and find a secure location to leave *Grace*. It was a plan overflowing with ambivalence. Leave *Grace*! Could we really *leave* her?

We continued our efforts to clean and organize the boat and restock it with fresh food. Knowing that we would soon be ending our full-time cruising status, we wanted to remove much of the boat's contents. We got several large boxes, and sorted through all our gear and supplies, saving some, sending other things home, and giving some to Goodwill. We also gave a large assortment of cruising items to George and Kay.

"They were so tickled to get those things. I think it made them feel like they really will go cruising."

"And we know they'll pass them on to someone else to use if they never do."

With the use of their car, we were pleased to be able to attend a Lutheran church a few miles down the road. We had been warmly welcomed and included in the family each time we visited. Also, since we had to wait for our engine part to arrive, I decided to see a doctor about a lesion on my lip. That resulted in having it surgically removed, as well as treatment for the rest of my face for many "precancerous" lesions. Despite our efforts there had been too much sun damage on the skin.

"Thank goodness I can just hide out here in the boat until all this heals," I said. "I look *terrible*."

"You'll always look pretty to me," said Fred with a big grin and a hug. My eyes were swollen, I had a huge black hole on my upper lip, and my face was blotchy red and brown. Pretty? *Right!*

Another big front had passed through the area and all the boats in the marina were bucking up and down in the water's swell. After a whole day of it, I was beginning to feel a little seasick, and we were glad for a chance to get off the boat by going to a nearby video rental store. We made it a regular stop for our evening's entertainment. We also began doing some car shopping, as we needed to buy a car when we returned to Oregon. It would be nice to know just what we wanted and the relative costs before we got there. I was content with and passed a good deal of time with my needlework. I had one Christmas stocking done and had started a second. Fred, however, was going "stir-crazy."

Finally, our engine part arrived from England. Fred spent many hours installing it. I was so proud of the way he attacked each task. His patience, thoroughness, and determination saw him through many difficult projects. He was proud of himself, too, when he had finished and celebrated with a glass of wine and a late lunch. We still needed to find a replacement for our windshield wiper. *Oh the joys of having an English boat in the U.S.*

We took George and Kay out to dinner at a Mexican restaurant, got our charts all in order, and were finally ready to leave Charleston. We waited for a favorable tide that came in the late morning as we planned to go only a short distance, and then made our goodbyes to everyone in the marina.

"On the road again...," I sang once again. "Oh how good it is to be underway."

"It sure is. I guess we haven't lost our wanderlust just yet. Hope it lasts until June."

"But I sure get nervous when we haven't been out sailing for awhile. It's the other boats, the docks, the currents—just maneuvering the boat around. It's almost like I'm afraid I've forgotten how to do it. Kind of crazy."

It was five-thirty in the evening before we got the anchor down, a much longer day than we had anticipated. When we came to the spot where I had planned for us to anchor, Fred thought it was too shallow. The second place seemed to be too open to the weather. Finally we found a place we could live with. Nothing is certain on a boat.

We had a relaxing trip down the ICW to Savannah, Georgia. Such a pace was a welcome change from our dash northward. We tried when possible to leave each anchorage with a favorable tide, as going against the strong current made for very slow progress. One day we laughed after we had anchored.

"A whopping 22 miles today. That's the way the 'beautiful people' do it—leisurely."

We stopped at an anchorage just shy of Savannah, so that we could arrive at a marina early the next morning and have the advantage of two full days for sightseeing, but only have to pay for a slip for one night. Although the city is seven miles up the Savannah River from the ICW, the currents were so strong to navigate it that most cruisers elected to stay at a marina near the waterway. There was good bus service into town.

Arriving at the dock the next morning, we first filled our tanks with fuel and water.

"Wow. These little gnats with the big teeth are something fierce this morning," I said.

I fanned Fred with a rag while he held the diesel nozzle in place in order to keep the little critters away from him. We hurried to get into a slip, cleaned up and on our way into the city.

Savannah was all we had been told—a lovely old southern city that exuded grace and charm. The "Savannah Jewels" were 22 beautiful squares or parks that were scattered around the old section of town, and spoke to a genteel society that relished beauty and refinement. The riverfront area had been developed in a tasteful way for tourists and recreation as well as providing good dining. We walked until our feet were sore and then found a great food buffet and Happy Hour in one of the big hotels. Afterwards, it was windy and had become cold so we hurried for the last scheduled bus to the marina. It was 30 minutes late and we were freezing by the time we got to the boat. What a difference from the warmth of the daytime.

For our second day in the city we took the Trolley Tour, which was greatly appreciated by our feet. It was informative and fun. We also went to some of the house museums for a close look at life in the old and elegant southern style. Finding a bench in one of the squares, we ate our lunch and admired the azaleas, as well as the dogwoods and tulips. Spring flowers were at their peak and the gardens exploded with vivid hues. Everywhere there were trees loaded with colorful blossoms and that graceful hanging Spanish moss.

In the afternoon we were intrigued by the Maritime Museum, before we finally gave up the tourist role and found a bus for our return. We got off at a grocery store to buy food items for the next leg of our journey, but were a little worried as it was more than walking distance to the boat. We had been told that the store manager would drive us to the marina with our purchases. Sure enough, he seemed glad to do that. But we got quite an earful and an interesting and unexpected view of history on that ride to the boat.

"Wow. Apparently the Civil War is still not over for some of these folks," Fred said.

"I'll say. He was really bitter about the actions of General Sherman and the Union Army. And what they did to his city. To hear him tell it, it sounded as though it all took place a month ago. I was afraid to say anything—after all, we're from the north."

"Well the city was pretty well devastated, all right. Nothing of war is pretty."

"I could stay at this marina for a month," I laughed. "*Six* glazed donuts and the newspaper delivered to your boat every morning. Now that's southern hospitality."

But it was time to move on. We had planned to go a short distance, but after turning into a small creek and winding our way upriver looking for a place to anchor, we saw a fixed bridge ahead with about three feet of vertical clearance.

"I'd say from the looks of things that we are *lost*. No such bridge on the chart, and we're definitely not going under it."

"We must have missed a marker somewhere. Time to turn around. When you're not familiar with the area, you can't lose your concentration for even a moment. I think I like ocean travel better."

It wasn't long before we found the correct entrance to the Moon River and a place to spend the night along with the local residents—at least 100,000 little gnats.

Page was planning to meet us in Florida for her spring vacation. From there, we hoped that we could take a trip to Greece with her if we were able to obtain flight passes. If that didn't happen we'd all do a little inland traveling in the Florida area. We had plenty of time before Page was to arrive, so if the tide turned strongly against us on the ICW, rather than fighting the opposing current, we simply pulled over to the side and threw out an anchor until the current was again more in our favor. It made for less frustration, and the sunshine was warm enough to enjoy the time to read a book and relax for a while.

While waiting at anchor one day, I realized it was Palm Sunday. We were a long way from any city or town.

"Darn. I had really wanted to go to church today, but there's no place around here," I complained. "Before cruising, I never realized how much I took for granted just the opportunity to worship in a church. It was always available. I guess we've learned a lot of unexpected things about ourselves as well as other places and boating."

"True. And learned to appreciate many of those things," Fred added.

After several days of plodding along the waterway, we came into a marina at the charming little town of Fernandina Beach. Friendly people greeted us at the dock. In town there were colorful flowers and benches along the sidewalks, and they even had music piped into the outdoor downtown area. It was a welcome change from the waterway. We tried to make phone calls to the kids and check the ticket loads for a flight to Greece.

"Daggone. There are flights with seats available for almost every day but the ones when we want to go. With Page having a tight schedule, we don't have the flexibility we need to use a pass. Guess we'll just have to tour Florida."

With the usual irritations of trying to make phone calls, the disappointment of not going to Greece, not being able to find what we needed in town, and a few bouncing hormones thrown in the mix, I was in a funk, and even mad at myself for being irritable. I heated a can of stew for Fred and went to bed at eight. Later, on reflection and in talking with Fred, I realized again that many of the things I like to do that are meaningful and satisfying to me, are difficult, and sometimes even impossible to experience when living on a boat. That included my professional work, church, music, exercise, private time, and social time. While I certainly had down times, or funky times when living at home, it seemed they were easier to shake off or put into perspective. Fred commented that for him right now, he just needed to get to some place and "stay put" for a while. The continual "on the go" lifestyle was becoming tiring for us. Perhaps, that after four years of traveling, we were becoming saturated with the vagabond experience.

"So—you think you've had enough?" Fred teased.

"Yep. At least for now. No promises about the future though."

"Well, I bet the moms will be glad to hear that," he added and we both had to laugh.

Daytona Beach was the city where we chose to stay for a time and we had a week to get there before our marina reservation began. It was early April, the sun was out and temperatures were warming. We were even able to put up a sail for a few days. Things were looking up. Once again we anchored off the old castle and fort at St. Augustine. We wanted to go ashore, but it would have meant setting up the dinghy for just a short time, and I was self-conscious being around folks as my face was still healing. A pretty sight I was not, and I was glad I didn't have to look at it often. (Poor Fred did.) So we decided to wait until we rented a car and would explore the town with Page.

After an early morning start to get through a bridge before they had restricted openings, and some favorable currents, we arrived at the huge Halifax Harbor Marina in Daytona Beach. It was warm enough to change into shorts and we relaxed in the sun and observed the bustle of the marina and town that surrounded it. The amenities in this place were numerous and even included a boat that came to your slip to pump out your head holding tank. You didn't even have to be onboard at the time, but simply call to request the service. That was a first for us. And it was a welcome task to hand over to others! It also kept the water clean and sparkling.

Exploring the area around the marina, we came upon a large Farmer's Market with lots of fresh produce and stocked up. Our "land legs" and feet were tired by the time we got back to the boat. Since Easter was the following day, we checked out a newspaper for ads of churches, and got a bus schedule. In the evening we called Page. Dawn had told her that although the flight loads to Greece were bad for us, Ireland looked very good. We were immediately excited. There was one small glitch—Page's passport had expired. She would check on Monday to see if she could get it renewed in time.

"Such a deal. Ireland. Can you believe it? Oh how I hope Page can get her passport updated."

"So once again we change gears in our thinking. Life is never dull with the benefits of our Delta Dawn, that's for sure."

On Easter morning we donned our "city clothes" and found the right bus to take us to a church whose location we had found on a map. It turned out to be a lot farther from the bus stop than it had appeared on the map, but we made it in time, and we were just grateful to be there to worship on this special day, as well as to *sit* after the long walk. Another very long walk was necessary to get to a nice restaurant afterwards, but we were again grateful for the activity to divert a twinge of homesickness.

"It's a nice day, but boy do I miss the family on these holidays."

"Me too. Won't be long now until they'll be close."

"Hot diggity! She got her passport. We're going to *Ireland*. Ah— the luck of the Irish. Well, I'm really Scotch. But that's close enough."

The following day we went to the local library to see what we could find out about Ireland. In less than a week, we met Page at JFK airport in New York. There were tense moments for a while as we anxiously awaited her arrival in the Domestic Terminal, not knowing she was waiting for us in the International Terminal. We tried having her paged, but she apparently had not heard it. As we neared departure time we headed for the International Terminal and were ever so glad to see her standing at the gate, worrying about where we were. Once onboard, we found that with parent passes we had Business Class seats, while Page, with a Buddy Pass, was in the coach section.

"Oh Dad. You don't need to do that," Page protested when Fred went back to change seats with her.

"But I *want* to. Go sit up front with your mom. Enjoy."

Now *that's* a Sweetie!

Despite the trauma of driving a rental car through the crowded streets of Dublin's Friday evening rush hour in the rain, being unable to turn onto the freeway where we planned, and then finding the key code of our brand new vehicle had not been set by the rental agency which necessitated a two hour wait for them to come to us so that we could restart the car, we had a lovely trip through Ireland. We were delighted with the charm and hospitality of the intimate home lodgings with their huge Irish breakfasts, and the warm friendliness of the people throughout the country. We hung by our heels upside down, high above the ground in order to kiss the Blarney Stone, tried Guinness beer, strolled along the banks of Galway Bay, and enjoyed shopping at the Waterford glass factory. We even found a sign to "Dardis Town"—perhaps the location of Steve's father's ancestors. Page was, as always, delightful company and a wonderfully good sport about both the mishaps and pleasures of travel abroad.

Back in Daytona Beach, Fred and I took time to explore the city itself before getting another rental car and driving to St. Augustine, and then on to Orlando, with all of it's many attractions.

"I can't walk another step. There's so much to see. You could spend a week just in Disney World."

"I think I enjoyed the Epcot Center the most. Everything was truly amazing—except for the crowds."

We were definitely enjoying ourselves while we waited for our return to Oregon. Of course there was also much to do in preparation for leaving the boat. Since we were flying back to Oregon we knew that we wouldn't be able to take much with us on the plane, so we continued our efforts to box things up and send them home via parcel post. One day we went by bus to a packaging and shipping store taking with us our precious crystal glasses that we had purchased in the Czech Republic. Because we feared they would be broken, we wanted them to be professionally packed. But when we found that the cost of packaging and sending 36 glasses would be astronomical, we were aghast.

"Thank goodness that clerk told us how we could safely pack the glasses ourselves. That was really nice of him."

"I'll say. He even told us where to purchase the bubble wrap that we needed."

We sat on the floor or the shipping store and carefully wrapped each glass, placing them in their original box, which the clerk had assured us was strong and safe enough for mailing.

For a break from the boat work, one evening we decided to take in a local baseball game in a park a few blocks from the marina. We had just finished taking 36 pictures on our camera. We had placed it and a jacket in a small black bag with a distinctive logo.

"Oh no. My bag is gone. Someone must have reached up through the bleachers and taken it."

"Let's go talk to the security staff."

We described our bag and found someone who said they had seen a young boy with such a bag. We ran around the park looking for him, until a security guard said a man and boy had just left with such a bag.

"The father told me that the boy always carried his catcher's mitt to the games in that bag," the guard said.

We ran to the parking lot just as a vehicle tore out onto the street.

"What chance in life does a kid have with a father that will lie to cover up his son's theft?"

"I just wanted the exposed film. I'd have given him the camera."

With one fully exposed camera stolen from our jacket in Ecuador, another, also completely exposed, left in a rental car in Guatemala, and now one stolen in Florida, we reckoned that picture taking (or keeping) was not one of our strong suits.

We had researched a number of safe places to leave our wonderful *Grace*, and had decided to use a small boatyard near Jacksonville, Florida. It was thirty miles inland up the St. John's River, so it would be somewhat protected from potential hurricanes and storms.

Finally, we once again entered the ICW and made our way northward. Our destination was not far from Daytona Beach, but for several days we took our time as we moved through the waterway and savored anchoring each afternoon along the way, knowing it would be one of the last days and nights of our incredible dream. At Jacksonville Beach we left the ICW, turned westward and made our way upriver to the city of Jacksonville, where we tied up at the long modern quay in the downtown area.

"Look around you. It's Saturday night, and this place is jumping. There's sure a lot happening around here," I said. "They really have developed this waterfront into an attractive and active place. Listen to that music. Sounds like a party."

"But I don't feel like partying or celebrating. Do you?"

"No...not really. Everything just feels a little sad to me. We're almost at the end of our dream and I don't want it to end. And yet I'm ready, too. It feels kind of crazy-making. It's almost like grieving. Let's just get a bite to eat, and then use our ear-plugs to try and get some sleep."

After traveling another day and a half, we arrived at the Green Cove Springs Boatyard.

"Well *Grace*. Here's your new home."

"Doesn't look too fancy, does it?" I looked around at the rather bleak surroundings.

"I guess if it's a safe place, that's the main thing."

We pulled up to a small dock to wait for our hauling out time the following day. Having hose, water and space available, we pulled out our heavy lamb's wool fleece mattress cover to wash it on the dock. It had been so useful in keeping us cooler in the tropics, and warmer in the cooler climes. Using our feet as well as our hands, we scrubbed and rubbed until we felt it was clean, and hung it over the boom to drip dry. It didn't take long in that strong Florida sun.

"No use washing the boat. That dusty, dry boatyard will have her caked in dirt in no time," I said grimly.

I hated the thought of our beautiful *Amazing Grace* propped up out of the water, standing for months in the dirt covered yard, looking more and more neglected.

It was with heavy hearts that we went about the final preparations for both our flight home, as well as the haul-out and moving *Grace* into the boatyard for a long-term stay. Everything possible was stripped from the deck. Electronics were disconnected. Water lines were drained. Through-hulls were plugged to prevent little critters from climbing aboard. Engines were winterized. Sails were removed and stored below. We passionately went about attending to all the little details to keep *Grace* protected as much as possible, almost like a parent that affectionately tucks in a sleeping child in the night.

This wonderful boat had taken us safely to so many places and through so many adventures. We had personified her in our minds, and she had become one of the family. We owed her so much. She, along with and through that amazing Grace of God, had allowed us to fulfill our dream, going even beyond our wildest imaginings. These four years had allowed us to learn, to grow, to appreciate, and to cherish not only the places and people we had met, but the times and experiences we had shared. And we realized with each passing day, that we had grown in appreciating and cherishing each other as well, sometimes in new and profound but simple ways. The bond between us was even stronger and more resilient than ever after having been tempered by wind and waves, joys and sorrows, delights and challenges. In many ways, we were no longer the person or the couple that had excitedly ventured forth into the dream. Truly, we had been blessed with amazing grace!

We had also come to appreciate and cherish our family even more, and realize that although our children were now adults, and no longer dependent on us, both we *and* they wanted to be where we could share our lives in the little everyday events, as well as the significant ones. It was *family* that had supported us and sent us off on this adventure four years ago, and it was *family* to whom we returned. Truly, we had learned anew that it was *family* that counted as one of God's richest blessings!

The family to whom we longed to return.

Indeed, the four years of living our cruising dream would forever be a time in our lives that we would never forget. And we would be forever grateful for having had it.

And now it was time to let go of the dream. Now the heartstrings and spirit pulled us in another direction. We were ready to return to our family, to our home—to new dreams and new adventures; knowing that truly amazing Grace would be in our hearts and lives—with us always, for whatever lay ahead.

Epilogue — Getting Grace Home

As the plane left the Jacksonville airport and flew upwards over the city, we tried in vain to see the boatyard and our beloved *Amazing Grace*, longing for one more opportunity to say our fond farewell. Leaving her, this beautiful boat that had taken us safely through so many adventures in so many places, was one of the most difficult things we had faced during our four-year journey. It would be almost six months before we would see her again, and there was a tug on the heartstrings each time we thought about her during those months, as she stood alone in the barren boatyard.

Once we were back in Dundee, Oregon, the months passed quickly as we worked to demolish the interior of our home and completely rebuild it. Totally new landscaping also took a heavy toll on aching backs, arms and legs. By October we were enjoying the fruits of our labor in our beautiful "new" home, and flew to Florida, courtesy of our "Delta Dawn," to make *Grace* ready for the upcoming winter weather.

"These long days of working on the boat aren't much fun when we know we won't be sailing her," I complained.

"Yeah, being in a boatyard is never easy. But we want *Grace* to be well protected for those cold nights ahead. At least we get to see Cindy and Reed. That's something to look forward to."

We had learned that our dear friends who had lost their boat, *Yobo*, were now in New Orleans and had purchased another boat. They were getting it ready to return to the cruising life in Panama, and we were delighted to visit them while we were in Florida.

"I'm beginning to wonder when we are ever going to get back

to go sailing in The Bahamas," I said as we flew back to Oregon. "I really don't want to be gone during the Holidays, and those Atlantic "northers" make it crazy to sail in January and February. And I *sure* don't want to be gone when Dawn and Jeff are getting ready for their wedding."

"And hurricane season goes from May to November. We sure don't want to try it then. Maybe we'll have to wait until next fall," Fred replied.

As the anticipated wedding day in early May approached, we were to receive more exciting news that didn't quite fit with the plan of returning to Florida in the fall *or* the following spring.

"So, Mom and Dad, how would you guys like to be grandparents?" Page said with a shy smile on her face. Steve stood beside her with a big grin.

"Really? *Really! Yahoo!*"

I shouted with glee and began to jump up and down, giggling and hollering and hugging our daughter. Fred glowed with happiness. The baby would be arriving in February. Our delight was uncontainable, and tears welled in our eyes as Fred and I held each other, knowing again, how *Blucky* we were.

"I'll take off twelve weeks when the baby is born, and then have to make up that last two months of my residency," Page said. "We were hoping you might be able to help out with some of the child care when I return to complete those final two months."

"Of course," I replied. "I'd be thrilled to do that. I can't wait!"

I turned to look at Fred, and smiled when I saw him give a slight nod of unspoken agreement as we shared the realization that it was time. Time to bring *Grace* home. There would be no more sailing in The Bahamas for *Amazing Grace*—we had been there and done that. We were now on to the thrills and adventures of new dreams—an expanding family and grandchildren! The original plan of returning for more exploration of those magical islands had been a good idea, but we had found an even better one.

Fred began to contact hauling agencies to make arrangements

for moving the boat across the United States by truck. Because of our swing keel, *Grace* was easier to fit on the flat bed of a vehicle than a fixed-keel boat, so there were more options. We were in no great hurry, so we arranged with one company to have them pick up the boat when they needed a cargo for their return to Oregon after they had made a haul to the east coast. That made the process less costly.

The boatyard staff in Florida completed all the preparations for being sure that *Grace* was ready to make the long trip overland. She was moved onto a truck and began the ride home. By October, 1997, we were standing in a boatyard in Portland, Oregon, looking at a very dirty, but none-the-less beautiful *Amazing Grace*. She showed the stress of the 3000 mile journey by truck, but there had been no significant damage enroute. It was not long before we had her polished and shined up, and back in the water. Our baby was finally home! *Gracias a Dios!*